# The Healing Virtues

## International Perspectives in Philosophy and Psychiatry

Series editors: Bill (K.W.M.) Fulford, Lisa Bortolotti, Matthew Broome, Katherine Morris, John Z. Sadler, and Giovanni Stanghellini

**VOLUMES IN THE SERIES**

**Portrait of the Psychiatrist as a Young Man**
*The Early Writing and Work of R.D. Laing, 1927–1960*
Beveridge

**Mind, Meaning, and Mental Disorder 2e**
Bolton and Hill

**What is Mental Disorder?**
Bolton

**Delusions and Other Irrational Beliefs**
Bortolotti

*Postpsychiatry*
Bracken and Thomas

**Philosophy, Psychoanalysis, and the A-Rational Mind**
Brakel

**Unconscious Knowing and Other Essays in Psycho-Philosophical Analysis**
Brakel

**Psychiatry as Cognitive Neuroscience**
Broome and Bortolotti (eds.)

**Free Will and Responsibility**
*A Guide for Practitioners*
Callender

**Reconceiving Schizophrenia**
Chung, Fulford, and Graham (eds.)

**Darwin and Psychiatry**
De Block and Adriaens (eds.)

**Oxford Handbook of Philosophy and Psychiatry**
Fulford, Davies, Gipps, Graham, Sadler, Stanghellini, and Thornton

Nature and Narrative
**An Introduction to the New Philosophy of Psychiatry**
Fulford, Morris, Sadler, and Stanghellini (eds.)

**Oxford Textbook of Philosophy and Psychiatry**
Fulford, Thornton, and Graham

**The Mind and Its Discontents**
Gillett

**The Abraham Dilemma**
Graham

**Is Evidence-Based Psychiatry Ethical?**
Gupta

**Thinking Through Dementia**
Hughes

**Dementia**
*Mind, Meaning, and the Person*
Hughes, Louw, and Sabat (eds.)

**Talking Cures and Placebo Effects**
Jopling

**Philosophical Issues in Psychiatry II**
*Nosology*
Kendler and Parnas (eds.)

**Philosophical Issues in Psychiatry III**
*The Nature and Sources of Historical Change*
Kendler and Parnas (eds.)

**Discursive Perspectives in Therapeutic Practice**
Lock and Strong (ed.)

**Schizophrenia and the Fate of the Self**
Lysaker and Lysaker

**Embodied Selves and Divided Minds**
Maiese

**Responsibility and Psychopathy**
Malatesti and McMillan

**Body-Subjects and Disordered Minds**
Matthews

**Rationality and Compulsion**
*Applying Action Theory to Psychiatry*
Nordenfelt

**Diagnostic Dilemmas in Child and Adolescent Psychiatry**
Perring and Wells (eds.)

**Philosophical Perspectives on Technology and Psychiatry**
Phillips (ed.)

**The Metaphor of Mental Illness**
Pickering

**Mapping the Edges and the In-Between**
Potter

**Trauma, Truth, and Reconciliation**
*Healing Damaged Relationships*
Potter (ed.)

**The Philosophy of Psychiatry**
*A Companion*
Radden

**The Virtuous Psychiatrist**
Radden and Sadler

**Addiction and Weakness of Will**
Radoilska

**Autonomy and Mental Disorder**
Radoilska (ed.)

**Feelings of Being**
Ratcliffe

**Experiences of Depression**
*A Study in Phenomenology*
Ratcliffe

**Recovery of People with Mental Illness**
*Philosophical and Related Perspectives*
Rudnick (ed.)

**Values and Psychiatric Diagnosis**
Sadler

**The Oxford Handbook of Psychiatric Ethics**
Sadler, Van Staden, and Fulford (eds.)

**Disembodied Spirits and Deanimated Bodies**
*The Psychopathology of Common Sense*
Stanghellini

**One Century of Karl Jaspers Psychopathology**
Stanghellini and Fuchs (eds.)

**Emotions and Personhood**
Stanghellini and Rosfort

**Essential Philosophy of Psychiatry**
Thornton

**Naturalism, Hermeneutics, and Mental Disorder**
Varga

**The Healing Virtues**
*Character Ethics in Psychotherapy*
Waring

**Empirical Ethics in Psychiatry**
Widdershoven, McMillan, Hope and Van der Scheer (eds.)

**The Sublime Object of Psychiatry**
*Schizophrenia in Clinical and Cultural Theory*
Woods

**Alternate Perspectives on Psyciatric Validation**
*DSM, ICD, RDoC, and Beyond*
Zachar, St. Stoyanov, Aragona, and Jablensky (eds.)

# The Healing Virtues
## Character Ethics in Psychotherapy

Duff R. Waring
Associate Professor of Philosophy
York University, Canada

OXFORD
UNIVERSITY PRESS

OXFORD
UNIVERSITY PRESS

Great Clarendon Street, Oxford, OX2 6DP,
United Kingdom

Oxford University Press is a department of the University of Oxford.
It furthers the University's objective of excellence in research, scholarship,
and education by publishing worldwide. Oxford is a registered trade mark of
Oxford University Press in the UK and in certain other countries



First Edition published in 2016



Published in the United States of America by Oxford University Press
198 Madison Avenue, New York, NY 10016, United States of America

British Library Cataloguing in Publication Data
Data available

Library of Congress Control Number: 2015948957

ISBN 978–0–19–968914–9

# Contents

# Acknowledgements

I am grateful to the following persons for their support, encouragement, and unwavering collegiality: Jennifer Radden, John Sadler, David Jopling, and Louis Charland, whose work raised the bar and inspired this book's conception. Eric Matthews has also been a notable influence. I've had the benefit of being exposed to the work of many other colleagues at meetings of the International Network of Philosophy and Psychiatry, and the Association for the Advancement of Philosophy and Psychiatry. My friend and copy editor Ted Killin brought his own virtues of focus to the book, as did Charlotte Green, Martin Baum, Matthias Butler, and the reviewers at Oxford University Press. I am especially grateful to Dr. Graeme J. Taylor, who listened to me think out loud over eight years of writing. His critical feedback and references for further study are still invaluable to me. Discussions with my friend and mentor R. Steven Turner continue to inform my thinking in too many ways to mention. As much of this book was written there, I thank my friends on the island of Hydra for their hospitality. There is finally one person whose contribution to my life surpasses every dedication I've ever tried to write for her: Jayne.

Chapter 1

# Introduction

## 1.1 Psychotherapy and Virtue Ethics

I want to explore the intersection of psychotherapy and virtue ethics with an emphasis on the patient's work in a healing project. I take the central idea of virtue ethics to be the following: instead of a paramount focus on evaluating the rightness or wrongness of actions in terms of consequences, rules, and duties, we maintain an important focus on evaluating the goodness or badness of persons in terms of their character and the virtues that define it. Virtue ethics is centered primarily on notions of virtue that encompass, but are not limited to the character of the agent. Virtue notions can also apply to acts (e.g., "generous" or "just" actions) and to rules of behavior (e.g., "Be Kind," or "Don't Be Callous").[1] Ethics is a generic term for various ways of understanding and evaluating the moral life.[2] As I define it, generic ethics includes moral considerations about how we ought to treat others and ethical considerations about how we ought to treat ourselves. Virtues can play a role in both other-regarding morality and self-regarding ethics.

Standard medical and reference dictionaries define psychotherapy as any number of theoretically based techniques for treating mental disorders and other problems in living by psychologic methods. The techniques rely mainly on establishing a supportive interpersonal relationship between a trained therapist and patient in which spoken conversation is used to encourage the communication of conflicts and to develop the patient's insight into the motivation behind her problematic patterns of thought and behavior. Persuasion, suggestion, reassurance, and instruction may also be used. The standard therapeutic aim is to change maladaptive coping patterns and to encourage personal growth.[3]

This change is effected in part by the efforts of the therapist. It is also effected by the patient's efforts at "working through" her problem. Her efforts are facilitated by the therapist but the patient is ultimately responsible for working on herself. The "working through" is a term that psychotherapy has inherited from psychoanalysis, where it referred to the analysand's ongoing efforts to overcome resistance to an analyst's interpretation. Those efforts supposedly allowed the analysand to incorporate the interpretation into her lived experience, to consciously accept certain repressed elements of her psyche, and to free herself from repetition mechanisms by which a conflict is perpetuated.[4] In broader terms applicable to a range of therapies beyond the psychodynamic, the "working through" means a persistent effort to resolve a problem by repeatedly confronting it and examining the ways by which one perpetuates conflict in current patterns of thought and behavior.

The problems include, but are not limited to, some conditions in the current nomenclature of mental disorder that can be plausibly construed as character faults. I refer throughout to the Cluster B Personality Disorders in the fourth and fifth editions of the American Psychiatric Association's *Diagnostic and Statistical Manual of Mental Disorders* (hereinafter DSM-4, DSM-5, or DSM).[5] Some psychotherapy cases, I will aver, illuminate much common ground between the working through and the cultivation of virtuous character in pursuit of a good life. This implicates the way of understanding and evaluating the moral life that we term virtue ethics. I focus on four psychotherapies that arguably aim at generic ethical self-improvement through the cultivation of virtues. I construe existential, Kohutian self-psychological, cognitive behavioral, and mentalization-based therapies as each presenting an intersection between virtue ethics and the talking cures.

This common ground between the working through and the cultivation of virtues can inform the praxis of both therapist and patient. The ethics of psychotherapy revolve partly around what therapists should or should not do vis-à-vis their patients: e.g., they should maintain confidentiality subject to a limited duty to warn if a patient threatens harm to self or specific other, and they should refrain from sexual relations with those who are or have been under their care.[6] But ethics can revolve as well around the sort of person that therapists should be: e.g., empathic, prudent, compassionate, respectful, and trustworthy. Contemporary practitioners have argued for therapist virtues that are vitally relevant to assisting the patient in the working through.[7]

I explore how this common ground relates to the patient. The ethics of a therapeutic dialogue can also revolve around the sort of person the patient should be. I think there is an argument for patient virtues that are crucially relevant to working through the problems in living that arise in psychotherapy, e.g., honesty, hopefulness, and perseverance. My central idea is not unfamiliar to some psychodynamic therapists: that treatment may need to build virtues while it ameliorates problems. The patient's work in psychotherapy can both challenge character strengths and result in their further development.[8]

Broadly defined, virtues are reliable and characteristic dispositions of a person to act, reason, and feel in certain ways. They require time, habituation, and experience to develop into actively and intelligently engaged abilities to respond appropriately to changing circumstances. Virtue involves acting on reasons with the right feelings and attitudes.[9] I use "virtue" in Swanton's sense to mean various modes of acknowledging and responding to a plurality of goods. These modes express generally stable traits of character that are multi-track dispositions involving complex mind sets of "fine inner states" that inform an array of emotional responses, desires, motivations, reasons, and values. Some contemporary conceptions of virtue ethics emphasize pluralist notions of both good lives and standards of virtue. The latter can be contextualized in their acknowledgement of psychological conflict.[10] The traditional ideal of the supremely virtuous exemplar can be supplanted by a moderately demanding threshold notion of virtue. Virtuous responses to the demands of the world can range from being good enough to supererogatory and can express a patient's efforts to improve by gaining greater psychological strength.[11]

Virtues are desirable for therapists and patients because they advance goods, like self-exploration, that are internal to the praxis of psychotherapy.[12] I regard them as desirable because they can (a) facilitate the patient's efforts in the working through and (b) constitute modes of recovery at which those efforts are aimed. Annas likens virtues to skills that require the need to learn from a trusted teacher and the drive to aspire to understanding, self-direction, and improvement. I posit the healing virtues in psychotherapy as requiring the same. Like the learner of a practical skill, the learner of virtue "needs to understand what she is doing, to achieve the ability to do it for herself, and to do it in a way that improves as she meets challenges, rather than coming out with predictable repetition."[13] Ditto the psychotherapy patient. Musical analogies are illuminative. One who achieves a practical mastery of the skills involved in playing piano has learned to do more than parrot her teacher's playing; she has learned to play expressively in a way that is characteristic of herself.[14] The patient who has sufficiently developed the healing and recovery virtues in psychotherapy has learned to do more than feign her therapist's influence; she has learned to live in a better way that is characteristic of herself. I term this mode of living authentic, and in some cases, psychotherapy might facilitate a patient's quest for it.

This definition of virtue accommodates Swanton's pluralistic conception of virtue ethics within which I develop my normative evaluation of psychotherapy.[15] Swanton's conception moves from "the standard virtue-ethical belief that virtues express fine inner states" to the claim that "the delineation of virtue needs to be informed by psychological theories of character which give a sufficiently deep account of those states."[16] Consequently, the task of delineating virtue acquires "the complexities of the task of understanding psychic health."[17] The aim of the virtues is to appropriately meet the demands of the world. This includes, but is not exhausted by, self-realization. Hence the acute importance to the virtuous life of striving for "psychological improvement."[18]

## 1.2 Chapter Synopsis

### Chapter Two: Psychotherapy and the Moderate Skeptic's Challenge

I begin with a schematic account of what psychotherapy is about and explain how psychotherapy can be understood as an ethically value-laden endeavor. At this point, I want merely to raise the idea that the talking cures inhabit overlapping epistemic and ethical spaces of normative appraisal. I then confront the pivotal epistemic issue of how we might know whether the insights that psychotherapy patients claim to achieve are veridical. Given the very real possibility that psychotherapy might foster self-deception as opposed to self-knowledge, we need to distinguish between veridical and placebo insights. Truth matters to the many psychotherapy patients who want insights about themselves that furnish an accurate understanding of who they are, how they came to be that way, and how they should change for the better. I regard the truth value of such insights as a cardinal issue and use Jopling's skeptical challenge as a point of departure.[19]

### Chapter Three: Epistemic Virtues in Psychotherapy: A Response to the Moderate Skeptic's Challenge

This chapter covers the epistemic space of normative appraisal. I argue that virtue epistemology can inform a reply to a moderate skeptic's challenge that is prefigured by certain aspects of psychodynamic thought. My response indicates an implicit set of epistemic virtues that can regulate psychodynamic explorations. I assume that patients can control whether they take insights seriously and how carefully they evaluate them. They can thus be held responsible for how well they exercise that control. I recast the challenge as a virtue epistemologist who relates justifiedness to the truth-conducive virtues by which persons can regulate inquiries and from which the warrant of beliefs is derived. I take the moderate skeptic's challenge as a motivational call to cultivate epistemic virtues that make patients responsible and conscientious aspirants to truth and self-understanding.

### Chapter Four: Reparative Ethics: The Nexus Between Mental Health and Moral Virtue

I begin my examination of psychotherapy's ethical dimensions. I examine the value-laden intersection of psychotherapy, positive mental health, and generic ethical values. I argue that these values permeate three points of a triadic analysis: (1) conceptions of mental disorder, (2) psychotherapeutic praxis, and (3) conceptions of positive mental health. After distinguishing between self-regarding ethical and other-regarding moral values I concentrate on how to cultivate responsibilities to develop and strengthen one's capacity for better responding to the demands of the world. One of these demands is to care for oneself. On my account, these responsibilities can be understood as the patient's striving to cultivate certain virtues in the dialogical process of psychotherapy. This striving implies a valued state or condition that one pursues and to some degree attains. It is here that I will argue for a connection between conceptions of positive mental health and ethical virtues. I begin exploring the virtue of self-love as a therapeutic goal which I elaborate further in chapter six, along with the responsibility to develop it in a healing project of self-regarding care. I introduce the Case of the Demoralized Woman to illustrate these claims.

## Chapter Five: Psychotherapy and the Virtuous Patient

I posit an application of Swanton's virtue ethical theory to clinical practice and argue for the relevance of patient-centered virtues to the working through. Psychotherapy cases that can be elucidated in virtue ethical terms have the triadic structure noted in chapter three. I approach the triadic structure of these cases in the following way: If (1) the problem can be elucidated in self- or other-regarding ethical terms, and (2) the goals of treatment involve any or all of the following: ethically desirable changes in (a) tendencies of affective/emotional response, (b) a better understanding of how one should treat oneself and/or others, and (c) better patterns of behavior, then (3) the efforts the committed patient makes to resolve the problem can involve the affective, cognitive, and practical facets of ethical self-improvement through the cultivation of certain virtues.[20] I argue that Swanton's "virtues of practice" can be cultivated by patients to meet the generic ethical challenges these cases present and introduce the case of Seneca's Angry Man to illustrate these claims. I challenge the notion that therapists must never pass moral judgement on their patients by blaming them. I suggest that there can be cases, however rare, in which therapists should hold patients accountable for unethical behavior and express carefully tempered ethical assessments in doing so. Negative emotions like guilt and shame might have a limited therapeutic application.

## Chapter Six: The Responsibilities of Patients in a Psychotherapeutic Healing Project

I set out the self-regarding ethical and other-regarding moral responsibilities that patients have in a psychotherapeutic healing project and the virtues that

I think patients should cultivate to meet them. The healing project begins with the patient's alliance with the therapist and becomes less dependent as the patient develops a stronger alliance with herself and works at recovery on her own. I expand upon the notion of self-regarding ethical responsibility outlined in chapter four in terms of a patient's independent project of self-regarding care. It reflects efforts to manage treatment and restore self-unity that the patient is responsible for making on her own behalf. I present the patient as cultivating specific virtues by which the project is conducted with the goal of recovery. These healing virtues can meet both other- and self-regarding responsibilities, as when the patient has to be perseverant in working with the therapist as well as herself. Once a threshold level of self-unity is restored, the patient continues to cultivate the recovery virtues by which it is sustained. These include virtues of self-respect and self-love that are focused largely on meeting the responsibility the patient has to herself. I conclude that some psychotherapy cases involve a patient's efforts to fashion an authentic way of living and suggest a notion of authenticity that emerges from the recovery virtues of self-love and empathic concern for others.

## Chapter Seven: Four Psychotherapies and the Triadic Analysis

I interpret existential, Kohutian self-psychological, cognitive behavioral, and mentalization-based therapies as generically ethical treatments in cases that fit the triadic analysis. Self-psychological and existential psychotherapies reveal generic ethical dimensions in their concerns with a patient's search for authenticity. I then show how cognitive behavioral therapy can be used to foster self-regarding ethical and other-regarding moral improvements in (1) tendencies of affective/emotional response, (2) a better understanding of how one should treat oneself and/or others, and (3) better patterns of behavior through the cultivation of healing virtues. I construe mentalization-based therapy as a quintessential generic ethical treatment that aims to foster the empathic concern for others that is a crucial facet of any moral perspective.

## Chapter Eight: Caveats, Summations, and Stones Left Unturned

I conclude by noting the parameters and limitations of my analysis and offer comments on some of the larger issues I touch upon, e.g., the situationist critique of virtue ethics and the emerging reservations about the positive psychology movement.

## 1.3 Psychotherapy and the Art of Living Well by Being Well

If there is an art to psychotherapy, then it pertains to ethics as the art of living. "Psychotherapy," claims Allen, cannot be conducted "without some sense of how life is best lived."[21] On my account, it can be conducted as a virtue ethical endeavor for therapist and patient alike. We live well in no small part by being well, and part of being well involves the psychic health that reflects the fine inner states of virtue. Where Radden and Sadler explored *The Virtuous Psychiatrist*,[22] I focus on the virtuous patient. My analysis explores the other side to their position that the psychiatrist's cultivation of certain traits "will be useful to therapeutic effectiveness."[23] I defend the position that the cultivation of certain virtues by the patient will enhance, and in some respects constitute, psychotherapeutic benefit. If so, then patients should cultivate them given their responsibility to care for themselves in a healing project. Or so I will argue.

## Notes

1. **Christine Swanton**, "The Definition of Virtue Ethics," in *The Cambridge Companion to Virtue Ethics*, ed. Daniel C. Russell (New York: Cambridge University Press, 2013), 329–336.
2. **Tom L. Beauchamp** and **James F. Childress**, *Principles of Biomedical Ethics*, 6th ed. (Oxford: Oxford University Press, 2009), 1.
3. Cf. *Compact Oxford English Dictionary* (2003), s.v. "Psychotherapy"; *Dorland's Illustrated Medical Dictionary* (1998; 2008), s.v. "Psychotherapy"; and *The American Heritage Stedman's Medical Dictionary* (2000), s.v. "Psychotherapy."
4. **J. Laplanche** and **J-B. Pontalis**, *The Language of Psychoanalysis*, trans. Donald Nicholson-Smith (New York: W.W. Norton and Company, 1973), 488–489.
5. **American Psychiatric Association**, *Diagnostic and Statistical Manual of Mental Disorders*, 4th ed. (Washington, DC: American Psychiatric Publishing, 1994), 649–661; **American Psychiatric Association**, *Diagnostic and Statistical Manual of Mental Disorders*, 5th ed. (Washington, DC: American Psychiatric Publishing, 2013), 659–672.
6. **William J. Winslade**, "Confidentiality," in *Encyclopedia of Bioethics*, ed. Stephen G. Post. 3rd ed. (New York: Thomson Gale, 2004), 494–500; Kevin V. Kelley and Peter Caws, "Psychoanalysis and Dynamic Therapies," in *Encyclopedia of Bioethics*, ed. Stephen G. Post. 3rd ed. (New York: Thomson Gale, 2004), 2182.
7. **Elliot D. Cohen** and **Gale Spieler Cohen**, *The Virtuous Therapist: Ethical Practice of Counseling and Psychotherapy* (Pacific Grove, CA: Brooks Cole, 1998).
8. **Richard F. Summers** and **Jacques P. Barber**, *Psychodynamic Therapy: A Guide to Evidence-Based Practice* (New York: The Guilford Press, 2010), 94, 259.
9. **Julia Annas**, *Intelligent Virtue* (Oxford: Oxford University Press, 2011), 5, 8, 9, 14.
10. **Christine Swanton**, *Virtue Ethics: A Pluralistic View* (Oxford: Oxford University Press, 2003), 3, 63.

11. **Swanton**, *Virtue Ethics*, 205–206, 210–211.
12. Cf. **Ernest Wallwork**, "Ethics in Psychoanalysis," in *Textbook of Psychoanalysis*, eds. Glen O. Gabbard, Bonnie E. Litowitz, and Paul Williams. 2nd ed. (Washington, DC: American Psychiatric Publishing, 2012), 357–358. As Wallwork notes, the idea that virtues can be crucial to realizing the goods internal to a practice like psychotherapy comes from Alasdair MacIntryre, who defined a practice as "any coherent and complex form of socially established cooperative human activity through which goods internal to that form of activity are realized in the course of trying to achieve those standards of excellence which are appropriate to, and partially definitive of, that form of activity." See MacIntyre, *After Virtue: A Study in Moral Theory*, 2nd ed. (Notre Dame, IN: University of Notre Dame Press, 1984), 187. The recovery virtues of self-love and empathic concern discussed in chapter six are expressions of the patient's psyche that are evaluated as therapeutic by standards internal to the praxis of psychotherapy: cf. Swanton, *Virtue Ethics*, 163.
13. **Annas**, *Intelligent Virtue*, 20.
14. Cf. **Annas**, *Intelligent Virtue*, 13–14.
15. **Swanton** has clearly expressed her agreement with "virtually all" of Annas' analysis in *Intelligent Virtue*, especially "the central claim that virtue is analogous to a practical skill." See Christine Swanton, "Comments on Intelligent Virtue: Rightness and Exemplars of Virtue," *Journal of Value Inquiry* 49 (2015): 307–315.
16. **Swanton**, *Virtue Ethics*, 6.
17. **Swanton**, *Virtue Ethics*, 10.
18. **Swanton**, *Virtue Ethics*, 14–15.
19. **David Jopling**, *Talking Cures and Placebo Effects* (Oxford: Oxford University Press, 2008).
20. **Brad K. Wilburn**, "Moral Self-Improvement," in *Moral Cultivation: Essays on the Development of Character and Virtue*, ed. Brad K. Wilburn (Plymouth, UK: Lexington Books, 2007), 69–84.
21. **Jon G. Allen**, "Psychotherapy: The Artful Use of Science," *Smith College Studies in Social Work* 78 (2008): 166.
22. **Jennifer Radden** and **John Z. Sadler**, *The Virtuous Psychiatrist: Character Ethics in Psychiatric Practice* (Oxford: Oxford University Press, 2010).
23. **Jennifer Radden**, "Virtue Ethics as Professional Ethics: The Case of Psychiatry," in *Working Virtue: Virtue Ethics and Contemporary Moral Problems*, eds. Rebecca L. Walter and P.J. Ivanhoe (Oxford: Oxford University Press, 2007), 115, 116, 117.

Chapter 2

# Psychotherapy and the Moderate Skeptic's Challenge

## 2.1 Introduction

I begin with a schematic account of what psychotherapy is about. We need a sense of what it means for a troubled person, whom I will classify as a patient, to be engaged in psychotherapy. How might we envision this engagement? My next step is to delineate the normative values that can inform insight-oriented psychotherapies. I define these as any psychotherapy in which a patient talks to a therapist in ways that help the former to understand the meaning of her problems and why and how she has perpetuated them. The understanding thus obtained should go some way toward ameliorating the patient's problems.[1]

I give a preliminary account of how psychotherapy can be understood as an ethically value-laden endeavor for both therapist and patient. In subsequent chapters, I refine this analysis with reference to cases and consideration of a virtue ethical approach to general normative theory. At this point, I want to raise the idea that the "talking cures" inhabit epistemic and ethical spaces of normative appraisal. I then address the epistemic question of how we might know whether the insights that patients claim to achieve in psychotherapy are veridical. Is there a theory of truth that would verify these insights as genuine self-knowledge about motivation and character, let alone knowledge that can be instrumental in resolving psychological conflicts? Psychodynamic therapy retains some emphasis on the healing potential of insight and, depending on how "insight" is defined, cognitive behavioral and existential psychotherapies also leave room for the acquisition of deep understandings of one's self or mode of being-in-the-world.

Given the very real possibility that psychotherapy might foster self-deception as opposed to self-knowledge, we need to distinguish between veridical and placebo insights. While placebo insights might be beneficial for some patients, they would not support claims to self-knowledge. I regard the truth value of such claims as a cardinal issue and use Jopling's skeptical challenge to the acquisition of self-knowledge in psychotherapy as a point of departure.[2]

## 2.2 The Secular Confessional

I start with the "what" of psychotherapy. What is it about, what does it do, and what does it address? Psychotherapy is treatment by talking and listening.[3] A person who begins psychotherapy assumes the role of a "patient" seeking care from a qualified professional who treats mental disorders or problems in living. A person who seeks care from a psychotherapist is essentially seeking treatment. A patient is one who receives any of various healing services or treatments. Thus, a person seeking healing care or treatment from a psychotherapist is plausibly termed a patient. All patients are clients insofar as they pay for goods and services rendered by a qualified professional. But not all professionals offer healing care to their clients and not all clients are patients who seek care from the professionals they consult.

A psychotherapeutic encounter is confidential and it is the patient who usually does most of the talking. Once committed to psychotherapy, the patient has an obligation to respond honestly to the therapist's questions.[4] This can be hard work insofar as a patient may not want to admit certain things about herself to herself, let alone to anyone else. The patient relates to the therapist a problem in living that causes her some degree of emotional suffering or distress. It might reflect symptoms of an officially recognized "mental disorder" such as those catalogued in the DSM.[5] It could also reflect a broader sense of existential malaise that does not translate readily into a DSM diagnosis. Either way, the therapist will attempt to situate the problem in the context of the patient's life. They can then attempt to figure out the origins, motives, and meanings of the patient's troubles.

We can expand this definition by thinking of psychotherapy as a dialogical encounter between two persons in the privacy of a secular confessional.[6] They usually sit facing each other. The therapist assumes the role of a healer who counsels, who offers some measure of guidance or assistance in an effort to help persons to better understand themselves and deal with their problems. The therapist can be a physician (e.g., a psychiatrist) who practices psychological healing techniques, or a clinical psychologist who practices the same. Regardless of profession, therapists attempt to remediate the mental disorders or problems in living for those who seek their care. Therapy is the treatment of illness, disability, mental disorder, or other problems in living. Psychotherapy is treatment of those problems by listening to and talking with the persons who have them. It sometimes involves bolstering insight by the inculcation of active techniques that aim to change entrenched patterns of feeling, thought, and behavior.

Therapists who are influenced by psychoanalysis may assume that the patient's troubles derive from what she does not know about herself. The therapist might seek to reveal repressed psychic realities, e.g., motives, wishes and conflicts that are causally potent and continuously existent. Fingarette calls this "the hidden reality view" of psychoanalysis. Therapists uncover what has been "present and invisible" in such a way as to enable patients to see these buried psychic realities for themselves.[7] If taken literally, the hidden reality view corresponds neatly to the idea that there are repressed psychic realities awaiting discovery of which patients are unaware (this view can also be applied to many post-Freudian psychodynamic therapies). Thus some insight-oriented psychotherapies can be seen as attempts to discover what is hidden but no less present and influential in the patient's life.[8]

In contrast, existential therapists may assume that a patient's troubles derive from what they do know about the human condition but aim to deny. Or perhaps a patient has lost touch with a life that is meaningful to her. A cognitive behavioral therapist might assume that patients' troubles derive from what they mistakenly think about themselves, from the cognitive errors they perpetuate through schemas of negative thinking. Thus in some cases, psychotherapy aims to enable patients to better deal with the troubling things they do know about themselves, e.g., a patient claims to know that he is an obsessive compulsive. In other cases, it aims to help patients who are troubled by what they do not know about themselves, e.g., a patient claims to not know who he really is. There can be all manner of troubles that fall between these claims, e.g., a patient knows she is disconnected from other persons but is not sure why.

I should clarify my three fundamental assumptions about insight-oriented psychotherapy (hereinafter psychotherapy). First, I think that the aim of psychotherapy, construed in the broadest terms, is to put patients in touch with the core aspects of their psyches, i.e., the predominant motivations and recurring patterns of emotional, cognitive, and behavioral response that inform their problematic ways of relating to themselves and others.[9] Therapist and patient do not contrive the patient's core aspects, as they might if they were fabricating a story with the patient as lead character. These aspects are rather discovered and confirmed in the course of therapy. I discuss core aspects in greater detail in chapter three. Second, psychotherapy aims to present options for change and to foster insights that enable patients to transform themselves, i.e., to change their modes of feeling, thinking, and acting. In some cases of psychotherapy, I will argue that these modes correspond to the affective, cognitive, and behavioral aspects of a patient's self-regarding ethical and other-regarding moral self-improvement (I further expand on this idea in chapter five).

My third fundamental assumption has been formulated by Charles Taylor: humans are self-interpreting beings.[10] Persons have a distinctive, fundamental disposition to increase the meaningfulness of their lives, or what Freud termed "the irresistible advance toward the unification of mental life."[11]

If persons are self-interpreting beings, then insight-oriented psychotherapy can enable them to create and discover the schemes of meaning by which they self-interpret. I argue in later chapters that motives are only part of what a patient's insights can illuminate but for now, suffice it to say that even if a therapist is committed to the idea that only motives count, the idea that feelings, thoughts, and behaviors are born of them compels us to think about what those feelings, thoughts, and behaviors mean.[12] The motives are at least part of their meaning. "This finally demands," says London, that psychotherapy "becomes an inquiry into the meaning of one's life."[13] We do not have to limit our sense of the meaningful to that which is hidden in the subconscious, the nature of which we can only infer. Why assume that hidden meaning must always be "coiled and ready to unwind" under probing by a therapist?[14] Rieff scored a telling point against classical psychoanalysis: "Motives easily and directly expressed, lying on the conscious surface of the mind, may be still more revealing."[15]

Psychotherapy thus inhabits a generic ethical space of normative appraisal. It cannot long avoid an exploration of the meaning and value systems by which patients live their lives. Patients may initially seek symptom relief without insight, says London, but many will aim further at greater self-awareness. Once undistracted by distressing symptoms, patients "see themselves as creatures of purpose—and worry about how to see themselves when they do not."[16]

Psychodynamic, existential, and cognitive behavioral therapies aim to change modes of emotional, cognitive, and behavioral response to demands of self and world. Behavioral change matters to existential and psychodynamic therapies insofar as insight and responsible choice inform the way we relate to ourselves and to others. Psychotherapy is connected intimately with self-improvement insofar as many patients wrestle with the gap between the persons they would like to be and the persons they are.[17] Indeed, it has been argued that since psychotherapy is concerned with effecting changes in a patient's actions and motivations, a concern that usually falls within the moral domain, it "clearly presupposes a set of values in the name of which the alteration of the lives of patients is undertaken."[18] This set of values can amount to an implicit conception of a flourishing life.[19] Virtues of character can arguably have a major role in a patient's efforts to work through the process of resolving, or at least modifying, the problem for which psychotherapy was sought. These efforts involve the patient's striving to realize the goals of therapy. Christine Swanton has provided an apposite rendition of dispositions relating to these efforts with her virtues of practice, which I discuss at length in chapter five. In short, psychotherapy can be a virtue ethical endeavor. As I discuss in chapter three, that endeavor can also be a virtue epistemological one.

This normative space of ethical/moral appraisal is not always acknowledged in psychotherapy. Freud's denial that psychoanalysis endorses a moral point of view has been soundly challenged by Phillip Rieff.[20] The proponents of cognitive behavior therapy do not present their approach as a means of ethical self-improvement whereas I think that, in some cases, it is precisely that. Existential psychotherapy might seem an unlikely candidate for the endorsement of self-regarding ethical values, let alone the transformation of other-regarding moral ones, but I think this assumption is too easy to make. On my account, its emphasis on authenticity opens up some interesting connections to virtue ethics. The line between psychotherapy and moral counseling may not be as bright as some would have us believe. There was a time when psychologists spoke of character as opposed to personality; when positive conceptions of mental health implied character traits conducive to a flourishing life as opposed to an absence of pathologic symptoms. Hence my abiding interest in Marie Jahoda's work, which I examine in chapter four.

This is not to suggest that all psychotherapeutic encounters involve generic ethical values. A patient seeking symptom relief from a compulsive need to wash his hands two dozen times after returning to his home may be an otherwise virtuous person. His self-regarding authenticity and other-regarding moral commitments may not be compromised by his obsession with personal hygiene. A schizophrenic in the grip of psychosis or a patient who is volitionally paralyzed by major depression can lack the capacity to appreciate a conception of the good life and the other-regarding obligations that go with it. The core deficit in these conditions is not an unethical way of relating to self or other but rather a debilitated ability to relate at all. A crucial aspect of treating such patients is attempting to restore their psychological capacities for autonomous and responsible decision-making. But in most cases we do not hold them responsible for the condition that eviscerates their mental capacity, although I will explore an argument that we may hold them to a self- and other-regarding responsibility to maintain their mental capacity once it has been restored. My focus will be on cases involving alleged mental disorders or problems in living that are more plausibly construed as ethical character flaws. In sum, I focus on cases where psychotherapy is involved in reframing a patient's ethical vision of a good life and reforming patterns of feeling, thought, and behavior that compromise self- and other-regarding responsibilities.

A psychotherapeutic encounter involves mutual obligations between therapist and patient. Aside from clear and specific threats of harm to self or other, or the sharing of anonymous data between consulting therapists, the patient entrusts his therapist with disclosures that the latter is obligated to keep between them. Patients are thus encouraged to be honest and unreservedly candid in revealing themselves. The encounter "is designed as an oasis in the desert of reticence in which the patient [usually] lives" and "the self-consciousness of ordinary conversations" is to be avoided.[21] It is understood that a patient's admissions of shame or guilt will not lead to expulsion from the secular confessional. Nor will those admissions usually lead to censure within it, although some therapists believe that they should challenge patients if a clash of values occurs (even then, the challenge stays in the confessional).

The encounter is also supposed to be dialogic, i.e., therapist and patient are supposed to converse. The patient relates a story from her life in which she tries to contextualize the problem for which therapy is sought. Therapist and patient interact with each other in assigning meaning to the problem in the context of the patient's story. Traditional Freudian psychoanalysts might have focused predominantly on listening and left most of the talking to patients, but most contemporary therapists engage in a mutual exploration of their patients' issues. There is a give and take, a to and fro in coming to explain by interpretation, to evaluate, and to reconfigure the meanings that are attributed to the patient's experience. We might say that an interpretation that a patient has unresolved guilt issues, the evaluation that she has entrenched patterns of thought that inculcate her sense of guilt, and the meaning reconfiguration that she is not such a bad person after all are mutual endeavors. Up to a point, we can say that therapist and patient work together on the latter's problems. Past that point, the patient has to rely more on her own resources and less on the therapist's. She must use what she has learned in therapy to work on her problems by herself. Or as I put it in chapter six, the patient has to assume responsibility for a project of self-regarding care. The patient's experience includes her sense of herself, her relations with others, and her manner of relating to the world at large.

This move towards reconfiguring the patient's sense of being-in-the-world can take various forms depending on the therapist's theoretical orientation. A psychodynamic orientation will incline the therapist to situate the patient's problem in terms of an extensive history of her past with particular emphasis on childhood development and early, perhaps traumatic relationships with parents or caregivers. This orientation assumes that the dynamics of past traumas can reverberate over time and be repeated and expressed in the present, i.e., that there are psychic causes of ongoing conflicts that, allegedly unbeknownst to the patient, are somehow buried in her mind. It also assumes the causal relevance of psychic material that is repressed in the patient's subconscious and perhaps expressed symbolically in dreams.

An existential orientation may involve a less comprehensive exploration of the patient's past and will eschew a focus on the subconscious. But it will require an attempt to understand the patient's present mode of being-in-the-world and the extent to which he embraces, or deceives himself about, his responsibility for making what he can of a free and open future. These orientations focus on the meanings that patients attribute to their experience and how they influence the choices behind their behavior. They are also insight-oriented. For a psychodynamic therapist, symptoms, complaints, conflicts, or confusions are "signs of covert maladies of [psychological] motive."[22] For an existential therapist, they indicate salient, ongoing motifs by which patients interpret their confrontation with the ineluctable givens of being-in-the-world: impending death, freedom and responsibility, isolation, and the challenge of finding meaning in an indifferent universe. Indeed, the patient may be avoiding, and hence lack, full reflective awareness of these givens, which can be seen in the way he responds or avoids responding to them.

A cognitive behavioral orientation would be concerned mainly with how the content of a patient's thinking influences his feelings and reactions and produces symptoms of distress. Thus patients become depressed who have cognitive schemas concerned with self-deprecation, where those who become anxious have schemas concerned with anticipating harm. The patient learns to master his problems by becoming fully aware of these schemas and then reevaluating and changing his thinking. The cognitive therapist teaches the patient to "think more realistically and adaptively, thus reducing symptoms."[23] The meaning of the patient's experience, i.e., the schemas by which he interprets the world and fashions his behavior, are again a predominant focus. One might classify cognitive behavior therapy as an action-oriented psychotherapy that disavows the relevance of insight. I think this would be a mistake. If insight is defined as "the acquisition of new understanding," then "insight is highly compatible with how cognitive behavioral therapies are currently practiced."[24] The attention paid by cognitive therapists to the influence of conscious thinking on behavior change "creates a domain of potential compromise and harmonious discourse between the earlier and more puristic insight and action orientations."[25]

Thus one of the aims of an insight-oriented psychotherapy is to bring hidden motives and unacknowledged patterns of behavioral and emotional responses to reflective awareness. During this process, the dialogue ebbs and flows. There are frequent pauses and long stretches of silence in the secular confessional. The therapist might use these intervals to engage in a reverie about how the patient's current disclosures relate to those made during other sessions. An ongoing facet of the therapist's attunement to the patient is keeping a vigilant watch for emerging or recurrent themes, reactions, or patterns of relating to self and others. These are expressive interactions of emotions and behavior that express the meanings patients attribute to their lived experience. Call these the core-aspect dynamics or themes of the patient's lived experience. One possibility is that the patient is quite familiar with these aspects but not sure what to make of them. The patient might be unsure of the meaning they express. He might also be conflicted about the meaning he thinks they should express. There can also be core-aspect dynamics, however repetitive, that the patient does not recognize and understand. It is crucial for the therapist to be both aware of the patient's core aspects and recognize whether or not the patient is aware of them. In some cases, a therapist must be both aware of core aspects of which the patient is unaware, and recognize that the patient is unaware of them. It falls to the therapist to make at least provisional sense of the core aspects and then share that sense with the patient. Call these the therapist's interpretations of the patient's core aspects.

The interpretations will depend to some extent on the theoretical orientation of the therapy. A therapist might work with one mode of psychotherapy or integrate ideas and techniques from various modes. Using one or various modes, there can be questions of fit: whether, and if so the extent to which, the patient accepts and appreciates the therapist's interpretations. This can depend partly on whether the therapist has tried to fit the patient to a mode of psychotherapy or tried to fit a mode of psychotherapy to the patient. It can also depend on the patient's credulity and the extent to which she is able and willing to reflect critically on the therapist's theoretical orientation and the interpretations that reflect it.

A normative premise that I defend is that patients ought to accept the epistemic responsibility for doing just that. Hence my argument that there are certain epistemic virtues that therapists and patients who care about aspiring to veridical insights and self-knowledge ought to cultivate in the working through of psychotherapy. Both should strive to cultivate intellectual dispositions of character that mitigate credulity and fortify the virtue of intellectual autonomy. This virtue is not a hyper-individual mode of solipsism; instead, it pivots on epistemic regulation by self and others. Nobody learns in a vacuum completely absent from some degree of dependence on or influence by others. Others influence our intellectual practices in various ways. They may provide us with information and training; guide us with their critical, probative questions; provide us with inspirational ideals and expectation; and encourage us with emotional support in our more difficult epistemic efforts.[26]

Hence the need for patients to be open to the challenge of evaluating a therapist's theoretical perspectives and interpretations rather than accept them uncritically.[27] They should develop an ability to think for themselves without being improperly dependent on or influenced by a therapist. This does not rule out the autonomous acceptance by a patient of various things she has learned from her therapist. There is even a sense in which a patient might internalize her therapist. Suppose the therapist offers the empathic support and understanding that the harshly self-critical patient denies herself. One can see this patient as needing to internalize what the therapist offers her so she can offer it to herself and, in effect, learn to become her own therapist.

The sessions between therapist and patient are time-limited, usually lasting about an hour. During that time, the patient is supposed to receive the therapist's sustained attention. This regard is unlike the attention the patient receives from most anyone else. The patient is the therapist's sole focus and is led to understand that, for the time involved, the therapist's world revolves around the patient's. The patient takes center stage in that the session is about him. This often results in a unilateral drift. Therapists can come away knowing more about their patients than most, but patients may learn much less if anything "personal" about their therapists. Therapists differ about whether, and if so the extent to which, they should reveal themselves to patients. Some view themselves as passive mirrors through which patients will self-explore, i.e., the less patients know about therapists, the better able are therapists to reflect patients' conflicts and the better able are patients to avoid divagation. Therapists also differ greatly on what they will do during a session. Some remain impassively detached from a patient's suffering, perhaps offering Kleenex when tears are shed, but some become more involved. Donald Winnicott once offered a distraught patient the solace of his family home.[28]

## 2.3 **Psyche and Life**

The lives of patients have an external dimension that can be observed by others and an internal one that cannot. I take the view that these dimensions interpenetrate as the patient's embodied being-in-the-world. Therapist and patient explore this mutual influence in the secular confessional. Still, it is not uncommon for people to think that psychotherapy is essentially an interior exploration of a patient's contained mind, of her inner terrain so to speak. We might think that the patient wants the therapist to trace channels of connection in her mind. These connections might explain how traumatic events in a patient's life have influenced troublesome thoughts and behavior, or how problematic patterns of thought have influenced the meaning that patients ascribe to certain events and the way they behave in response. A therapist might think that her theory and praxis allows her to do that, i.e., to find these connections, not to create them. As if a pre-existing set of tunnels through which emotional signals can pass were somehow laid out beneath the mind's quotidian topography. The therapist digs through the surface, brushing away layers of topsoil until the rooted channels of connection are revealed.

There might be some cases where these channels are fairly clear-cut. Imagine a set of occurrences with traumatic impact that a young child internalizes. A boy is repeatedly humiliated by his father for minor infractions: he does not come home on time, he loses a new scarf, or does a poor job cutting the lawn. The father's temper is overpowering. He secludes the boy in a room, and forces him to strip from the waist down. He makes the boy watch as he removes his belt and carefully doubles it before beating him. Suppose these repeated episodes incise a neural pathway to the boy's amygdala. His "fight or flight response" becomes switched on at the slightest provocation. He comes to see the world as a threatening place in which he is ever vulnerable to attack and abasement. Others see him as anxious, easily agitated, and lacking self-esteem. The traumas result in a pattern of emotional and behavioral reactions that the boy perpetuates into adulthood. He learned to smother his anger at an early age for fear of his father's retaliation. But as he grew older, he learned to express it in pre-emptory retaliation. His own temper became a protective suit of armour. Nobody would get close enough to humiliate him again. He becomes Seneca's Angry Man and we will meet him again in chapter five.

There will be other cases where the channels of connection are not clear. What links will therapist and patient trace then? A historical connection of facts is part of the exploration. Things have happened to the patient: failures, triumphs, and accidents. She has done unto others and others have done unto her: loves won and lost, people who have come and gone but left lasting effects that color her thoughts. These are the facts and occurrences of her life, the record of births, deaths, times, dates, people, and places. If she knows, then she knows these things have happened. Some of these occurrences have set her back. She has not been able to take them in her stride and move on. Far from having long since occurred, they infiltrate her present and get in her way. She worries that her future will be stunted by her past. But where to begin?

Thus the first order of business for the therapist is to get a sense of why the patient has sought treatment. This initially involves finding out what things have happened to the patient and what things she has done. The patient's grasp of the facts may not be pristine. Even if we assume that she does not want to deny their occurrence, the events of her life may have been dimmed or modified in myriad ways by memory. This can make connections hard to discern. We cannot assume that therapist and patient will discern the same channels of connection. The therapist might regard the connections traced by the patient as part of what gets in her way. The patient might see the different connections traced by the therapist as obstructive. Or perhaps the patient wants the therapist to do all the work, i.e., to trace definitive connections through which her vexed emotions and behavior will be explained by the relevant historical events. In that case, credulity is arguably an epistemic disposition that responsible therapists and patients should strive to avoid. I hope to show that there are cases in which epistemic and ethical responsibility is built into the goals and methods of psychotherapy.

Note that I have referred so far to the facts of what folk psychologists might call the patient's external life. It would be sufficiently complicated if these were the only facts of concern but they are not. There are also the facts of the patient's inner life, the life of his psyche. Psychodynamic, existential, and cognitive behavioral therapies all acknowledge this terrain, although they differ in the depth and detail with which they attempt to map it. This is the life of memories, private desires, wishes, and phantasies. It is also the life of the patient's object relations: of the people and images he carries around in his head, the significance they assume for him, and the way he relates to them. Memories can be distorted: conversations might be remembered accurately as what was said, or imagined as what we wanted to say. Thus the conversations imagined can become the conversations remembered. These internal dialogues can continue for years and be re-imagined as what we would say now of certain persons and the ways in which we interacted with them. The things that have happened to people and the people involved become objects of phantasies that can have a transformative effect on both memories and the way the patient views the world. Phantasies of persecution can render the world a threatening place. This terrain is much harder to map. Hence the reliance of psychotherapy on some theory of mind, self, or personality structure.

Psychodynamic therapy digs deepest in attempting to explore this terrain. Existential and cognitive behavioral therapies avoid exploring the patient's subconscious and thus stay closer to the surface. But the patient's responsibility for sustaining meanings, values, and patterns of thought, as well as her ability to change them, are no less relevant to each of these psychotherapies. The responsibility cannot fall on the therapist alone because there is no guaranteed epistemic privilege by which therapist or patient can claim a definitively accurate mapping of this psychic topography. Problems can arise if one or the other believes they have that privilege. As we'll see, Jopling's conceptual analysis of placebo response in psychotherapy is a testament to what can happen if a confused patient buys into a therapist's uncritical belief that their theoretical orientation offers the only key to the patient's problem, or that they have the only tools and compass by which a patient's psychic terrain can be accurately mapped.

Occurrences from psychic and external worlds are only part of the terrain. We cannot detach them from the emotions and meanings with which the patient invests them. If a person knows herself, then she knows how she feels about these occurrences and what they mean to her. Channels of connection relate external facts and psychic events to emotional resonance and reverberant meanings. But some people become patients because they do not know themselves and are troubled by it. They are, in various ways, pained by emotional resonance and reverberant meanings. Coming to know the origin and development of their problems is not enough to change them. If we think of the mind as like an interconnected set of software programs, then knowing how one of them is structured is at best a first step toward redesigning it. Therapists who do cognitive behavioral therapy are well aware of this. But think of a patient who lacks a sense of connectedness to her life. She might be falling apart because she lacks the channels through which events, emotions, and meaning are connected in a way that enables her to live well. She may not know what to make of what she has done or of what has been done to her. She could be dissociated from or mystified by her experience. She might be deceiving herself about the meaning of things, as when a woman convinces herself that her husband's beatings are motivated by love and concern. I will explore a case in which a patient feels that her experience lacks a meaning that she can live by. This is the Demoralized Woman and we meet her in chapter four.

If only memory was a depository that would reliably furnish the essential experiences that could digest the problems that plague the patient's present.[29] But the most accurate remembrance is not necessarily curative. Even the woman who allegedly could not forget suffered continually from depression. The most exact visualization of past events did not furnish her with transformative insights.[30] A memory that eidetic would recall every painful experience with its original force and vivacity. And that is precisely what patients with post-traumatic stress disorder want to stop doing. For many other patients, there can be gaps in memory and lacunae in meaning; empty craters and canyons in the terrain. This means that some patients will have to map their own channels and formulate their own meaningful connections.

Novelists are well aware of the reciprocal relation between fiction and fact. Referring to the tactics of interpretation in psychoanalysis, Rieff notes that the creation of meaning in therapy for the patient's "random acts indeed resembles literary creation ... [and that] meaning does not emerge out of the raw material of incident and language in a piece, at once."[31] Facts do not resonate by themselves; facts are what the patient responds to. Facts are felt, and become more or less meaningful, or perhaps assume different meanings, as a patient's sense of how his life is unfolding changes over time. Emily Fox-Gordon claims that the need to render our lives into narrative form is writ on our genes.[32] This is an assumption that is not distant from the experience of many patients. Over time, the imagination transmutes facts into a narrative that offers up personal connections. Norman Mailer spoke of having to examine, reduce, and refine an amalgam of facts to create a record of the given that breathes with the life of those who experienced it.[33]

If this creation is a joint venture between therapist and patient, then the possibilities of a placebic folie à deux will ramify. How do we navigate the veracity of these insights? How should this exploration of self be epistemically regulated? If we could write up a factually exact record of the events of a life in perfect sequence, we would still have to formulate a meaningful story line. Some aspects of that story will emerge from the facts, others will be imputed to them. One can construct a narrative going forward by making our lives conform to a fundamental, identity-conferring project, as an adolescent Jean Genet committed himself to being a thief.[34] Or one can claim to discern the narrative arc of one's life by looking back on it. Either way, we will edit with varying degrees of self-awareness; some experiences will be thematized and others ignored or rendered tangential. The objective facts do not do all of the work. We shape them and they shape us. But we need some criteria by which a meaningful and coherent narrative is formulated as more or less true. We also need to distinguish justified and possibly true insights about ourselves and others, discerning between insights and self-serving deceptions or rationalizations that can alienate a patient from the self she wants to explore.

Hence the concern philosophers can have about the veridicality of the insights that patients acquire in psychotherapy. This concern is not unique to the secular confessional. It can apply to any dialogue by which persons aim to "get to the bottom" of a mutual concern. The vagaries of memory, the shifting meanings that we attribute to the events in our lives, our capacity for self-deception, and our limited ability to track and verify the truth of another person's factual claims are unavoidable. The possibilities for missing the point, for not hearing what we should, and for believing what we should not are immeasurably great. And yet we do not paralyze ourselves with bewilderment. We address instead the ethics of belief. If we aim to be responsible and reliable seekers of truth, then we should cultivate those dispositions of character that are conducive to responsible and reliable inquiry.

I think a case can be made that the pertinence of psychotherapeutic theory and praxis is to some extent patient-relative. I cautiously offer an analogy to psychopharmacology. Psychiatric drugs do not always exert uniform effects on patients with the mental disorders they are designed to treat. They can induce minimal, no, or even paradoxical effects. They might work on a given patient only if titrated to an idiosyncratic dosage or used in combination with other compounds. Neurochemical adjustments do not conform to a one-size-fits-all model. The characteristic factors of psychotherapies that might be shown superior to placebos in some random control trials could also have variable effects on different patients. Psychological adjustments might have to be suitably tailored to the unique contours of the patient's psyche. Psychotherapy may have to be suitably tailored to the patient. In fact, there is a psychotherapeutic integration approach that aims to do just that.[35] This can also be a matter of prospective patients deciding whether their problems fit a psychotherapy's theory, aims, and praxis. For instance, if I want only to quell my anxiety about temporary confinement in small spaces, or dispel my compulsive urge to wash my floor whenever I have stepped on it, I may well have little interest in a psychodynamic exploration of my childhood and family relations.

Frank construed psychotherapy as a healing relationship in which technical procedures and background theory were incidental. He concluded that the ideas behind different modes of psychotherapy were largely irrelevant and "suggested that almost any theory will do if the patient is willing to accept it."[36] Those ideas would not be irrelevant to epistemically critical patients who are only motivated to acquire insights that have a strong warrant for being true. Indeed, I argue that patients should approach the working through of psychotherapy with just that motivation. Credulity would be an epistemic vice that might further self-deception. Debates about how the talking cures induce therapeutic benefit do not obviate the notion that a patient's efforts to work through problems and strive for a greater self-understanding can be an epistemically normative endeavor. Psychotherapy might offer the committed patient an exercise in character development that is best elucidated in virtue epistemic, as well as virtue ethical terms. Debates about the mechanisms by which psychotherapy works might ignore this idea in favor of stressing biomedical analogies to drug effects and generic anthropological paradigms of healing relationships.

## 2.4 A Tincture of Pyrrhonism

Let me summarize Jopling's skeptical challenge. On what he calls "the standard view," a link between self-exploration, insight, and healing is commonly assumed in psychodynamic therapy. It allegedly provides a valid method of exploration and discovery that enables patients to acquire bona fide insights and veridical self-knowledge. A therapist's interpretations reframe a patient's self-exploration and assist her in acquiring her own insights. As such, those interpretations are assumed to be specific, effective, and non-suggestive instruments of therapeutic change. The standard view also assumes that a patient's acquisition of insight is a primary agent of therapeutic change. The motivating agency of these insights is not held to depend on suggestion, persuasion, or expectancy effects. It is rather an intrinsic property of the insights themselves.[37] Patients "who have acquired insight," says Jopling, are supposedly "well on the way to achieving" higher degrees of "self-acceptance, emotional maturity, and self-responsibility than before they began psychotherapy."[38] But Jopling notes that there is little discussion about the criteria that evaluate interpretations and insights as true or false. As between correspondence, coherence, and pragmatic theories of truth, the epistemic questions of what makes interpretations and insights true or false and the criteria for specifying good or bad evidence for their truth or falsity are often left unaddressed. Interpretations and insights "may need to be graded on an epistemic scale of better to worse, or more truth-tracking and less truth-tracking."[39]

This point is not lost on contemporary psychodynamic theorists. Eagle notes the "formidable challenge" of determining the degree to which, if at all, interpretations and insights enhance self-knowledge.[40] Jopling notes that there are currently no definitive answers to questions about the truth criteria by which this challenge might be met. Absent such criteria, Jopling claims we have good reason to not take the standard view at face value. Although he affirms that many patients benefit from psychotherapy, he questions the assumption that they always benefit from veridical insights based on a therapist's truth-tracking interpretations of their psychic lives.[41] Jopling offers an alternative hypothesis of therapeutic change that revolves around the conceptual possibility of placebo effects in psychotherapy. It might be the case that psychotherapy works instead by elaborate explanatory fictions. These are false explanations of the patient's emotions, psychology, behavior, and personality that "when offered as interpretations or acquired as insights are powerful enough to rally the mind's native healing powers."[42]

Jopling propounds a moderate skepticism that does not rule out the possibility that psychodynamic interpretations and insights can lead to self-knowledge. But if therapists and patients are going to claim that interpretations and insights are true, then they bear the onus of adducing a theory of truth by which those claims can be confirmed. Jopling gives no indication as to what theory of truth would meet his challenge, but without one we might just as well mistake false interpretations and insights for true ones or vice versa. Patients run the risk of acquiring false beliefs about their psychic lives and becoming estranged from themselves through self-deception.

One of the strengths of Jopling's analysis is that its critical bite is not limited to the "fractionated field" of psychodynamic therapy.[43] The moderate skeptic's challenge raises a host of questions that can easily be extended to other psychotherapies that place therapeutic value on a patient's acquisition of insight. This extension depends, of course, on how we define insight. Jopling acknowledges the different meanings and contents of insight across psychotherapies, e.g., the meaning and contents of Jungian insights differ from those of classical Freudian psychoanalysis, which can differ in turn from those of short-term psychodynamic therapy. There are nonetheless shared constituent ideas that encompass these meanings in a concept of insight.[44]

The following is Jopling's formal delineation of the common elements that link this concept across a range of therapies.[45] Insight is a condition that occurs when a patient acquires an emotionally resonant, action-guiding comprehension of four conditions. Patients must comprehend (1) the kinds and symptoms of the disorders (or problems in living) from which they suffer; (2) the causes and/or meanings of those disorders or problems; and (3) the relation between those causes and/or meanings "and their overall life processes," e.g., "their behaviors, emotions, and personality". As per condition (4) the insight can occur when patients believe that their comprehension of (1)--(3) is valid "and when they *believe* that the validity of their understanding is measured against and confirmed by the relevant psychological, behavioral, and historical facts."[46] The fourth condition only applies once (1)–(3) have been satisfied. As a "notional or belief-indexed state," condition (4) is satisfied even if in fact a patient's comprehension of (1)–(3) has no such validity.[47]

This formal definition can be applied, with minor modifications, to existential and cognitive behavioral psychotherapies. The former aims to catalyze patients into facing the unacceptable givens of existence (e.g., impending death, freedom and responsibility, isolation, and the challenge of finding meaning in an indifferent universe). The aim of existential psychotherapy is to help patients to liberate themselves "from the disturbing consequences of denial, evasion and distraction by enabling them to change their response to the existential givens."[48] Patients may deny, evade, or distract themselves from facing up to their responsibility to assume their freedom and provide their life with meaning through identity-conferring commitments. These denials are the source of disturbance and conflict.The existential therapist focuses on what the patient does not want to know and cannot open up to. The patient is challenged to realize the nature and extent of her denials and confront the ineluctable givens of existence.[49] This enables her to begin the work of formulating the purpose and meaning of her life. Cognitive behavioral therapy aims to help patients see through and reject their negative patterns of self-defeating thought. Patients come to understand how life events led to the development of their core beliefs and behavioral coping strategies as they learn to test and evaluate them. On these definitions, it is hard to see how existential and cognitive behavioral psychotherapies can avoid placing therapeutic value on insight. Thus Jopling's skeptical challenge applies to them as well.

Although I concede the skeptical challenge to self-knowledge in psychotherapy, I argue that responding to it does not require a theory of truth that would do the kind of verificatory tracking that Jopling would endorse. The attainment of true propositions about states of factual affairs might be less important to patients than attaining a prescriptive sense of how they ought to live and who they ought to be. Jopling's argument suggests that acquiring something less than veridical self-knowledge may not dissuade prospective patients from committing themselves to a talking cure. Why should responsible patients forego benefit that does not meet strict conceptual standards of propositional truth, when they can virtuously acquire epistemically and practically justified beliefs that enable them to better deal with, or perhaps even resolve, their problems in living? These beliefs could at least be plausibly and possibly true.

Accordingly, we can imagine therapists and patients working together to devise interpretations (leading to insights) through the cultivation of epistemic virtues that will regulate the inquiry. I posit three main "epistemic goods" that can arise from these insights: (1) some of these interpretations plausibly amount to justified true beliefs about the patient, which can be expressed in propositional truth claims that could be confirmed outside the secular confessional; (2) other interpretations may amount to justified beliefs that are worth holding given the epistemic quality of the inquiry that produced them; and (3) others might transmute into the non-propositional good of a patient's holistic self-understanding. I discuss these three epistemic goods in the next chapter. Thus a therapist can say to a patient: "We have applied reliable epistemic virtues in our inquiry and can be confident that our interpretations are worth holding because they are true to your core aspects. We can also be confident that your insights into how you should change and reconfigure yourself are worth living by." These are cases in which we arguably have less reason to be burdened by the skeptic's challenge given our confidence in the personal qualities by which we regulated our inquiry.

## 2.5 **Conclusion**

Jopling's formal definition of insight is not specifically psychodynamic. It does, I suggest, require a clear and engaged awareness of illuminative and motivational meaning. Insight must first be transparent to the patient. He must be aware that he has gained a new understanding. Insights must then clear things up for him. This can be done in a variety of ways. Insights can dispel confusions, answer uncertainties, resolve doubts, assuage anxieties, dispel fears, and acknowledge and evaluate denials, faults, personal strengths, and weaknesses.

It is often thought that insight involves a greater awareness of what motivates a patient, what drives or causes him to think and act in certain ways. Insight can also involve a greater awareness of how a patient's schemes of meaning influence his lived experience of being-in-the-world and how that lived experience can be changed by the creative choice of new schemes of meaning. Insight can involve a new sense of meaning that reconfigures a patient's previous understanding of himself. Insight should also, I argue, reflect a grasp of the "core aspects" of a patient's being. This term encompasses the central facets of his life that define his personality and way of being-in-the-world. We can thus speak of discovering and identifying a patient's interactional patterns and the wishes and expectations associated with them.[50] We can also identify his predominant thematic attitudes and views of the world—how he views himself and his relation to others.

Problems with acquiring a veridical sense of a core self are widespread, although their ethical nature is not always acknowledged. In the context of psychotherapy, insight also requires the patient's engagement; it is derived from a searching inquiry of self in which truth matters. Thus therapist and patient ought to conduct this inquiry in a way that reflects a commitment to obtaining insights that, to the best of their abilities and knowledge, are plausibly true. Insights must also reveal directions for self-transformation and inspire the patient to change for the better.

Finally, there may not be one stand-alone theory of truth that will answer the skeptic's challenge. I aver this for reasons both conceptual and empirical, the latter reasons being related to what is actually possible in psychotherapeutic practice. Therapists must take much of their patients' disclosures on trust. Freud insisted that psychoanalysis would not work unless the patient was completely honest, but therapists are limited in their abilities to track and verify even the external facts of a patient's life. Granted, there are steps therapists can take, especially if they suspect deception. Newman and Strauss recommend that therapists gather information from numerous sources, such as family members, previous clinicians, and clinical records.[51] But we do not expect therapists to leave their offices in an exhaustive search for either documentary evidence or for witnesses who can provide credible testimony about a patient's version of what happened. This task could ramify the longer the therapy lasts. Empirically verifiable facts aside, no therapist can verify the accuracy of a patient's memories of how she felt about what happened. As a rule, a therapist will not know what a patient remembers accurately, let alone how the patient has modified her feelings over time. The patient herself might be unaware of how far her recollections stray from what actually happened or what she felt when it happened, if it happened. Therapists might be even less able to reliably know when patients are deceiving themselves.

Therapists have to work mainly with what the patient discloses here and now on the assumption that he is telling the truth or recollecting to the best of his ability. The therapist can be alert for indications that the patient is being deceptive but there is no reliable method of verification, no failsafe way to confirm the truth or falsity of much of what a patient says. Many therapists concede that while intuitive and inferential skills at detecting deception can be developed to varying degrees, they must still become accustomed to living with ambiguity, confusion, and uncertainty about the extent to which patients are being truthful. Kottler notes that most of what therapists know about their patients is based on their own self-reporting, which can be "notoriously unreliable, distorted, inaccurate, biased, selective, and self-serving." Patients will often present themselves in the best or worst possible light in order to gain "sympathy, respect, or validation." They sometimes enjoy the power of deceiving therapists who occupy a position of authority and expertise as "truth-seers."[52] No small wonder that some therapists argue for a robust degree of skepticism about much of what patients disclose.[53] In sum, the truth-tracking abilities of therapists are limited ab initio in ways that no practical method of distinguishing true statements from false ones can completely surmount.

A formal theory of truth may only take us so far down the road of empirical truth-tracking, i.e., checking and verifying the truth of a patient's account of her life. I maintain that it is a mistake to think that the relevant empirical issues of truth-tracking will be settled once we resolve our conceptual questions about the apposite theory, or theories, of truth. While I think that some version of a correspondence theory of truth may, to a limited extent, inform the activities of recounting a narrative, compiling case histories, and verifying therapeutic insights, I am not convinced that it is always relevant to the ethical self-understanding that some patients seek in psychotherapy. An objective relation to truth by which the standards for self-knowledge are detached from the person who seeks it does not, I suggest, capture the transformative relation to meaning and behavior at which insight-oriented psychotherapy aims.

I offer a virtue epistemological response to the skeptic's challenge. Psychotherapy can and ought to be guided by certain epistemic commitments that may better enable therapists to offer interpretations and patients to acquire insights that are possibly true. In striving to know ourselves, we need more than a theory by which we can distinguish true from false propositions. We need to cultivate the intellectual virtues that can optimize the epistemic capacities of those who must regulate the inquiry. Psychotherapy should involve the responsible reflective agency of patient and therapist alike. This is my argument in the next chapter.

## Notes

1. Cf. **Perry London**, *The Modes and Morals of Psychotherapy*, 2nd ed. (New York: Hemisphere Publishing Corporation, 1986), 47.
2. **David Jopling**, *Talking Cures and Placebo Effects* (Oxford: Oxford University Press, 2008).
3. **London** takes a similar approach to delineating the common features of insight-oriented psychotherapy sessions. See *The Modes and Morals of Psychotherapy*, 51–52.
4. Cf. **Phillip Rieff**, *Freud: The Mind of the Moralist* (New York: Anchor Books, 1961), 364.
5. **American Psychiatric Association**, *Diagnostic and Statistical Manual of Mental Disorders*, 4th ed. (Washington, DC: American Psychiatric Publishing, 1994); American Psychiatric Association, *Diagnostic and Statistical Manual of Mental Disorders*, 5th ed. (Washington, DC: American Psychiatric Publishing, 2013).
6. Cf. **Michel Foucault**, *A History of Sexuality: An Introduction* (New York: Vintage Books, 1978), 56-59.
7. **Herbert Fingarette**, *The Self in Transformation: Psychoanalysis, Philosophy and the Life of the Spirit* (New York: Harper and Row, 1965), 18–19.
8. **Fingarette**, *The Self in Transformation*, 57.
9. **Morris N. Eagle**, *From Classical to Contemporary Psychoanalysis: A Critique and Integration* (New York: Routledge, 2011), note 3.
10. **Charles Taylor**, "Self-Interpreting Animals," in *Human Agency and Language: Philosophical Papers 1* (Cambridge: Cambridge University Press, 1985), 45–76.
11. **Sigmund Freud**, "Identification," in *The Standard Edition of the Complete Works of Sigmund Freud*, ed. James Strachey (London: Hogarth Press, 1953), 105.
12. **London**, *The Modes and Morals of Psychotherapy*, 55–56.
13. **London**, *The Modes and Morals of Psychotherapy*, 56.
14. Cf. **Rieff**, *Freud: The Mind of the Moralist*, 84, 110.
15. Cf. **Rieff**, *Freud: The Mind of the Moralist*, 84. According to Rieff, Freud narrowed his idea of the meaningful in these very ways.
16. **London**, *The Modes and Morals of Psychotherapy*, 119.
17. **Alan C. Tjeltveit**, "The Good, the Bad, the Obligatory, and the Virtuous," *Journal of Psychotherapy Integration* 14 (2004): 158–159.
18. **John Margolis**, *Psychotherapy and Morality* (New York: Random House, 1966), 21.
19. **Robert L. Woolfolk** and **Dominic Murphy**, "Axiological Foundations of Psychotherapy," *Journal of Psychotherapy Integration* 14 (2004): 179.
20. **Rieff**, *Freud: The Mind of the Moralist.*
21. Cf. **Rieff**, *Freud: The Mind of the Moralist*, 364–365. Rieff was referring specifically to the classic psychoanalytical session in which the therapist sits behind the patient who is prostrate on a couch. Many of the ideas that informed these sessions are relevant to other modes of psychotherapeutic encounter. Rieff's eloquent descriptions can thus be seen as having a broader application.

22. **London**, *The Modes and Morals of Psychotherapy*, 72.
23. **Augustus J. Rush**, "Cognitive Therapy," in *The Psychotherapy Handbook*, ed. R. Herink (New York: New American Library, 1980), 91–94.
24. **Martin Grosse Holtforth** et al., "Insight in Cognitive-Behavioral Therapy," in *Insight in Psychotherapy*, eds. Louis G. Castonguay and Clara E. Hill (Washington, DC: American Psychological Association, 2007), 57.
25. **London**, *The Modes and Morals of Psychotherapy*, 118.
26. Cf. **Robert C. Roberts** and **W. Jay Wood**, *Intellectual Virtues: An Essay in Regulative Epistemology* (Oxford: Oxford University Press, 2007), 285, 258–261.
27. Cf. **Roberts** and **Wood**, *Intellectual Virtues*, 260–267.
28. **Brett Kahr**, *D. W. Winnicott: A Biographical Portrait* (London: Karnac Books, 1996), 85–86.
29. Cf. **Norman Mailer**, *The Spooky Art: Thoughts on Writing* (New York: Random House, 2004), 206–207.
30. **Jill Price**, *The Woman Who Can't Forget: The Extraordinary Story of Living with the Most Remarkable Memory Known to Science—A Memoir* (New York: Free Press, 2009).
31. **Rieff**, *Freud: The Mind of the Moralist*, 131.
32. **Emily Fox Gordon**, *Book of Days: Personal Essays* (New York: Spiegal & Grau, 2010), 222.
33. Cf. "**Norman Mailer**: The Art of Fiction," in *The Paris Review Interviews*, vol. III, ed. Philip Gourevitch (New York: Picador, 2008), 418–419.
34. **Jean-Paul Sartre**, *Saint Genet: Actor and Martyr*, trans. Bernard Frechtman (New York: George Braziller, 1963).
35. **Rutger Willem Trijsburg**, **Sjoerd Colijn**, and **Jeremy Holmes**, "Psychotherapy Integration," in *The Oxford Textbook of Psychotherapy*, eds. Glen O. Gabbard, Judith S. Beck, and Jeremy Holmes (Oxford: Oxford University Press, 2005), 95–110.
36. **Joel Paris**, *Prescriptions for the Mind: A Critical View of Contemporary Psychiatry* (Oxford: Oxford University Press, 2008), 25; Jerome D. Frank and Julia B. Frank, *Persuasion and Healing: A Comparative Study of Psychotherapy*, 3rd ed. (Baltimore: Johns Hopkins University Press, 1993).
37. **Jopling**, *Talking Cures and Placebo Effects*, 72–77.
38. **Jopling**, *Talking Cures and Placebo Effects*, 77.
39. **Jopling**, *Talking Cures and Placebo Effects*, 48.
40. **Eagle**, *From Classical to Contemporary Psychoanalysis*, 227.
41. **Jopling**, *Talking Cures and Placebo Effects*, 21, 23.
42. **Jopling**, *Talking Cures and Placebo Effects*, 19.
43. **Jopling**, *Talking Cures and Placebo Effects*, 68.
44. **Jopling**, *Talking Cures and Placebo Effects*, 68.
45. **Jopling**, *Talking Cures and Placebo Effects*, xxi–xxii. Jopling lists the following as insight-oriented, psychodynamic psychotherapies: "psychoanalysis in its many incarnations, Jungian analysis, short-term psychodynamic psychotherapy, and the newer psychodynamic theories of ego psychology, object relations theory, self-psychology, and interpersonal psychology." In his earlier paper, he included

existential psychotherapy. See Jopling, "Placebo Insight: The Rationality of Insight-Oriented Psychotherapy," *Journal of Clinical Psychology* 57 (2001): 21.

46. **Jopling**, *Talking Cures and Placebo Effects*, 68.
47. **Jopling**, *Talking Cures and Placebo Effects*, 69.
48. **Hans W. Cohn**, *Existential Thought and Therapeutic Practice: An Introduction to Existential Psychotherapy* (London: Sage Publications, 1997), 24.
49. **Cohn**, *Existential Thought and Therapeutic Practice*, 24, 121.
50. **Eagle**, *From Classical to Contemporary Psychoanalysis*, 217, note 3.
51. **Cory F. Newman** and **Jennifer L. Strauss**, "When Clients Are Untruthful: Implications for the Therapeutic Alliance, Case Conceptualization, and Intervention," *Journal of Cognitive Psychotherapy* 17, 3 (2003): 224–252.
52. **Jeffrey Kottler**, "How Well Do We Know Our Clients?" in *Duped: Lies and Deception in Psychotherapy*, eds. Jeffrey Kottler and Jon Carlson (New York: Routledge, 2011), 10.
53. **Helen K. Gediman** and **Janice S. Lieberman**, *The Many Faces of Deception: Omissions, Lies, and Disguise* (New York: Jason Aronson, 1996).

Chapter 3

# Epistemic Virtues in Psychotherapy: A Response to the Moderate Skeptic's Challenge

## 3.1 Introduction

Psychotherapy raises normative questions about the qualities of patients who aspire to know themselves. I think this aspiration is relevant to the patient's cultivation of epistemic virtues. Hacking reminds us that we value the way people can fulfill themselves by gaining a realistic self-understanding that enables them to face the past as well as the present.[1] Eagle argues forcefully that the pursuit of self-knowledge and truth is emblematic of psychotherapy.[2] Saks concedes that psychotherapist and patient might never learn anything true about the patient's psyche, and have to be satisfied with "less-than-certain" interpretations, but they are still committed to finding the truth. Indeed, neither therapist nor patient should be satisfied with interpretations that do not "make a claim to possible truth."[3] When therapists aim for knowledge of their patients, and patients aim for knowledge of themselves, I believe that epistemic virtues might denote therapeutically desirable qualities that those who aspire to truth should have. Thus psychotherapy can raise questions about the kind of aspirants to truth that therapists and patients should be.

Yet Jopling propounds a moderate skepticism: if therapists and patients are going to claim that interpretations and insights are true, then the onus is on them to adduce a theory of truth by which those claims can be confirmed. Although patients run the risk of acquiring false beliefs about their psychic lives and becoming estranged from themselves through self-deception, we cannot rule out the possibility that some psychodynamic interpretations and insights can lead to self-knowledge. But how to distinguish true insights from false ones? And Jopling has yet another concern: therapists can resort to an "interpretive force-fitting" by which the patient's experience is made to fit the theoretical framework of the therapy.[4] Responding to the skeptic's challenge on Jopling's terms requires a theory that would track the truth of interpretations and insights while avoiding the distortion of a patient's experience through theoretical force-fitting.

I understand Jopling to be posing his challenge in such a way as to make justification a property of beliefs. Since I think we ignore the skeptic's challenge at the risk of self-deception, I do not attempt to refute it. Instead, I recast the terms by which it is posed. My response to the challenge indicates an implicit set of epistemic virtues that can regulate psychodynamic explorations. I argue that virtue epistemology can inform psychotherapy and is prefigured by certain aspects of psychodynamic thought. I assume that some patients can control whether they take interpretations and insights seriously and how carefully they evaluate them. As such, they can be praised or blamed for how well they exercise that control. I elaborate these ideas with two principal arguments from which a number of ancillary ones are developed.

I argue first that it is constructive to recast the challenge as a virtue epistemologist who relates justifiedness to the truth-conducive virtues by which persons regulate inquiries. The warrant of beliefs is thus to some extent derivative from those virtues. This recasting will not address, let alone rebut, every skeptical concern. But it can invite a response that has normative implications for the agency of patients who aspire to the epistemic goods of psychotherapy, i.e., for how they ought to conduct themselves in working through the treatment process. Thus I take the skeptic's challenge as a motivational call to cultivate epistemic virtues that make patients responsible and conscientious aspirants to truth and self-understanding.

Working from a hybrid approach to virtue epistemology that is broadly responsibilist, I make the second principal argument that patients ought to cultivate epistemic virtues, and I attempt to show that these virtues are implicit in psychodynamic theory. These dispositions of inquiry better enable them to attain the epistemic goods of psychotherapy, of which I posit three: (1) justified true beliefs about the "core aspects" of their motivations, defenses, and behavior; (2) justified beliefs about their motivations, defenses, and behavior that are possibly true to the extent that they are generated by truth-conducive virtues; and (3) a holistic, partly normative self-understanding that, while not a propositional belief state, can amount to one's own vision of living well.

I claim that the cognitive attainment of justified true beliefs (good 1) is but a first step in coming to know oneself by working through a normative process of changing one's life for the better, and that justified beliefs (good 2) can be worth holding if conscientiously acquired. Holistic self-understanding (good 3) might be of cardinal importance to patients who aim to better meet the challenge of living well by reconfiguring their vision of a satisfactory life that reflects their character. A virtue epistemology that is not focused exclusively on true propositions and the states of believing in them is arguably well suited to helping us understand the normative aspirations to good 3.

## 3.2 **Definitional Parameters**

I have already defined psychotherapy as an ethically value-laden endeavor that does not deal exclusively with the truth or falsity of claims about the extra-linguistic facts of patients' lives—it also deals with evaluating the meanings they attribute to those facts, and those evaluations are often ethical. Psychotherapy is connected intimately with ethical self-improvement insofar as many patients wrestle with the gap between the persons they would like to be and the persons they are.[5] It can thus revolve crucially around ethical issues of how the patient ought to relate to self and others and what changes of personality or character are most worth cultivating. Indeed, the "everyday work" of psychotherapists can involve them unavoidably in the formation of value judgments on the patient's ways of relating to self and others. Ramzy, for instance, thought it "preposterous" to deny that the accumulated evidence of psychoanalysis had begun to "show that certain patterns of psychic organization are more conducive to a better way of life than others."[6] I note as well Matthews' claim that psychotherapy can facilitate a patient's efforts to live by a more satisfactory vision of life.[7]

Jopling's skeptical challenge sets some of the parameters of my analysis. As he specifies psychodynamic therapies as quintessentially insight-oriented, I will refer only to insight-oriented therapies and only to patients who engage with them to seek greater self-knowledge. Although I believe that therapists must bring intellectual virtues to psychotherapy, I will concentrate on how the working through is a virtue-epistemological endeavor for the patient. I define insight-oriented psychotherapy as representing a category of approaches that assume that a patient's behavior is disturbed due to a lack of awareness of underlying motivations, feelings, beliefs, fears, and desires. Psychotherapy thus involves the elucidation of these internal dynamics and the development of a better sense of self-understanding that facilitates more satisfactory, adaptive behavior.[8]

A principal goal of psychodynamic therapy is to expand the patient's awareness of unconscious conflicts, feelings, desires, motivations, and behavior patterns.[9] Eagle broadly defines current psychodynamic approaches as means of enabling patients' reflective capacity to think about their own mental processes and those of others. This capacity enables patients to be aware of their "core aspects," i.e., their recurrent problems, motivations, and patterns of emotional response and behavior. These core aspects are the basis on which we infer any "hidden expectations, assumptions, anxieties, desires . . . wishes [and] defenses . . . underlying . . . [one's] habitual relationship patterns . . . that have governed important aspects of one's cognitive, affective, and interpersonal life."[10] The aim is for patients to make meaningful connections among different aspects of their thoughts, feelings, and reactive behaviors, but these connections are often blocked by repression.

To overcome these mental blocks, the therapist's interpretations supposedly generate insights into the assumptions and defenses that underlie a patient's habitual attitudes and relationship patterns. I define "interpretation" as a "communication by the [therapist] aimed at expanding the patient's self-knowledge by pointing out connections in the patient's mental life of which he or she was previously unaware,"[11] and I use the word "insight" to mean the patient's development of new knowledge or understanding that is related to the issues she presents in therapy.[12] As such, a patient's insight into how her mind works might take the form "this is how I act and think when I am anxious, or conflicted, or worried that I might offend someone."[13]

Jopling's reservations about our capacities for self-deception indicate his concern with the process by which such patients form beliefs based on psychodynamic theory. Jopling wants interpretations and insights to follow the true course of a patient's life as opposed to the predetermined dictates of theory. Jopling does not use truth-tracking in Nozick's sense of a process that would eschew justification and produce true beliefs in suitably described counterfactual conditions.[14] He uses it in the broad sense of connecting beliefs correctly with extra-linguistic facts about the world or the psychic life of the patient and wants graded evidence and justificatory reasons for believing interpretations and insights. Belief-based epistemologists may acknowledge intellectual virtues, but define them as dispositions that enable one to attain knowledge where knowledge is defined as tracking the truth. They do not define knowledge as a normative accomplishment of a person who regulated her inquiry with truth-conducive intellectual virtues.[15]

I take the skeptic's challenge to be formulated in the traditional terms of an epistemologist who focuses on static belief states. These are evaluated as either justified or justified and true—if true, then the belief state amounts to knowledge. Jopling criticizes the standard view of psychodynamic therapy from the standard view of epistemology: the latter view holds that knowledge is essentially a mode of belief with a focus on propositional knowledge, i.e., knowing-that-p, transcribed as isolated statements in which a predicate or object is affirmed or denied regarding a subject. Philosophers who see knowledge as adequately grounded, justified true belief usually propose a conception of, or supplement to, that grounding in order to specify the logically necessary and sufficient conditions of any belief being an instance of knowledge.[16] In other words, epistemic inquiry aims essentially to explain what knowledge and justified belief are and to determine the extent to which we are able to acquire belief states about true propositions.[17]

## 3.3 First Argument: Recasting the Moderate Skeptic's Challenge as a Virtue Epistemologist

I consider the skeptic's challenge, and formulate my response to it, in virtue epistemological terms. I argue first that it is constructive to recast the challenge as a virtue epistemologist who relates justifiedness to the truth-conducive virtues by which persons regulate inquiries. I have three reasons for thinking this. First, this recasting can motivate the consideration of other resources besides the justificatory properties of detached belief states. When the primary focus of evaluation is on those properties, the person who inquires after knowledge is overlooked. If that person can significantly shape the quality of the inquiry (i.e., how well it is conducted), and that quality is to some extent truth-conducive, then we might want to focus on the kind of personal engagement that cultivating that quality involves. We can think of knowledge as a normative achievement of the person who responsibly seeks it.

Hence my second reason for recasting the skeptic's challenge: a focus on justifiedness as based in part on the epistemic virtues of persons can highlight the responsible and qualitative contribution that patients ought to make to a psychotherapeutic inquiry. I offer the cautious claim that the truth conduciveness of these virtues will go some way to making beliefs worth holding as at least possibly true to the extent that they have been conscientiously acquired.[18] My third reason for recasting the skeptic's challenge is that a focus on discrete belief states will not accommodate the kind of holistic self-understanding which might be important to some patients.

For a virtue epistemologist, the primary focus is not the largely third person "evaluation of states of belief as 'justified' or as 'knowledge.'" It is rather the regulation of deliberation and inquiry. We will only understand how well we can regulate inquiries, control the formation of opinions, and inquire well to the extent that we should "by giving a central role to states such as [epistemic] virtues."[19] Success in inquiry depends in no small part on our epistemic character. A patient's intellectual honesty, for instance, will influence whether she generally comes to doubt interpretations or insights when she is presented with sufficient counter-evidence. This focus might have its own relevance to psychotherapeutic inquiries. As I noted in chapter two, an objective relation to truth by which the standards for self-knowledge are detached from the person who seeks it may not apprehend the transformative relation to meaning and behavior at which psychotherapy aims. If I am right about this, then at least virtue epistemology puts the person back in the picture, i.e., it re-engages the standards for self-knowledge with the qualities of the person who seeks it.

Some virtue epistemologists hold that being intellectually virtuous is essentially about having the cognitive faculties or dispositions that reliably report the truth. Epistemic virtues are dependable cognitive tools that enable the inquirer to attain the truth more often than not—this is the reliabilist approach.[20] Others "decentralize" epistemic questions about the status of beliefs and focus instead on relating intellectual habits and dispositions to the active agency of those who seek truth through inquiry. As such, aspiring knowers can be assessed as responsible or irresponsible and traits like impartiality and courage are intellectual virtues that persons who desire the truth should want to have—this is the responsibilist approach.[21] My response to the skeptic's challenge owes much to Linda Zagzebski's hybrid conception of virtue epistemology. Although it undercuts a strict division between camps, she feels that her theory is foundationally "closer" to responsibilism, but not quite as different from reliabilism as might be implied. It posits virtues as having a motivational and a success component that might connect the internal and external aspects of epistemic virtues and epistemically virtuous acts.[22]

Zagzebski defines a virtue as "a deep and enduring acquired excellence of a person, involving a characteristic motivation to produce a certain desired end and reliable success in bringing about that end."[23] Each virtue has two components: a motivational component and a component of reliable success in attaining the motivational component's aims. Epistemic virtues are defined by a general motivation for knowledge, which clearly includes a desire to acquire true beliefs and avoid false ones. This motivation leads one to follow rules and belief formation procedures that are known to one's epistemic community to be truth-conducive, i.e., it leads us to be aware of the reliability of some belief-forming processes and the unreliability of others. It also leads one to acquire the motivational components specific to the individual epistemic virtues, e.g., open-mindedness, fair-mindedness, and intellectual flexibility. The virtue of open-mindedness, for example, involves both the specific motivation to be receptive to new ideas, which derives from the general motivation for truth and understanding, and reliable success in forming undogmatic beliefs. The general motivation for knowledge generates the specific motivation to be open-minded because being receptive to new ideas is truth-conducive and recognized by the epistemic community as being so.[24]

This specific motivation leads one to acquire behavior patterns characteristic of the open-minded "even if it means overcoming contrary inclinations."[25] It is insufficient to be merely aware of epistemic rules and procedures. One will not use them reliably without the general and specific motivational components of epistemic virtues. A person has the epistemic virtue of being open-minded when he has the specific motivation to inquire in a receptive way and is reliably successful in actually conducting unprejudiced inquiries. We observe that open-mindedness is "truth-conducive in the long run."[26] This is truth-conduciveness in the "weak sense that behavior of this sort usually leads to the truth," i.e., if we examine a large number of a person's beliefs formed over time, then we see that open-mindedness is generally truth- conducive. We should take "a very large class of instances of the virtue as the set of cases against which reliability is measured."[27] Being closed-minded tends to prevent persons from having true beliefs and knowledge as it obstructs the motivation to go through the reliable processes of belief formation.[28] We see the blend of internal and external elements here: epistemic virtues are in part internal dispositions to attain true beliefs and in part reliable external mechanisms for attaining them.

In sum: if epistemic virtues can (1) motivate the following of rules and procedures that can exclude bad grounds for belief, (2) are generally truth-conducive, and (3) are incorporated into psychodynamic praxis, then one has some support for thinking that an epistemically virtuous psychodynamic praxis can be truth-conducive and a better means of psychic inquiry than a crystal ball. I accept Saks' concession that therapists and patients might never learn the truth and have to be satisfied with "less-than-certain" interpretations.[29] However truth-conducive epistemic virtues might be, their application in psychotherapy does not guarantee the truth of interpretations and insights. But it arguably strengthens the plausibility of a claim to their possible truth.

There is an interesting parallel to epistemic responsibility in contemporary psychodynamic thought. Morris Eagle writes of an "epistemological stance" that is reflected in a "devoted and truth-seeking attitude" that therapist and patient must share in their efforts to guide the patient to "an understanding of who he or she is and has the potential to be."[30] He views this attitude as incompatible with an instrumental reliance on confabulated "narratives" and explanatory fictions.[31] Although Eagle focuses on the therapist, the internalization of this attitude by the patient is crucial. Greenson wrote of the importance of the patient's identification with the exploring, truth-seeking analyst.[32] A key aspect of the therapeutic alliance is the patient's incorporation of the practice of "seeking the truth and telling it as fairly and accurately as possible."[33] The truth-seeking attitude does not guarantee self-knowledge. Indeed, there are daunting challenges to attempting to provide definitive answers to questions about the validity criteria for enhanced self-knowledge in psychotherapy.[34] But the application of this truth-seeking attitude might make an understanding and appreciation of the patient's psychic reality more likely. On a virtue epistemological account, therapists and patients can be assessed as responsible or irresponsible and a devoted, truth-seeking attitude is a central intellectual virtue that therapists and patients who aim for veracious insights would want to have.

Jopling refers to epistemic responsibility, although he does not expand on its implications. He claims that those who evince "little epistemic caution" by making apathetic "efforts of corroboration and evaluation" are more culpable than those who aim for comprehensiveness and rigor in their "knowledge-seeking" activities. He thus implies that therapists have some degree of epistemic responsibility to avoid "blinding theoretical dogmatism" and "narrow-minded prejudice" against certain types of patient. He also implies that patients can bear some degree of onus to avoid "bad faith" epistemic practices for which they can be held accountable, such as "self-deception, willful ignorance, quasi-rational selective attention, and selective forgetting."[35] These are ways by which patients can lead themselves astray. But Jopling does not imply that acting in epistemic good faith will guarantee veridical interpretations and insights—even the most well-intentioned therapists and patients acting responsibly and with epistemic good faith might be mistaken. The point implied is to regulate the inquiry with epistemic practices that aim to avoid "misdiagnoses, misinterpretations, misprognoses, and misapplied treatment methods."[36]

One implication of Jopling's reference to epistemic responsibility is that patients should understand their vulnerability and suggestibility in the psychotherapeutic context. He also implies that they are responsible for understanding and satisfying "consensually endorsed epistemic norms about the nature, range, and relevance of therapeutic evidence . . . [and norms of] practical reason and inductive inference in matters psychological."[37] A virtue epistemologist would argue that these norms of evidence and practical reasoning are not applied by rote. Their best application reflects the epistemic qualities of the person who puts them to use and these are the intellectual virtues that should regulate the inquiry into grounds for belief.

## 3.4 **Second Argument: Psychotherapy and the Cultivation of Epistemic Virtues**

The following virtues highlight the regulative contribution that the patient's epistemic character can make to a psychodynamic inquiry. The central virtue of epistemic conscientiousness, or responsibility, is a disposition to try one's best to arrive at the truth. Ways of being epistemically responsible and conscientious might involve the regulative traits of impartiality, open-mindedness, intellectual sobriety, courage, and perseverance.[38] All of these traits would be applied in service to a devoted and truth-seeking attitude. They would motivate epistemic good faith and inform the application of the norms of evidence and practical reasoning to which Jopling arguably holds therapists and patients responsible. While much work is required to give a robust account of these traits, there is renewed interest in elucidating the intellectual virtues that can inform a regulative epistemology.[39] My own outline is thus provisional.

Courage and perseverance denote dispositions to repeatedly confront aspects of oneself that one usually wants to avoid. It also speaks to the "working through," or the effort the patient has to make to overcome the resistances that prevent insight from leading to therapeutic change. Impartiality denotes an effort to avoid unreflective bias, a disposition to weigh and assess interpretations and insights for cogency, fit, and (insofar as possible) fidelity to relevant facts. Impartiality can also denote a disposition to critically evaluate the extent to which psychodynamic interpretations and insights can distort, as well as articulate, one's lived experience. For instance, given her traumatic past, a patient may feel too sympathetic toward a specific psychodynamic approach that aims to explore it. She may also feel unduly sympathetic to any plausible interpretation that seems to explain her problems and affords her a quick flight into a superficial psychic health. This implies that open-mindedness, or a disposition to acknowledge and evaluate ideas that can challenge or apparently confirm the assumptions that a patient has about herself, is an essential epistemic virtue to cultivate.

Intellectual sobriety denotes a disposition to be habitually free from inordinate, uncritical, and credulous enthusiasms for theories and ideas. In sum, the patient should strive to cautiously appraise appealing interpretations and insights. These traits are as much about epistemic autonomy as they are about responsibility. This connection is not lost on Roberts and Wood. On their conception of a regulative epistemology, the virtue of intellectual autonomy is an appropriate, self-regulating ability to think for oneself without being improperly dependent on or influenced by others. It involves a dispositional awareness of the extent to which our epistemic life is influenced by others as well as a disposition to evaluate this influence as intelligent laypersons. It can thus be a reasonable, active, and motivated use of guidance from another. Intellectual autonomy is expressed in one's careful choice of the appropriate person from whom guidance is sought, the humility of being open to help, a modicum of skill for posing questions and raising the issues to be explored, enough understanding to grasp and evaluate what others contribute to the dialogue, and "the self-confidence to venture judgments" on what they say. In other words, it is the antithesis of obsequious acceptance. When combined with a willful orientation to "the more serious epistemic goal of truth," this dialectical versatility enables the person who seeks help to assimilate the other's input and make it her own.[40] There is a similar versatility in psychotherapy if we allow for the patient's internalization of a devoted and truth-seeking attitude. This attitude can enable patients to emotionally avow interpretations and insights as their own as they come to understand who they are and have the potential to be.[41]

We see other interesting parallels to the virtues of intellectual responsibility and autonomy in psychodynamic thought. On Meissner's account, bilateral negotiation is a core component of the process by which therapist and patient achieve mutually satisfying and meaningful interpretations. The patient's openness to therapeutic influence must be balanced by increasing degrees of "circumspection, independence, and judgment."[42] This dialectic stands in marked contrast to "any form of indoctrination, compliance, or submission."[43] Meissner regards the patient's autonomous evaluation of interpretations and insights as a key responsibility in psychoanalysis. Excessive trust in a therapist or mode of psychotherapy is an impediment to this exercise of independent judgment. Part of the analytic work with such overly compliant patients is the effort "to enable them to find a more balanced position that avoids the difficulties of naïve and willing compliance, or unwillingness to evaluate or criticize the analyst's contributions."[44]

The patient who seeks self-understanding displays an initiative that psychotherapy aims to strengthen by having the patient assume increasing degrees of responsibility, e.g., bringing material for the therapy to work on and associating, processing, and even interpreting it. Given a balanced trust in the therapist and a stable sense of intellectual autonomy, the patient is gradually more willing and able "to undertake, on his own recognizance, . . . the interpretation and application of his own therapeutic material."[45] Levy and Inderbitzin have also stressed the therapist's efforts to enable "the patient's capacity for independent (autonomous) self-observation" and "post-treatment self-analysis." Psychotherapy can thus promote intellectual responsibility and autonomy by expanding the patient's ability to recognize intra-psychic conflicts "and to utilize the signal function generated by dysphoric affect to activate self-observing capacities rather than automatically resort to regression and defense."[46]

I posit these traits as epistemic virtues that a patient who aspires to self-knowledge should want to have. The probative dialogue and exploratory reflection by which patients might attain well-justified and possibly true remedial beliefs about themselves arguably requires their cultivation. At the very least, the seeker after truth should be a seeker after justified belief and self-understanding that has been conscientiously acquired through the regulative application of truth-conducive virtues. The responsibility for cultivating these virtues in the working through of psychotherapy is ultimately the patient's.

## 3.5 What Virtuous Epistemic Regulation Aims to Avoid: Interpretive Force-Fitting

A virtue epistemologist argues that while self-knowledge is not guaranteed, we foreclose on its very possibility if we make a less than virtuous effort to attain it. One aspect of this effort is to make therapy accurately fit the suitable patient instead of resorting to what Jopling terms an "interpretive force-fitting" by which the patient is made to fit the theoretical framework of the therapy.[47] This refers to the long-standing criticism that psychoanalysts "stuff the unconscious with all manner of things which to no one's surprise they then find there when they look."[48] The history of psychoanalysis affords some illustrative examples. One thinks of Freud's insistence that Dora's disagreements about the accuracy of his interpretations were actually covert avowals. When she denied being in love her father, Freud took this as proof that his interpretation was correct. "If one takes this 'No' not as the expression of an impartial judgement, of which the patient is in fact not capable, disregards it, and continues the work, proofs will soon appear that 'No' in such a case signified the desired 'Yes.' "[49] Gay notes that "Freud thus opened himself to the charge of insensitivity, and worse, of sheer dogmatic arrogance: . . . he was not listening now, but forcing his analysand's communications into a predetermined pattern."[50] A virtue epistemologist need not deny the dynamic of resistance to claim that we need more than a patient's disagreement with an analyst's interpretations to confirm it.

Consider as well the recollections of psychoanalyst Sandor Rado, who was analyzed in 1910 as part of his clinical training. He claimed that analysis in those early years "was not the study of the life of a person, digging out what the turning points, what the problems were. ... It was a search for the opportunities to apply certain Freudian insights . . . [e.g.,] castration complex, Oedipus complex, narcissism, oral eroticism, anal eroticism . . . the patient's production was very soon oriented by that, because he saw that what is fruitful is if he talks about these matters."[51] It might be argued that Rado was not above some interpretive force-fitting of his own. Some of his later work on female masochism revolved around claims that any woman who expresses castration fantasies is reflecting the "salient, precipitating" trauma that allegedly follows "with striking frequency" after a young girl first "catches sight of a penis."[52] She experiences the "humiliating reflection" that she lacks one, which "produces severe psychic pain, and terminates in something like a paralysis of feeling."[53] These ideas provoked an interesting debate about evidentiary standards and the assessment of evidence. Rado's claims were criticized by Karen Horney as "unwarranted generalization[s] from limited data" that did not account for the influence of broader factors inherent in "the culture-complex or social organization in which the particular masochistic woman has developed," e.g., "social conditioning" and stereotypical attitudes toward females.[54] Horney notes that Rado assumes this trauma to be the cause of female masochism, as opposed to its expression, without offering "evidence of its factual occurrence."[55] While Horney conceded that Rado's ideas might be theoretically "stimulating," she objected to the assumption that they are the exclusive links "in a chain of proof."[56] In resisting this effort to make patients fit what she took to be a limited theory, Horney warned against overestimating the importance of "anatomical-psychological-psychic factors" in the analysis of women.[57]

One might well be wary of therapists who do not think beyond the limits of their own theories and of patients who are unwilling to question them. Donald Winnicott's wife Claire became enamored with Melanie Klein's theories after reading one of her papers. She sought a Kleinian analysis and expressed frustration with her first analyst when she did not receive "Kleinian interpretations" of her dreams. Of her later analysis with Klein herself, Winnicott recalled the predominant application of theory over clinical exploration: "She implanted her own theory on what you gave her. You took it or left it."[58] Claire Winnicott was capable of leaving it. She recalled her disillusionment with Klein when she related a "thoroughly Kleinian dream" that it took the formidable analyst twenty-five minutes to interpret. A number of Klein's colleagues felt that her lengthy interpretations were "too coloured by a wish to defend the accuracy of her theories" at the expense of exploring the material that her patients presented.[59]

It is tempting to speculate on the extent to which Claire Winnicott might have colluded with Klein in an uncritical acceptance of her theories. And yet it appears that she retained a sense of her epistemic autonomy and could question the relevance of the Kleinian interpretations she sought. I concede Jopling's point that there can be cases in which a patient starts having psychodynamic dreams after being inculcated in psychodynamic theory by a therapist.[60] But that does not negate the possibility that a patient might be having dreams that she only comes to understand after reflecting on a psychodynamic interpretation. One can just as easily imagine philosophy students having moderately skeptical thoughts after reading skeptical theory. We cannot endorse a view from nowhere. Surely any person engaging in self-inquiry through dialogue with another brings a truckload of assumptions and beliefs about her motivations and behavior to the encounter. It is difficult to imagine a revelation of self-knowledge occurring in isolation or absent the background context of these assumptions. Even if it could so occur, the subject of this revelation would have to re-contextualize her newfound insight in either the background assumptions she had before the revelation, a new set of background assumptions that she would somehow create after the revelation, or some combination of the two. If motivations and behavior are the objects of inquiry, then they are connected intimately to the inquirer and affected by the process of inquiry. As Code might put it, neither self-knowledge nor justified true beliefs would be a product of inquiry "that stands alone in the sense that details of the processes of its production are irrelevant to its structure, content, and/or evaluation."[61]

The anecdotes about interpretive force-fitting indicate a deliberate effort by therapists to subordinate patients to the predetermined dictates of theory. They implicate credulous patients who might be duped into theory adherence. Others might collude in this subordination while others might question it. A virtue epistemologist would argue that interpretive force-fitting does not constitute an intellectually conscientious attempt at accurately understanding the patient. There is arguably no epistemic virtue in Freud's admission that "Quite often we do not succeed in bringing the patient to recollect what has been repressed. Instead, we produce in him an assured conviction of the truth of the construction, which achieves the same therapeutic result as a recaptured memory."[62] This is precisely the type of remark that raises a red flag for the skeptic, and well it should. Interpretations made on the basis of persuasion can amount to the kind of self-serving explanatory fictions that so concern Jopling. They would epitomize the idea that the warrant for a patient's holding any belief *p* would reflect nothing more than the fact that it makes him feel better.[63] Again, this is to eschew the requirement for being motivated to settle for nothing less than critically discerning, credible grounds for belief.

We may yet succeed in showing that psychodynamic interpretations and insights can never be good grounds for either self-knowledge or justified true beliefs. But we have not shown that their formulation requires the distortions of interpretive force-fitting. I think we have succeeded in showing that we have reason to be skeptical of their uncritical acceptance by therapists and patients alike. Insight-oriented psychotherapy may yet go the way of phrenology but, in the meantime, we ought to do nothing less than rely on intellectual virtues and good faith epistemic practices to regulate these psychic explorations. If justifiedness follows from a belief's source in intellectual virtues, which are properties of persons, then how might we evaluate the three epistemic goods of psychotherapy? I will consider each in turn.

## 3.6 Epistemic Goods in Psychotherapy

### 3.6.1 Justified True Beliefs

It might be thought that an ideal solution to the epistemological vagaries of interpretations and insights would be some version of a correspondence theory of truth, at least insofar as it expresses an important and, for some, enduring feature of the concept of truth: that a statement is true only if there is some extra-linguistic thing in the world in virtue of which it is true.[64] Psychotherapy depends significantly on autobiographical memory and we might question whether a correspondence theory could accommodate its shifting, protean nature. Not all such memories are pristine copies of the original experience. Crucial details can be forgotten or re-imagined. Memories can be reconfigured to incorporate new information or new interpretations acquired through hindsight. Plus, therapists are limited in their abilities to independently verify many of the claims their patients make. Hence the epistemic responsibility placed on patients to be ruthlessly honest in the therapeutic encounter. This is a demanding virtue to cultivate. Do Rousseau's *Confessions* indicate unsparing frankness or engaging guile and mounting paranoia? Rousseau wants us to believe the former, and he insists that while he might omit facts, he cannot be mistaken about what he has felt. Yet he is well aware that recurrent fictions can acquire great consistency over time and become definitively fixed in his mind.[65]

But there is surely some room for knowledge of extra-linguistic facts in psychotherapy. Zagzebski defines knowledge as "a state of belief arising out of acts of intellectual virtue."[66] If the inquiry is regulated by epistemic virtues, there are bound to be some very basic, true, and definitive things we can say about a patient, about who she is and how she lives; about how she regards herself and relates to others. Call these the "core aspects" of the patient.[67] Again, this term encompasses the central, relatively stable structures of the patient's psyche that have governed important facets of the patient's cognitive, affective, and behavioral life. We can thus speak of discovering and identifying a patient's recurrent relationship patterns and the assumptions, anxieties, wishes, conflicts, and expectations associated with them.[68] We can also identify a patient's predominant thematic attitudes and views of the world, how she views herself and her relationships.

Consider how a patient's core aspects can be captured in the following prototypical interpretations: "You react with anger when your masculinity is threatened"; "You avoid commitment in relationships (avoidant attachment pattern) because you've repeatedly experienced rejection"; and "The central function of your anger at your sister is to avoid experiencing the anger you feel towards your parents." For the latter interpretation to be a justified true belief that is true to a core aspect of the patient, it must be based on "the discovery and awareness that the patient has been angry at her parents and defended against becoming aware of that anger and owning it as hers."[69]

The core aspect interpretations noted above are not especially deep or thick with speculative theory. They are theory-thin descriptions that could plausibly be confirmed with evidence about the patient's relationship patterns gathered outside the therapeutic encounter and evaluated according to Jopling's "standard norms of practical reason and inductive inference in matters psychological."[70] If core-aspect interpretations are arrived at responsibly through the virtuous application of these norms and procedures, then intellectual virtues might influence our attitude about the relevance of meeting every skeptical challenge. Skeptical challenges can arise even when epistemic responsibility motivates us to reflect on the grounds of our beliefs and to control the standards we employ in the course of that reflection. But this deliberation can enable us to have confidence in a virtuously conducted inquiry and to resist the claim that responding to skepticism is *always* central to the epistemological task.[71] If the function of interpretations is to be true to the patient's core aspects, then some of them will not have to be evaluated in Hume's study.

Psychotherapy does not stop at core-aspect interpretations, as if a therapist were supposed to say: "We have verified that, as a matter of fact, you carry a lot of guilt and hostility. Our work is done." As Lear would put it, psychotherapy is an extended practical deliberation and there is always the further question of how the patient should live with these facts.[72] If patients need to cultivate honest attentiveness and care in their self-reflective inquiries, then responsible agency is implicated in the development of the best reflective selves and our evaluations of the best ways to explore them. Patients' commentaries on their actions and beliefs can also be used to "generate verifiable and falsifiable hypotheses" about their behavior, about their values, and the kinds of reasons they find compelling.[73]

### 3.6.2 **Justified Beliefs**

Zagzebski regards justified beliefs as "what a person who is motivated by intellectual virtue, and who has the understanding of his cognitive situation a virtuous person would have, might believe in like circumstances."[74] Patients can acquire justified but tentative beliefs about their motivations, defenses, and behavior that are based on limited evidence and serve as starting points for further investigation. These suppositions can be reported in hypothetical statements after surviving cautious and critical reflection involving epistemic virtues, norms of practical reason, and inductive inference.

Truth is not guaranteed here. Jopling argues that interpretations will not induce therapeutically beneficial insights unless patients believe them to be true, i.e., that interpretations track the facts.[75] He does not discuss patients who evaluate interpretations and insights with intellectual sobriety. Such patients might find the supporting evidence to be limited, or regard the interpretations as being too theory-thick and speculative. Other interpretations might fare better. To varying degrees, the truth-conduciveness of the virtues that generated these beliefs can provide a warrant for truth. Indeed, if Jopling is right that patients can derive therapeutic benefit from willfully believing interpretations they initially know to be false, then there seems to be no reason why patients could not derive some therapeutic benefit from believing that they have conscientiously acquired a promising hypothesis about their conflicts.

If we define justification in terms of epistemic character, such that one has justification if and only if one is exercising one's intellectual virtues, then success in psychotherapeutic inquiry depends on the regulative virtues, the cognitive skills of practical reasoning, and the evaluation of evidence. If we are confident that our psychotherapeutic inquiries reflect our epistemic virtues, then we can be confident that they have been regulated toward truth-conduciveness.[76] Virtuously acquired beliefs that are less than certain can still be worth holding.

### 3.6.3 **Holistic Self-Understanding**

Our epistemic aspirations in psychotherapy might transcend the acquisition of true propositions. Knowledge might have broader and richer modes of awareness than propositional belief states. A primarily responsibilist theory has the advantage of holding that valuable epistemic states include holistic states of understanding.[77] This is a mode of knowledge which is not propositional in the sense of being reducible to, or synonymous with, a statement in which a predicate or object is affirmed or denied regarding a subject. Understanding does not focus on a discrete object. It focuses instead on the relation of parts to other parts and the relation of a part to a whole. The object of understanding is not a discrete proposition about a belief, but rather the relatedness of part to whole.[78]

Propositions corresponding to individual belief states are not the only way reality can be made intelligible. Understanding is an appreciation of order, pattern, fit, and function. It is an awareness of how the parts of something hang together, the role each one plays in the context of the whole, and of the role that whole plays in ever-larger schemes of things. Understanding can be a holistic grasp of complex systems of propositions (e.g., stories, theories, and books) or things other than propositions (e.g., works of art, musical compositions, or the character and psychic lives of persons). While the component pieces are propositional, the structure of the whole is not. One can write out the proof of a mathematic theorem as a sequence of propositions, "but understanding the proof involves seeing the relations between the propositions, and that is not itself the knowledge of a proposition."[79]

Understanding comes in degrees of grasping connections and fitting things together. While we think propositions are true when they match the state of affairs they are about, we say that understanding has to be more or less adequate to what it is about. One can have a highly intelligent, coherent, but inaccurate interpretation of something that would not qualify as an understanding, e.g., one can comprehend a creationist theory of the universe without that theory being true. Understandings can be more or less deep, insightful, and penetrating. They aim at comprehensiveness as opposed to exactness and we often have to sacrifice the latter for the former.[80] Deeper understandings require long and arduous effort. Roberts and Wood put it this way: "Understanding often emerges only with concerted intellectual activities like exploring, testing, dialectical interchange, probing, comparing, writing, and reflecting. These practices require virtues for their best prosecution."[81] As a matter of degree, understanding can be close enough to the truth without being misleading. Patients who attain self-understanding would have a holistic grasp of the coherence relations of their core aspects, values, and personal history.

I assume much the same thing about a patient's psyche that Zagzebski assumes about "reality." It has a structure of core aspects the propositional comprehension of which is an important therapeutic goal. I also assume that it is unlikely that the structure of a psyche is exclusively propositional. I propose holistic self-understanding as a nonpropositional comprehension of one's psyche. It is a property of persons as opposed to propositional belief states.[82] I also think it is an epistemic good of some importance to psychotherapy. Just as one might know many individual propositions that make up a body of knowledge without understanding how they cohere, we might know many facts about ourselves without understanding how we cohere.

Patients arguably want a broad appreciation of how their lives "hang together," a coalescent grasp of the order and patterns of their experience.[83] They also want a normative sense of how the facts and values of their lives should cohere. Patients can aspire through psychotherapy to having their lives coalesce in ways that better reflect their sense of who they want to be and how they want to live. Holistic self-understanding can unify their values in a vision of a more satisfactory life. One might express component parts of this vision as a sequence of propositions, e.g., "I have an identity-conferring commitment to overcoming my guilt and acquiring greater self-respect." But understanding the vision involves seeing the relations between the components, which is not in itself the knowledge of a proposition.

Eagle notes that propositional insights about one's core aspects have to be avowed and integrated into the psyche's great mass of associations and ideas.[84] Avowal is an expression of the patient's assumption of responsibility for the thoughts and feelings by which she owns the insight and the influence it will have on her deliberations.[85] As facilitative of therapeutic change, the integration of avowed insights into one's "dominant mass of ideas" can be seen as "making meaningful connections among different aspects of one's thoughts, feelings, and behaviors."[86] This can deepen a holistic grasp of how the facts and values of our lives not only do, but also *should* "hang together." It can help to organize and reconfigure what patients already know about themselves with an emergent sense of how they ought to change for the better. This enables the patient to bring her dominant mass of associations into a "mutually reinforcing network of ideas," a "larger web of value"[87] by which they understand themselves in a vision of a more satisfactory life; a vision of what it would mean for them to live well by being well. A responsibilist account is open to exploring the relevant kinds of agency by which holistic self-understanding might be attained. One attains it by developing the virtues by which one inquires skillfully about oneself. As I have defined it, the normative aspects of self-understanding implicate ethical values. This raises the question as to whether, and if so the extent to which, self-understanding is also an ethical as opposed to epistemic good.

## 3.7 **Limitations of a Virtue Epistemic Response**

There are limitations to my attempt at responding to the moderate skeptic's challenge with a primarily responsibilist virtue epistemology. Indeed, these limitations are well-known to leading responsibilists. My attempt does not provide "an easy calculus for assessing knowledge and belief claims nor [does it] provide a decision-making scale against which specific knowledge claims can be measured for validity."[88] There is much room for practical epistemic judgment in making such assessments. We have to assess more than whether norms of evidence and practical reasoning have been applied in a psychotherapeutic inquiry. We have to assess the merit of that inquiry by delineating the epistemic qualities of the persons who pursued it. These qualities have bearing on how well those norms were applied. We need a robust and thorough account of the intellectual virtues and a better idea of how they are acquired. More to the point, how are they inculcated in psychotherapy?

We should also be cautiously sober in our estimation of virtue epistemology and its potential to reorient the standard approach to theories of knowledge. Crisp avers that the way forward is not entirely clear: if we want to distinguish epistemic and ethical virtues, and ethical knowledge from knowledge of other kinds, then we need a better sense of how the two kinds of virtues might interact in an inquiry with normative dimensions related to the well-being of the inquirer.[89] I do not think that virtue epistemology can avoid, let alone resolve, every dispute over the meaning of justification. However much virtue epistemologists might claim to depart from traditional theories of knowledge, any plausible virtue epistemology will have to say a lot about beliefs and their grounding and justification.[90]

I have not determined which philosophical theory of truth might best resolve the moderate skeptic's challenge to the veridicality of psychotherapeutic interpretations and insights. I have suggested instead that the transformative, remedial beliefs and self-understandings that patients aspire to might be justified and understood as having a crucial relationship with the intellectual virtues. Justifiedness can be partly understood as being rooted in dispositional qualities of persons. We ought to bring a special self-regarding care to psychotherapeutic inquiry as our sense of ourselves and of what life is best for us may hang in the balance. Perhaps the best way to respond to the skeptic's challenge and avoid explanatory fictions is to acknowledge our propensity for self-deception and then cultivate epistemic virtues that aim to avoid it.

## 3.8 Further Thoughts on the Moderate Skeptic's Challenge

Psychotherapy can be a daunting challenge for both the faint of heart and the faint of mind. And so it should be if self-knowledge or remedial self-understandings are valued by those who commit themselves to working through their problems. Jopling's critique does not foreclose on the ethically value-laden nature of psychotherapy. "Part of our conception of what it is to be a responsible moral agent is that we place a high value on being cognizant of who we are, where we are going in our lives, what moves us to action, how we affect others and how others regard us." Although Jopling does not endorse virtue epistemology, aspects of his analysis may not be incompatible with it. He avers that the question "Who am I?" can be investigated in a "searching and fundamental manner" that reflects a critical self-evaluation of "core desires, beliefs, motives, emotions, and character traits." He notes that we ascribe genuine self-knowledge to those who pursue this question in that way and acquire greater action-guiding insight into their values and motives. An inquiry that aims to achieve this increased awareness entails "a greater degree of [epistemic] responsibility."[91]

Jopling does not shut down the possibility that psychotherapy has the potential for enabling greater action-guiding insight in each of these facets of our being-in-the-world. Most of us have the ability to become responsible epistemic and moral agents. We foreclose on that ability if epistemological skepticism leads us to conclude that a conscientious evaluation of our core aspects cannot lead to greater degrees of action-guiding insight into our values and motives.

In our striving to both know ourselves and to become responsible ethical agents, I think we need more than a theory by which we can distinguish true from false propositions. We need to cultivate the intellectual virtues that can improve the self who must regulate the inquiry. If self-evaluation through psychotherapy can lead to more than a superficial awareness of oneself, then our best assumption is that it requires much more than a superficial effort; it arguably requires a greater degree of responsibility to shoulder the commitment of cultivating the epistemic and ethical virtues by which that increased awareness can be achieved.

I think patients should engage with a mode of psychotherapy that offers a theoretical foundation that is meaningful to them. It is often claimed that some psychotherapies work better than others for certain problems. We can imagine cases in which some psychotherapies work better than others for certain persons. There should be some degree of sympathetic fit between a patient and the perspective on well-being that a talking cure assumes. Psychodynamic therapy would not fit a patient who has no interest in exploring her past but wants symptom relief from an obsessive-compulsive preoccupation with hand washing. Insofar as a patient should know what the psychotherapy is about and how it supposedly works, theoretical foundations should be part of the informed consent process.

But here is where I think that process should dispel an erroneous and counter-therapeutic assumption that patients might make about a talking cure, especially an insight-oriented one, i.e., that psychotherapy will exert specific remedial effects on patients analogous to those exerted by a drug that aims to correct a biochemical imbalance. The assumption is that psychotherapy is an intervention that is given to patients who must then let the process work on them. There is an implicit passivity to this assumption that obfuscates a link between a patient's active agency and healing. This link is best preserved when patients understand that they must work on psychotherapy. On my account, this "working through" stresses the patient's active agency in cultivating and applying intellectual virtues to both regulate and pursue a rigorous and responsible self-inquiry. A therapist can guide and inspire this effort but patients must cultivate their own virtues with diligence. If these virtues best enable patients to attain justified and possibly true beliefs about themselves, and greater self-understanding, then developing them is tantamount to developing their potential as self-healers.

Self-healing is not about complacent or passive acceptance. Patients have to be ruthlessly honest in disclosing the information about their lives on which a therapist's interpretations will be based. Those interpretations are not to be swallowed like pills. They have to be assessed by patients for their probative value, veracity, and the extent to which, if at all, they illuminate the meanings of their motivations and behavior in a way that makes their problems tractable. Insights acquired by a patient may sometimes occur like the proverbial "aha!" experience. More often than not, even that revelation will have to be preceded by an arduous and critical inquiry in which the patient is ever alert to the tendency to settle for self-serving rationalizations.

Epistemologists often fashion thought experiments in which they propose evil demons who deceive those who think they know. Given our proclivity for avoidance and denial, patients can be their own evil demons and deceive themselves. There is a sense in which epistemically responsible patients have to be vigilant in working against a disposition to credulity, aiming for dispositions like impartiality and open-mindedness as intellectual virtues that a person who desires the truth should want to have. The intellectual virtues they ought to cultivate in order to regulate their self-exploration will also be conducive to their healing. The responsibility for cultivating these virtues in the working through of psychotherapy is ultimately their own.

It might seem that I place too great a burden on patients to become knowledgeable about psychotherapeutic theory and praxis. I concede that burden, but the question is whether it is too great. Do they have to become authorities on psychotherapeutic theory? No more than they would have to be a certified mechanic to satisfy themselves that they are not buying a faulty second-hand car. My conception of patients' responsibility here is at least moderately demanding. An authentic exercise of their capacity for self-healing means that patients are responsible for acquiring a sufficient grasp of its theories and methods such that they are equipped to evaluate any interpretation that seems implausibly distant from their experience or sense of the problem. Of course, they have to evaluate their experience or sense of the problem as well. If patients are likened to client-consumers of medico-psychological services, then they should strive to be informed, knowledgeable, and critical ones. Patients should not be acquiescent dupes and not all of them want to be. Therapists should be vigilant for the ones who are too acquiescent. This is one of the edifying benefits of Jopling's skeptical challenge. One can respond to it by cultivating the intellectual virtues.

## 3.9 **Conclusion**

If the epistemic virtues are truth-conducive and regulate the application of reliable "norms of practical reason and inductive inference in matters psychological,"[92] then Zagzebski's reliability component to the virtues could apply. If therapists and patients justifiably believe in their possible truth, then these interpretations and insights might become more effective in stimulating the patients' native healing powers in the service of psychic restoration.

In insight-oriented psychotherapy, truth still matters to therapists and patients, even if patients have to resign themselves to never obtaining the whole truth about themselves, in which case they should not resign their care for and commitment to responsibly pursuing it. Saks can be read as making an epistemic virtue out of a disposition to aim for the truth. Wisdom lies in part in not losing sight of what one cares about. If a defining feature of psychoanalysis "is that it proceeds via the acquisition of beliefs about oneself" then responsible patients should settle for beliefs that have been virtuously cultivated.[93]

## Notes

1. **Ian Hacking**, *Rewriting the Soul: Multiple Personality and the Science of Memory* (Princeton, NJ: Princeton University Press, 1988), 265.
2. **Morris Eagle**, *From Classical to Contemporary Psychoanalysis: Critique and Integration* (New York: Routledge, 2011), 239; Morris Eagle, "Psychoanalytic Interpretations: Validity and Therapeutic Effectiveness," *Nous* 14 (1980): 411, 421.
3. **Elyn Saks**, *Interpreting Interpretation: The Limits of Hermeneutic Psychoanalysis* (New Haven: Yale University Press, 1999), 126.
4. **David Jopling**, *Talking Cures and Placebo Effects* (Oxford: Oxford University Press, 2008), 102.
5. **Alan C. Tjeltveit**, "The Good, the Bad, the Obligatory, and the Virtuous," *Journal of Psychotherapy Integration* 14 (2004): 158–159.
6. **Ishak Ramzy**, "The Place of Values in Psychoanalytic Theory, Practice, and Training," in *Moral Values and the Superego Concept in Psychoanalysis*, ed. Stephen C. Post (New York: International Universities Press, Inc., 1972), 218, 221–222.
7. **Eric Matthews**, "Moral Vision and the Idea of Mental Illness," *Philosophy, Psychiatry, & Psychology* 6 (1999): 373–388.
8. **Douglas J. Scaturo**, "Insight-Oriented Psychotherapy," in *The Corsini Encyclopedia of Psychology*, eds. I.B. Weiner and W.E. Craighead (New York: John Wiley and Sons, 2009), 1–3.
9. **Glen O. Gabbard**, "Major Modalities: Psychoanalytic/Psychodynamic," in *The Oxford Textbook of Psychotherapy*, eds. Glen O. Gabbard, Judith S. Beck, and Jeremy Holmes (Oxford: Oxford University Press, 2005), 10.
10. **Eagle**, *From Classical to Contemporary Psychoanalysis*, 279, 285.
11. **Richard B. Zimmer**, **Peter M. Bookstein**, **Edward T. Kenney**, and **Andraes K. Kraebber**, "Glossary," in *Textbook of Psychoanalysis*, eds. Glen O. Gabbard, Bonnie E. Litowitz, and Paul Williams. 2nd ed. (Washington, DC: American Psychiatric Publishing, 2011), 576. There has been a "sea change" in psychodynamic thought on the function of interpretation. In Freudian terms, the analyst was a kind of psychic detective who deciphered repressed desires and oedipal conflicts in the patient's mind by using interpretations to reveal "the latent meaning" in what

the patient says and does. See Goldberg, "Process, Resistance, and Interpretation," in *Textbook of Psychoanalysis*, eds. Glen O. Gabbard, Bonnie E. Litowitz, and Paul Williams. 2nd ed. (Washington, DC: American Psychiatric Publishing, 2011), 295. In Freudian terms, interpretation "reveals the modes of the defensive conflict and its ultimate aim is to identify the wish that is expressed by every product of the unconscious." See J. Laplanche and J.B. Pontalis, *The Language of Psychoanalysis*, trans. Donald Nicholson-Smith (New York: W.W. Norton and Company, 1973), 227. Perhaps the most radical contemporary account views interpretation as an implicit, ongoing, and largely unconscious conjoint process of dreaming that unfolds in the intersubjective field of therapist and patient. This process enables the "not-yet-thinkable elements of emotional and psychical experience" to be transformed through symbolization into "thinkable qualities of self-experience." See Goldberg, "Process, Resistance, and Interpretation," 295–296. Less recondite accounts still inform therapeutic practice. According to Eagle, interpretation has lost its elevated status as the principal mode of therapeutic action and has been replaced largely by various types of corrective emotional experience arising in an empathic therapeutic relationship. Hence the central contemporary tension on whether insight-generating interpretations or the therapeutic relationship "is the primary carrier of therapeutic action and the main agent of therapeutic change." See Eagle, *From Classical to Contemporary Psychoanalysis*, 272, 277, 281. The classical view that the therapeutic relationship is the background factor that facilitates the work of interpretations has been "reversed" by the view that interpretation is a background factor that functions to strengthen and facilitate the therapeutic relationship through the patient's corrective experience of feeling understood by the empathic therapist. However, insofar as much current praxis views the identification and analysis of the patient's relationship patterns, hidden expectations, assumptions, anxieties, defenses, desires, and wishes as significant—even if only as revealed by the patient's reactions to the therapist—then I think it can accommodate the definition provided. "Interpretations are statements made by the therapist that attempt to [identify and] explain the patient's thoughts, feelings, behaviors, or symptoms . . . the primary modes of therapeutic action . . . [are the] fostering of insight and the therapeutic relationship . . . " See Gabbard, "Major Modalities: Psychoanalytic/Psychodynamic," 9–10.

12. **Messer** and **McWilliams** posit the following criteria for insight in psychodynamic therapy: (1) Recognition of patterns or connections in behaviors and emotional responses as might be manifest in past and present relationships; (2) Ability to observe one's own internal processes, personality, or psychopathology, e.g., a patient who realizes she is being defensive in a therapy session; (3) Revision of pathological beliefs, e.g., the patient who realizes that it might not be his fault that his mother is so depressed; (4) Recognition of motivations of the self, e.g., the patient who realizes that she avoids writing because she fears she has no talent; and (5) Recognition of motivations of others, e.g., the patient who blamed his mother for his misfortunes comes to see her good intentions towards him. An insight has depth the closer it gets to the core of a presenting problem. It has conviction when it is fully accepted or, as I will argue below, emotionally endorsed. See Stanley B. Messer and Nancy McWilliams, "Insight in Psychodynamic Therapy: Theory and Assessment," in *Insight in Psychotherapy*, eds. Louis G. Castonguay and Clara E. Hill (Washington, DC: American Psychological Association, 2005), 21–22.

13. Cf. **Eagle**, *From Classical to Contemporary Psychoanalysis*, 279, 290. Gabbard notes that the goals of psychodynamic therapy are numerous. Psychodynamic therapists look for patterns in relationships and ask how past patterns of relatedness get repeated in the present, both in and outside the consulting room. For instance, are there recurrent conflicts that inhibit the patient in social settings? Once delineated, the therapist aims to formulate interpretations of these repetitive patterns. Another goal is to make the patient aware of problematic attachment patterns so more satisfactory modes of attaching to others is made possible. An overarching goal is to help patients "live in their own skin." This can involve therapists helping patients to understand how they lie to or hide from themselves and project their own feelings and conflicts on others. It can also involve helping them to strengthen their self-esteem. See Gabbard, "Major Modalities: Psychoanalytic/Psychodynamic," 10. Goldberg claims that the aims of analysis are no longer exclusively or even primarily focused on "uncovering the inner conflicts of patients." They pertain as well to "facilitating or fostering patients' psychical capacities (emotional flexibility, tolerance of a variety of self-states, broadened symbolic capacities, greater mobility in object relationships, and . . . an ability to deal flexibly with the complexity of psychosocial experience." See Peter Goldberg, "Process, Resistance, and Interpretation," 285–286.
14. **Robert Nozick**, *Philosophical Explanations* (Cambridge, MA: The Belknap Press of Harvard University Press, 1983).
15. **Heather D. Battaly**, "Thin Concepts to the Rescue: Thinning the Concepts of Epistemic Justification and Intellectual Virtue," in *Virtue Epistemology: Essays on Epistemic Vice and Responsibility*, eds. Abrol Fairweather and Linda Zagzebski (Oxford: Oxford University Press, 2001), 110.
16. **Robert C. Roberts** and **W. Jay Wood**, *Intellectual Virtues: An Essay in Regulative Epistemology* (Oxford: Clarendon Press, 2007), 9.
17. **Christopher Hookway**, "How To Be a Virtue Epistemologist," in *Intellectual Virtue: Perspectives From Ethics and Epistemology*, eds. Michael DePaul and Linda Zagzebski (Oxford: Oxford University Press, 2007), 192. Until the advent of Gettier problems, the standard view was associated with the idea that knowledge has three conditions: it is (1) belief that is good in the senses of being (2) justified and (3) true. Post-Gettier, there is an ongoing but unresolved debate about a fourth condition that would rule out situations where the truth corresponds to a justified true belief by accident. Much of the analysis that is unpacked from the standard view concerns the justification or warrant of beliefs, i.e., how and by what are beliefs justified?
18. Cf. **Michael DePaul** and **Linda Zagzebski**, "Introduction," in *Intellectual Virtue: Perspectives From Ethics and Epistemology*, eds. Michael DePaul and Linda Zagzebski (Oxford: Oxford University Press, 2007), 10.
19. **Hookway**, "How To Be a Virtue Epistemologist," 199.
20. **Guy Axtell**, "Introduction," in *Knowledge, Belief, and Character: Readings in Virtue Epistemology*, ed. Guy Axtell (New York: Rowman and Littlefield Publishers, 2000), xiv, xvii.
21. **John Greco** and **John Turri**, "Virtue Epistemology," *The Stanford Encyclopedia of Philosophy* (Spring 2011Edition), Edward N. Zalta (ed.), URL = <http://www.plato.stanford.edu/archives/spr2011/entries/epistemology-virtue/>.Accessed August 25, 2015.

22. **Linda Zagzebski**, *Virtues of the Mind: An Inquiry into the Nature of Virtue and the Ethical Foundations of Knowledge* (Cambridge: Cambridge University Press, 1996), 25 (note 17), 299, 334.
23. **Zagzebski**, *Virtues of the Mind*, 137.
24. **Zagzebski**, *Virtues of the Mind*, 181.
25. **Zagzebski**, *Virtues of the Mind*, 176.
26. **Zagzebski**, *Virtues of the Mind*, 176, 186.
27. **Zagzebski**, *Virtues of the Mind*, 186.
28. **Zagzebski**, *Virtues of the Mind*, 188–189.
29. **Saks**, *Interpreting Interpretation*, 126.
30. **Eagle**, *From Classical to Contemporary Psychoanalysis*, 238.
31. **Eagle**, *From Classical to Contemporary Psychoanalysis*, 238–239.
32. **Ralph Greenson**, *The Technique and Practice of Psychoanalysis* (New York: International Universities Press, Inc., 1967).
33. **Martin H. Stein**, "A Clinical Illustration of a 'Moral' Problem in Psychoanalysis," in *Moral Problems and the Superego Concept in Psychoanalysis*, ed. Stephen C. Post (New York: International Universities Press, Inc., 1972), 237–238.
34. **Eagle**, *From Classical to Contemporary Psychoanalysis*, 227.
35. **Jopling**, *Talking Cures and Placebo Effects*, 213–214.
36. **Jopling**, *Talking Cures and Placebo Effects*, 214.
37. **Jopling**, *Talking Cures and Placebo Effects*, 215.
38. **James Montmarquet**, "An 'Internalist' Conception of Epistemic Virtue," in *Knowledge, Belief, and Character: Readings in Virtue Epistemology*, ed. Guy Axtell (New York: Rowman and Littlefield Publishers, 2000), 137–138; James Montmarquet, "Epistemic Virtue," *Mind* 96, no. 384 (1987): 484–485. Although I use the virtues listed by Montmarquet, I apply them in terms of Zagzebski's hybrid approach rather than Montmarquet's pure responsibilism. The latter approach eschews any semblance of reliabilism, i.e., Montmarquet does not make truth-conduciveness a defining feature of an epistemic virtue. Like Zagzebski, I see these virtues as truth-conducive where Montmarquet does not. For a concise account of the differences between Zagzebski and Montmarquet on the issue of truth- conduciveness and epistemic virtues, see Zagzebski, *Virtues of the Mind*, 174–176.
39. **Roberts** and **Wood**, *Intellectual Virtues*, 8-9.
40. **Roberts** and **Wood**, *Intellectual Virtues*, 259, 261, 265–267.
41. **Eagle**, *From Classical to Contemporary Psychoanalysis*, 238, 287–288.
42. **William W. Meissner**, *The Therapeutic Alliance* (New Haven: Yale University Press, 1996), 176.
43. **Meissner**, *The Therapeutic Alliance*, 6.
44. **Meissner**, *The Therapeutic Alliance*, 175, 184.
45. **Meissner**, *The Therapeutic Alliance*, 185.
46. **Stephen T. Levy** and **Lawrence B. Inderbitzen**, "Neutrality, Interpretation, and Therapeutic Intent," *Journal of the American Psychoanalytic Association* 40 (1982): 1010.
47. **Jopling**, *Talking Cures and Placebo Effects*, 102.

48. **Norman Zinberg**, "Value Conflict and the Psychoanalyst's Role," in *Moral Problems and the Superego Concept in Psychoanalysis*, ed. Stephen C. Post (New York: International Universities Press, Inc., 1972), 179. Zinberg attributes this remark to one J.C. Whitehorn.
49. **Sigmund Freud**, "Fragments of an Analysis of a Case of Hysteria," in *The Standard Edition of the Complete Psychological Works of Sigmund Freud*, vol. 7, trans. and ed. James Strachey (London: Hogarth Press and the Institute of Psycho-Analysis, 1953), 1–22.
50. **Peter Gay**, *Freud: A Life for Our Time* (New York: W.W. Norton and Company, 1998), 250.
51. **Susan Quin**, *A Mind of Her Own: The Life of Karen Horney* (New York: Summit Books, 1987), 161.
52. **Sandor Rado**, "Fear of Castration in Women," *Psychoanalytic Quarterly II*, nos. 3–4 (1933): 433, 435.
53. **Rado**, "Fear of Castration in Women," 433; cf. Quin, *A Mind of Her Own*, 270.
54. **Karen Horney**, "The Problem of Feminine Masochism," *The Psychoanalytic Review* 22 (1935): 241, 248–250.
55. **Horney**, "The Problem of Feminine Masochism," 247; cf. Rado, "Fear of Castration in Women," 435.
56. **Horney**, "The Problem of Feminine Masochism," 249–250; cf. Quin, *A Mind of Her Own*, 271.
57. **Horney**, "The Problem of Feminine Masochism," 257.
58. **Phyllis Grosskurth**, *Melanie Klein: Her World and Her Work* (Cambridge, MA: Harvard University Press, 1987), 451.
59. **Grosskurth**, *Melanie Klein*, 451–452; Wilfred Bion, *Bion in New York and Sao Paulo* (Perthshire: Cluny Press, 1980), 86.
60. **Jopling**, *Talking Cures and Placebo Effects*, 102, 172.
61. Cf. **Lorraine Code**, *What Can She Know? Feminist Theory and the Construction of Knowledge* (Ithaca, NY: Cornell University Press, 1991), 110.
62. **Sigmund Freud**, *The Standard Edition of the Complete Psychological Works of Sigmund Freud*, vol. 23, trans. and ed. James Strachey (London: Hogarth Press and the Institute of Psycho-Analysis, 1953), 265–266.
63. Cf. **James Montmarquet**, "'Pure' Versus 'Practical' Epistemic Justification," *Metaphilosophy* 38, no. 1 (2007): 72–87.
64. **Michael Dummet**, *Truth and Other Enigmas* (Cambridge, MA: Harvard University Press, 1978).
65. **Jean-Jacques Rousseau**, *Confessions*, trans. A. Scholar (Oxford: Oxford University Press, 2000), 269–270, 421.
66. **Zagzebski**, *Virtues of the Mind*, 271.
67. **Eagle**, *From Classical to Contemporary Psychoanalysis*, 217 (note 3), 237–238.
68. **Eagle**, *From Classical to Contemporary Psychoanalysis*, 279, 284.

69. **Eagle**, "Psychoanalytic Interpretations: Validity and Therapeutic Effectiveness," 405; Eagle, *From Classical to Contemporary Psychoanalysis*, 288, 273.
70. **Jopling**, *Talking Cures and Placebo Effects*, 215.
71. **Hookway**, "How to be a Virtue Epistemologist," 196–198.
72. **Jonathan Lear**, "Avowal and Unfreedom," *Philosophy and Phenomenological Research* LXIX, no. 2 (2004): 452–454.
73. Cf. **Christine MacKinnon**, "Knowing Cognitive Selves," in *Intellectual Virtue: Perspectives From Ethics and Epistemology*, eds. Michael DePaul and Linda Zagzebski (Oxford: Oxford University Press, 2007), 233, 252.
74. **Zagzebski**, *Virtues of the Mind*, 241.
75. Note that Jopling uses "veridical" as meaning justifiable by the extent to which an interpretation corresponds accurately to the real world. A valid interpretation is a veridical one. Veridical interpretations give rise to veridical insights and non-veridical interpretations give rise to non-veridical insights. Veridical insights track the truth of veridical interpretations: *Talking Cures and Placebo Effects*, 76, 78. But this need not be so, as patients might acquire veridical insights into how their minds work on the basis of inaccurate interpretations. Zen koans are neither true nor false but can allegedly trigger satori. Eagle argues that since true interpretations might provoke defensive reactions, and inexact ones might have therapeutic effect, it is the veridicality and authenticity of the insight that the interpretation generates which is more important than the veridicality of the interpretation. See Eagle, "Psychoanalytic Interpretations: Validity and Therapeutic Effectiveness," 405–424.
76. Cf. **Hookway**, "How to be a Virtue Epistemologist," 200.
77. **Linda Zagzebski**, "Recovering Understanding," in *Knowledge, Truth, and Duty: Essays on Epistemic Justification, Responsibility, and Virtue*, ed. Mathius Steup (New York: Oxford University Press, 2001), 248.
78. **Zagzebski**, "Recovering Understanding," 241.
79. **Zagzebski**, "Recovering Understanding," 244; Julius Moravscik, "Understanding and Knowledge in Plato's Philosophy," *Neue Hefta fur Philosophie* 15/16 (1979): 53–69.
80. **Roberts** and **Wood**, *Intellectual Virtues*, 42–50; Wayne D. Riggs, "Understanding 'Virtue' and the Virtue of Understanding," in *Intellectual Virtue: Perspectives From Ethics and Epistemology*, eds. Michael DePaul and Linda Zagzebski (Oxford: Oxford University Press, 2007), 216–221; Zagzebski, "Recovering Understanding," 242–244.
81. **Roberts** and **Wood**, *Intellectual Virtues*, 50.
82. **Zagzebski**, "Recovering Understanding," 242, 245.
83. **Riggs**, "Understanding 'Virtue' and the Virtue of Understanding," 216–221.
84. **Eagle**, *From Classical to Contemporary Psychoanalysis*, 288, 290; cf. **Richard Moran**, *Authority and Estrangement: An Essay on Self-Knowledge* (Princeton, NJ: Princeton University Press, 2001).
85. **Moran**, *Authority and Estrangement*, 89, 93, 131, 164.
86. **Eagle**, *From Classical to Contemporary Psychoanalysis*, 288, 290.
87. **Ronald Dworkin**, *Justice for Hedgehogs* (Cambridge, MA: The Belknap Press of Harvard University Press, 2011), 192.

88. **Lorraine Code**, *Epistemic Responsibility* (Hanover: University Press of New England, 1987), 63.
89. **Roger Crisp**, "Virtue Ethics and Virtue Epistemology," in *Virtue and Vice, Moral and Epistemic*, ed. Heather D. Battaly (New York: John Wiley and Sons, 2010), 29.
90. **Crisp**, "Virtue Ethics and Virtue Epistemology," 34.
91. **David Jopling**, "Placebo Insight: The Rationality of Insight-Oriented Psychotherapy," *Journal of Clinical Psychology* 57 (2001): 34.
92. **Jopling**, *Talking Cures and Placebo Effects*, 215.
93. **Saks**, *Interpreting Interpretation*, 134 (note 12), 212.

Chapter 4

# Reparative Ethics: The Nexus Between Mental Health and Moral Virtue

## 4.1 Introduction

Meeting the skeptic's challenge introduced the notion that cultivating virtues of inquiry can lead to beliefs and self-understandings that have a credible warrant on possible truth. I extend this notion to focus on the cultivation of virtues of character that inform an ethical way of living, and here begin the transition from virtue epistemology to virtue ethics. I take the central idea of virtue ethics to be the following: goodness or rightness (which are properties of actions) is explained in terms of the action's source in generic ethical virtues (which are properties of persons, i.e., the rightness of an action follows from its source in a moral virtue and not the other way around). I start with the same broad definition of a virtue noted in the Introduction: a virtue is a multi-track character trait or disposition to perform desirable self- or other-regarding acts of a certain type, e.g., benevolent ones. These dispositions involve a complex mindset of fine inner states that inform an array of emotional responses, desires, motivations, reasons, and values. I will argue over this and the next two chapters that psychotherapy can entail a reparative ethics of virtue; in certain cases, the motivated patient strives to develop dispositions to better respond to the generic ethical demands of the world. These demands can be context-specific and thus unique to a psychotherapeutic healing project. With reference to the type of healing project I will describe, psychotherapy can be understood as a form of moral engagement between therapist and patient.[1] It can also be understood as a means of helping a patient to develop an ethical engagement with him or herself. Psychotherapy can thus be understood as an "intrinsically ethical endeavor"[2] involving other-regarding moral and self-regarding ethical responsibilities.

It has long been argued that psychiatric, psychological, and psychotherapeutic discourses are value-laden. I will argue that ethical and moral values are especially relevant to three points of reference that I will explore below: (1) conceptions of mental disorder; (2) psychotherapeutic praxis; and

(3) conceptions of positive mental health. I will attempt to show how ethical and moral values can permeate all three points of reference. This triadic analysis will be connected to a pluralistic virtue ethics in chapter five. After distinguishing between self-regarding ethical values and other-regarding moral values I concentrate on how to cultivate ethical responsibilities to develop and strengthen one's capacity for better responding to the demands of the world. These responsibilities can be understood as the patient's striving to cultivate certain virtues in the dialogical process of psychotherapy. This striving implies a valued state or condition that one pursues and to some degree attains. It is here that I will argue for a connection between conceptions of positive mental health and ethical virtues. While I do not deny that the terms "mental health" and "ethical virtue" can be distinguished, I contend that their overlap is sufficient to make some notions of ethical virtue pivotal to conceptions of positive mental health. For instance, a balanced disposition of self-love is one such notion that is arguably crucial.

There is much in positive mental health and virtue ethics that can involve efforts at self-improvement. These efforts can encompass both the ways we ought to relate to ourselves and the ways we ought to relate to others. In some cases, patients who commit to a healing project will have to develop certain virtues in their striving for symptom relief. Maintaining recovery from a major mental disorder can also involve the ongoing exercise of ethically valued character traits. In some cases, patients' characters are developed to the point at which they have rudimentary traits or dispositional capacities that can be then built up to the level of virtues. We might see them as bringing nascent virtues to psychotherapy. In other, more difficult cases, these basic dispositional capacities are much less developed but have some potential for realization in a good enough way. Working through the psychotherapeutic process can be tantamount to strengthening the dispositional capacities from which virtues can emerge.

## 4.2 **The Distinction Between Ethics and Morality**

Ethics is used often as a generic term for various ways of elaborating the moral life. Used thus, it can be understood as including both self- and other-regarding concerns and responsibilities. Hence my occasional use of the terms "generic ethics" or "ethical/moral." But I distinguish ethics and morality along Dworkinian lines in most of what follows. Dworkin uses the term morality to include principles about how persons should treat others. He uses the term ethics to include convictions about which kinds of lives are good or bad for persons to lead. Ethics pivots on the question: "What life would be a good and successful life for me?" The answer depends on one's "critical interests," or those convictions, deep evaluations, and identity-conferring commitments, however inarticulate or submerged, by which one defines a good life. My critical well-being is improved by my achieving, or having what it takes, to make my life a better life to have. By contrast, morality can provide standards for conduct that differ from the standards of my own well-being. Dworkin endorses a "challenge model" of ethical value. He holds that living a life is a challenging performance that demands skill. This is our most "comprehensive and important" challenge and our critical interests are comprised of the achievements and experiences that mean we have met the challenge well. Ethical integrity, or authenticity, is gained through effort. It is achieved when a person lives by the conviction that her life, in its central features and defining critical interests, is an appropriate one for her, and that no other life she might live would be a plainly better response to her situation. Thus, to live with ethical integrity is to live an authentic life. Ethical integrity can fail when a person "lives mechanically" and lacks a sense of having and responding to ethical convictions. It can also fail when a person deliberately avoids cultivating and responding to such convictions when she is otherwise able to do so. This can be accompanied by "a vague and persistent sense" that the person is not living as she should.[3] That vague and persistent sense might lead one to psychotherapy.

The distinction between ethics and morality might be seen as separating other-regarding obligations and duties from self-regarding ideals by which one aspires to improve one's own life. We can admire persons who fulfill these ideals in an excellent or sufficiently good way, but persons who satisfy the moral minimum of other-regarding obligations cannot be faulted for not cultivating higher standards of personal excellence.[4] I am not so sure of this, as I think there are some cases in which persons can be so faulted. If aspirations do not have to be supererogatory, then failure to live up to my chosen aspirations might make me unethical. We expect people to have a modicum of ambition to make something of their lives, and we can even speak of a self-imposed responsibility for making efforts to realize that ambition and live with ethical integrity. There is clearly an aspirational component: one has to want to live this way and we might think it a good thing that this motivation be expressed in concerted efforts and strengthened with resolve and perseverance. But this aspiration is arguably not supererogatory. There is an intuitive, quotidian sense in which we hold persons responsible for themselves, not just for the way they treat others. We morally criticize persons who take advantage of others but we also think less of those who take advantage of themselves. We disapprove of someone who willfully squanders his potential, who backs down from every challenge, and who refuses to evince the initiative to get his life in order. At the very least, we feel sorry for those who do not regard themselves as worthy of living well. We find it difficult to respect those who do not respect themselves, even when this deficit does not adversely affect others. We hold persons responsible for maintaining a modicum of self-worth. We feel that this is something persons should be taught as children to cultivate for themselves; that there is something wrong with the way they value themselves if they expect others to cultivate it for them. I speak interchangeably of self-worth or self-regard. I elaborate below that it is comprised of two profile virtues: self-respect that is delimited by self-love.

So intuitive is our disapproval of diminished self-worth that we reflexively look for reasons not to hold persons responsible for abusing, disadvantaging, or otherwise devaluing themselves. Thus the substance abuser is enslaved by the disease of addiction, a condition that diminishes autonomy and decimates self-control. This despite the fact that many addicts willfully assert both when they quit on their own. I will argue in chapter five that blaming, or holding a victim responsible, need not amount to intemperate censure. It can amount to an exhortation to be a better friend to yourself, a virtue ethical effort for which you are ultimately responsible.

Lack of self-worth is a standard symptom of major depression. If one lacks it, then one will not feel worthy of being responsible for oneself. However sorry we might feel for such persons, we also think it wrong to hold them accountable for their condition, which many regard as an afflictive brain disease. An ascription of responsibility for cultivating ethical integrity might be otiose in such cases if not presumptuously naïve. Yet the self-worth that is a necessary condition of ethical integrity is precisely what we want such persons to have. We might see the capacity for self-worth to be completely extinguished until the person's neurochemistry is rebalanced. But we cannot deny that we encourage depressed persons to assert themselves against their depression and cultivate a better life. I want to explore the extent to which, if at all, we can reasonably, compassionately, and supportively expect people to assume ethical responsibility for themselves, especially those who initially lack the self-worth that very assumption requires. Lack of self-worth can be seen as more than a symptom of a brain disease. We might also see it as indicating the normative project of self-renewal that depressed persons should make of themselves if they can. If they cannot, then a cardinal therapeutic goal is to enable that ability and inspire the motivation to assume that responsibility. If that ability is restored, then further recovery from depression can be an exercise in self-regarding care, a virtuous cultivation of self-respect, and appropriate measures of self-love.

The distinction between self-regarding ethics and other-regarding morality is not meant as a bifurcation. It does not dichotomize two realms of normative reflection and praxis. Conceptions of the good life are not eremitic. They include others and a conception of how we ought to treat them. Indeed, other persons, e.g., our friends or loved ones, can be our critical interests. Dworkin endorses the "Kantian principle" that we cannot adequately respect humanity in ourselves unless we respect it in others, and that our reasons for thinking it important how our own life goes are reasons for thinking it important how anyone's life goes.[5] The idea that concern for others develops from self-concern has an ancient provenance in Aristotle. He posited a psychological primacy to a self-love that opened outward to others, i.e., the ways we relate to friends are first the ways we relate to ourselves. The decent person relates to her friend as to herself since the friend is another self. Such people are "concerned with themselves and each other" since they all seek a good life that is lived according to the virtues.[6] They extend their self-love to others and "care about their good for their own sakes."[7] Persons who strive to achieve a good life by living virtuously will not live at the expense of others because living virtuously "just is" doing things like acting out of concern for oneself and for others.[8] Nor are conceptions of the good life developed in a social vacuum. Critical interests and values worth living by cannot, as a rule, exclude others. Few of us aim for self-fulfillment by becoming anchorites. I turn now to an examination of how self-regarding ethical and other-regarding moral values can inform 1) conceptions of mental disorder, 2) psychotherapeutic praxis, and 3) conceptions of mental health.

## 4.3 **Ethical and Moral Values in Conceptions of Mental Disorder**

We can start by thinking about the DSM's Cluster B personality disorders. These are not disorders, like psychotic depression, that destroy the patient's mental capacity. They are disorders that have been cast as other-regarding moral conditions that require an apposite, but as yet unspecified form of moral treatment. Louis Charland makes an eloquent case. Persons diagnosed with Cluster B personality disorders exhibit "morally objectionable and reprehensible behavior toward others," e.g., (1) "the pervasive pattern of disregard for and violation of the rights of others" evinced by those with antisocial personality disorder; (2) the "inappropriate, intense anger" and "instability in interpersonal relationships" evinced by those with borderline personality disorder; (3) the "inappropriate sexually seductive and provocative behavior" evinced by those with histrionic personality disorder; and (4) the "lack of empathy" evinced by those with narcissistic personality disorder. The "central issue" for treatment is whether the patient has a "moral willingness to change" and a "sustained readiness to make the moral effort to make and sustain that change."[9]

A successful therapy would presumably replace immoral character flaws with morally desirable character strengths. Set aside for a moment the debate about whether there is an effective treatment for these disorders and imagine a mentally capable patient who moves in psychotherapy from having such a personality disorder to being mentally healthy. I argue that she must strive to transform herself in ways that do not just closely resemble, but actually involve ethical and moral growth through the attainment of self- and other-regarding virtues. This entails that the personality disorder is a normative deficiency for which we can hold the patient responsible in a way that we should not hold the schizophrenic responsible for his inability to distinguish fact from delusion. Treatment reflects ethical value to the extent that it requires a patient's responsible efforts to improve his affective, cognitive, and behavioral makeup. This involves changing the way he thinks and feels about himself, and transforming his holistic understanding of the kind of person he wants to be. Treatment reflects moral value to the extent that it requires his responsible efforts to improve the way he treats others.

If a Cluster B personality disorder is essentially a set of character flaws, then the patient needs to transform and strengthen his character to be rid of it. These would be cases in which patients have to develop certain virtues in both their efforts to meet, and then sustain, therapeutic goals. Patients can bring undeveloped capacities for cultivating virtues to psychotherapy. Some might bring nascent virtues of focus to psychotherapy that can enable them to acquire other virtues of care and concern for others. One can lack certain virtues and be internally constrained from cultivating them through no fault of one's own. Or not, depending on the condition afflicting the patient. One can, however, attain a character stronger in certain virtues by striving to overcome a condition that diminishes one's abilities to treat oneself and others in ethically desirable ways. The Cluster B personality disorders are the most obvious examples of how generic ethical values can define the three factors of clinical pathology, the proposed treatment, and the desired therapeutic outcome.

Charland posits a commonsensical distinction between medical and moral kinds of disorder. Identification and treatment of the latter require "articulation in moral terms and concepts."[10] Identification and treatment of the former presumably require articulation in medical terms and concepts. As such, they could be morally neutral. There is no doubt that this distinction can be made. For instance, the identification of cystic fibrosis does not require articulation as an ethical or moral deficit and its treatment does not consist in ethical or moral improvement. By contrast, the identification and treatment of the DSM-5's Cluster B personality disorders, as well as the disruptive, impulse control, and conduct disorders (oppositional defiant disorder, intermittent explosive disorder, conduct disorder, kleptomania, and pyromania) would require articulation in moral terms.[11]

The latter five disorders are most plausibly articulated as moral ones, involving as they do difficulties in controlling the hostility of emotional and behavioral responses that aggressively impinge on the moral and legal entitlements of others.[12] If these disorders turned out to reflect a neurochemical imbalance, then there would be a medical/moral overlap. We cannot discount this possibility. We should thus be wary of assuming that this medical/moral distinction will neatly apply to mental disorders on an either/or basis. There are many cases that do involve medical/moral overlap. Standard symptoms of major depression include neutral clinical symptoms like decrease in appetite, weight loss, insomnia, and fatigue. These are conjoined with other symptoms that have generic ethical resonance, like feelings of worthlessness and disengagement from others.[13] Major depressive disorder can thus have a corrosive effect on one's ethical and moral capacities.

In sum, the identification and treatment of numerous mental disorders can be expressed to varying degrees in both generically ethical and clinical terms. More complex examples include "substance-related and addictive disorders."[14] If one subscribes to the theoretical model that posits addiction as a disease whereby the drug takes control of the user's brain, then drug addiction can seem initially to be a medical disorder. But even on that strong assumption, notions of moral responsibility and strength of character can inform the articulation of treatment. There are unresolved issues about whether the identification and treatment of, say, heroin or alcohol addiction requires articulation in terms that are either strictly medical, strictly moral, or a combination of both.[15] I will return to the generic ethical/medical overlap below.

The fact that a set of diagnostic criteria do not, as in the Cluster B personality disorders, directly employ self-regarding ethical or other-regarding moral terms does not mean that such terms cannot be implied, as Charland acknowledges.[16] He apparently thinks the Cluster A and C disorders are morally neutral because, for instance, persons with avoidant personality disorder need not dislike or hate those whom they avoid, persons with dependent personality disorder need not intend to annoy those to whom they cling, and persons with obsessive-compulsive personality disorder need not intend to embarrass or ignore others as a result of their condition.[17] But even if negative moral terms are part of a diagnostic criterion, they need not imply disapprobation of the person to whom they are applied. It is a negative and ethically value-laden judgment to claim that a severely depressed person lacks self-respect or a sense of moral worth. I might go so far as to say that she is ethically impaired by her condition. Indeed, I might say that she lacks the ethical capacity to care about risks to herself of which she is cognitively aware.[18] But I do not thereby hold her culpable for the deficit, nor do I imply that she is bad for being that way; I can be expressing moral compassion and insist that she needs help. In other words, using generic ethical terms in the identification of certain disorders, even those thought to be diseases of the brain like major depression, need not equate the corrosive ethical impact of the disorder with a patient's willful badness.

Charland notes rightly that the treatment of Cluster B disorders requires of the patient a "moral willingness and effort" that the Cluster A and C disorders do not. You can be fully cured of obsessive-compulsive disorder, avoidant, or schizoid personality disorder but still have a bad character and commit immoral acts. But you cannot be fully "cured" of antisocial, borderline, histrionic, or narcissistic personality disorder and persistently intend to be cruel, dishonest, and indifferent to how you make others feel. Successful treatment involves a moral commitment to a significant character change, a kind of moral "conversion."[19] The "cured" Cluster B patient would have to not only behave, but would also have to see herself and others much differently. The treatment would consist of interventions designed to awaken and stimulate the development of a sufficiently stable ethical character, a different way of living with oneself and others. This would involve much more than symptom relief. Indeed, one aim of the treatment would be to bring the patient to an understanding that he ought to feel uncomfortable about treating others the way he habitually does. Better values and behavioral habits are called for. Presumably, a "cure" would mean that the patient cultivates better values and behavioral habits; that she wants to actually be a better person. This kind of personal transformation would involve more than an intellectual cognizance of moral rules based on duties or consequences. Mere conformity to the prescriptions of deontological and consequentialist ethics does not capture the kind of radical personal transformation envisioned here. I think this transformation is best captured by the basic thrust of an ethics of virtue by which the patient is encouraged to cultivate a better character as the basis for a better life.

The cultivation of certain virtues can be understood as both the means and the goal of successful treatment. A successful treatment of the Cluster B personality disorders leading to a full cure would be, on Charland's account, a predominantly or perhaps even an exclusively "moral" treatment. The "moral willingness and commitment to change" this treatment requires is held to be "typically absent in consent to therapy for other sorts of mental and behavioral disorders." Two such moral "milestones" are "willingness and commitment to developing the capacity for empathy" and the "willingness and commitment to relate honestly in the therapeutic alliance."[20] The extensive degree of moral willingness and commitment to change in such treatment might be absent in therapies for other disorders, but I would argue that some degree of self-regarding ethical and other-regarding moral willingness and commitment to change are typically present in a psychotherapeutic alliance.

Charland would contrast moral treatments with standard psychotherapies in a way that I do not. "Strictly speaking," he writes, "the moral treatment of the Cluster B disorders falls in the province of what psychiatrist David Healy calls the quest for *authenticity*."[21] Standard psychotherapy may help and sometimes even be required for moral recovery, but according to Charland it can never be sufficient on its own. He thinks that moral treatment and standard psychotherapies diverge, and that "for the Cluster B disorders at least, moral treatment must form the core of any successful treatment and recovery."[22] By this account, resolving past traumas, repressed conflicts, and changing negative schemas of thinking are goals of standard psychotherapy. They are quite distinct from the goal of assuming one's authenticity. That goal is thought by Charland to relate to moral treatment as a non-standard psychotherapy, e.g., dialectical behavior therapy. Healy is even less accommodating. He takes the position that the quest for authenticity has nothing at all to do with standard psychotherapy.[23] I contest this idea in chapter seven, in which I show that notions of authenticity as a goal of treatment are not limited to the existential psychotherapies.

Here is where I differ from Charland. I find the psychotherapy cases that are best elucidated in virtue ethical terms to have a triadic structure. The three parts of this structure are (1) the problem for which psychotherapy is sought; (2) the desirable outcome or goal of the psychotherapy; and (3) the psychotherapeutic praxis that aims to bring that outcome about. In cases that fit this triad, I see standard psychotherapies as generic ethical treatments in which psychodynamic or cognitive behavioral techniques can be used for both self-regarding ethical and other-regarding moral ends. Standard psychotherapies for a variety of disorders can be at least partially articulated in generically ethical terms, as can the disorders themselves. Freud saw the articulation of psychoanalysis in at least one generic ethical term: the analysand's commitment to relate honestly to herself and to the analyst was of axial importance to the therapeutic alliance. Freud spoke of the patient's promise "to be absolutely honest and never leave anything out because for some reason or another it is unpleasant to tell it."[24] Luhrman notes that a crucial facet of psychodynamic therapy is teaching a patient to take responsibility for dealing with her problems. This involves a self-regarding ethical commitment of "trying to see yourself clearly, with your inadequacies, your awkwardnesses, your discomfort,

[and] your own dishonesty about the very process of coming clean."[25] We need not stop with psychoanalysis. One can imagine other psychotherapies in which the patient has to make significant efforts to be honest, in ways that she would rather avoid, about aspects of her life that make her quite uncomfortable. If honesty is a virtue of character, then patients may have to cultivate it in psychotherapy. Where Healy regards the quest for authenticity as falling outside the scope of psychotherapy, I posit cases where supporting that quest is key to the praxis of these therapies and where living an authentic life is an implicit goal of treatment.

The triadic cases begin with mental or behavioral disorders that involve character faults which the patient can sensibly be held capable of and responsible for changing. Hence the disorder can be articulated in generic ethical terms. We can then move easily to a treatment that involves a concerted effort to replace character faults with strengths or virtues. The treatment can then be articulated in virtue ethical terms. This entails a state of mental health that transcends symptom relief—it involves at least a threshold state of being virtuous. Hence the desired treatment outcome, or mode of mental health, can also be articulated in virtue ethical terms. My aim in the next chapter is to present a psychotherapy case that shows how a mental disorder, a psychotherapeutic mode of treatment, and a desired state of mental health can be articulated by a pluralistic theory of virtue ethics.

I want now to present a psychotherapy case that broadly reflects this triadic scheme, but without reference to an obvious mental disorder. I want to illustrate a problem in living that turns instead on a deficient relation to oneself. I will relate this problem below to deficits in positive mental health. I call this the case of the Demoralized Woman. Conceivably, an ethical willingness and commitment to change can be present in a patient's psychotherapeutic efforts to surmount the unyielding residuum of a major depression. I imagine a case where the resolution of an "officially" defined mental disorder might leave one with a problem in living that can seriously impair one's positive mental health, without resulting in the symptoms or functional impairments of the disorder that preceded it. There is a trivial sense in which mental disorders are problems in living, but we may want to hold that not all problems in living are mental disorders.

## 4.4 The Demoralized Woman

A female patient has spent the better part of the past two decades dealing with major depression. Assume that the best available evidence indicates that the depression resulted from a neuropsychological brain defect, perhaps a congenital biochemical imbalance of neurotransmitters that was aggravated by psychologic and situational factors beyond the patient's control. She finally responds to an adjusted dosage of the right antidepressant and experiences some noticeable symptom relief without adverse side effects. Her appetite returns and she stops waking up in the early hours of the morning. Her psychomotor retardation is gone, as is her pervasive sense of nonspecific guilt and impending doom. And yet she complains of still not feeling right, of a persistent state of desuetude. She has emerged from a black despair to a grey zone. Given her response to the drugs, she believes that this residual demoralization stems from what the depression depleted in her. The depression has left her with less of herself to come back to. She lacks hope and vision for a fulfilling and useful life. What the drugs have not given her is a sense of self-esteem and purpose with which she can identify.[26] She begins psychotherapy, but in an attempt to do what? Trilling's assessment of Madame Bovary can be reconfigured here. The woman aims "to overcome the nullity of her existence and to make, or seize, what is called a life. Doubtless something is lacking in her temperament, but not everything."[27] Trilling assesses Emma as having this developed will. I assess the Demoralized Woman as someone who ought to develop it.

What might we say is wrong with this woman? Some might argue from a clinical perspective that aspects of her depression persist. Others might claim that the depression overlaid unresolved psychological conflicts that eventually tipped the biochemical balance. That balance has been restored, but the conflicts remain. Different interpretations can be applied. It turns out that she had importunately critical and emotionally distant parents who did not "mirror" her in a positive way. As a child, she did not see acceptance, pride, and encouragement in their responses to her. A psychodynamic therapist might aver that an intrapsychic conflict between her ego and her excessively harsh and demanding superego makes her feel that she does not deserve deeper goods. She does not feel worthy of greater potential and so belittles it. One psychodynamic goal is to confront this condemnatory superego and replace it with a more accepting one. We might see as implicit in this terminology a call for the woman to repair herself, to be a better parent to herself than her parents were. A cognitive psychotherapist might be less interested in her developmental years and concentrate on the negative thought schemas that she habitually resorts to. Aiming to shift her focus to more positive schemas is yet another way of sounding the call for her to repair herself. This call will resonate with various theoretical intonations in most "humanistic" approaches to psychotherapy.[28]

From a self-regarding ethical perspective, she persists in disempowering herself. But I should be clear: while she is not responsible for ending up in this condition, she is arguably responsible for working her way out of it. Nor is behavior toward others of concern: she keeps her promises, tells the truth, and is not violent or manipulative. She is not, in the other-regarding sense defined above, an immoral person, and her clinical depression was not a moral fault. Thus her demoralization would not fit in Charland's category of interactive moral disorders. On my account, her malaise is self-regarding and ethical. Still, I do not want to speak of an ethical wrong here. What then might we say is ethically problematic about her case?

We might portray her problem as a self-regarding lack or absence, an ethical worm in the heart of her being. She is not completely lacking an imagination that kindles to the idea of self-defining purpose.[29] She can understand that her life could be worthwhile but she has no idea of what she is, or ought to be, worthy of. She lacks a sense of the person it would be worthwhile for her to be. I aver that she lacks critical interests. We can further refine this idea. As Taylor would have it, she lacks a sense of "strongly valued goods" in her life. These are goods to which one cannot help but have recourse in determining the purposes of one's *own* life, e.g., "deliberating, judging situations, deciding how you feel about people, and the like."[30] Taylor also refers to these "goods" as our "deepest evaluations"; our own-most, often inchoate sense of what is important to us, what is "worthy or higher, or more integrated, or more fulfilling." In sum, they are the "convictions by which we define our identity."[31]

Our deepest evaluations comprise a moral topography; a space of aspiration and assessment that orients us to life by demarcating what we consider meaningful and desirable.[32] This can also be seen as the space of holistic self-understanding. Through reflection and self-interpretation and "strong evaluations," we add detail to this topography. This involves "defining what it is we are really about, what is truly important to us," and our conception of the good life. It can also involve contrasting "higher" motivations with "baser, more self-enclosed and troubled one[s], which we can see ourselves as potentially growing beyond, if and when we can come to experience things from the higher standpoint."[33] These are the values that we try to define and to realize through a way of living that is faithful to our identity-conferring convictions.[34] I do not use the term "identity" in a static sense, but rather in a temporally dynamic sense that encompasses fidelity to both who we are and to whom we strive to be. Our identity, claims Taylor, is defined by these strong evaluations, which are connected intimately with ourselves as agents. A self decides and acts out of these fundamental evaluations. "[35] They inform our sense of authenticity, our unique way of being true to ourselves. In lacking a sense of self, the Demoralized Woman lacks ethical identity.

We can now begin to articulate the Demoralized Woman's problem in ethical terms. The black hole of depression has exsanguinated her "deepest evaluations" and drained her capacity for agency. Her sense of self is atrophied. She lacks identity-conferring convictions and the resources to be a "strong evaluator." Taylor claims that if we fall out of alignment with our "moral space," if we lose our deepest evaluations, then we would break down as persons and lose our grip on who we are. This can induce a crippling experience of disaggregation.[36] This experience can be expressed conceptually in numerous ways: "as being lost … unintegrated, or without meaning, or insubstantial, or empty."[37] It is apparently not uncommon for this sense of being out of joint to bring persons into psychotherapy.[38] Eagle observes that "typical neurotic problems … of an oedipal nature" do not pose a major challenge for contemporary psychotherapists. That challenge is posed by the many patients who seek help for "problems of self" that are "experienced as *feelings of meaninglessness*, feelings of emptiness, pervasive depression, *lack of sustaining interests, goals, ideals and values*, and feelings of unrelatedness" (italics mine). He sees these problems as illuminating "the importance of goals and guiding values as both a reflection of and a maintainer of psychic health."[39]

Taylor proposes a corollary to this experience by which we have a sense, however dim, about what it would mean for us to be back on track, integrated, and in alignment with ourselves. He claims that we have a feel for the internal resources, strengths, or virtues that we need to cultivate in the process of integral realignment.[40] The woman might start existential psychotherapy, in an attempt to "remoralize" herself.[41] Taylor's portrayal of identity crisis and breakdown goes some way to capturing this woman's problem. The real life case of Linda Logan comes even closer.

Logan lived for three decades with bipolar disorder that culminated in psychotic depression. She is well poised to write now of the self-diminution that her condition imposed. There were periods when she felt that she had a depressed self and a manic self, both of which competed with a traumatized self that could discern the differences between them. The psychotic depression imploded whatever sense of cohesion she had left. She became unable to see where she ended and where other persons and the environment began. This would be the ground-zero point of demoralization. The cumulative effects of depression led to a depletion of self-worth, a sense that her "self" was slowly vanishing as the disorder wore on. While her psychiatrist felt that a new regime of drugs would reinstate her as a happier self, she was uncertain as to whether she retained a self that treatment could revive. A pharmaceutical focus on medication and symptom relief obstructed her treatment team from helping her to deal with the experience of losing her identity. The notion that she needed help dealing with philosophic questions about who she is and who she wants to become, about cultivating a vision of a satisfactory life, was quite redundant to the clinical business of symptom reduction and the monitoring of her sleep patterns, appetites, and drug responses. When it came to self-restoration, Logan was on her own.[42]

Once her bipolarity petered out, she was stabilized on medication and discharged from the hospital. She felt salvaged but not yet regenerated. That would take years of "small changes" in a secure and facilitative holding environment (Logan calls it a "cocoon") that enabled her to start rebuilding and consolidating herself as a distinct person. Only some aspects of her former self were resuscitated during recovery. New interests in writing, painting, and honest dialogue in a support group began to define her efforts to reconstruct herself. Logan reminds us that for many persons with mental disorders, "the transformation of the self is one of the most disturbing things about being ill. And their despair is heightened when doctors don't engage with the issue, don't ask about what parts of the self have vanished and don't help figure out strategies to deal with that loss."[43] These cases show that an exsanguinated, demoralized self is a problem that can be articulated in self-regarding ethical terms.

## 4.5 **Ethical and Moral Values in Psychotherapeutic Praxis**

In the Demoralized Woman's case, praxis involves the therapist and patient's efforts to work through her malaise. This is not something he can do to or for her so much as it is something he can challenge and motivate the woman to do for herself. From a virtue ethical perspective, I see her problem as a lack of self-regard and a habitual disposition to perpetuate it. She lacks the self-love of a healthy bond with herself and has difficulty seeing herself as potentially growing beyond it. She lacks a sustained motivation to tend to the work of defining herself. Indeed, she doesn't know how or where to begin. We can also speak of a flattened sense of self-respect. Not that she lacks it entirely, since she respects herself enough to seek therapy. But she is seriously limited in her present ability to tap into an inarticulate but powerful sense of the importance of her life and equally powerful beliefs about what achievements would give it value.[44] I will argue below that self-love is delimited by self-respect and that both forms of self-regard play a crucial and consolidative role in the development of one's ethical identity.[45]

The psychotherapist can offer an empathic and supportive alliance that is respectful of her person. He would reinforce three ideas: (1) that she is worthy of an ethical identity; (2) that she will discover herself through creative, identity-conferring efforts; and (3) that she can and ought to attend to herself with love and respect. It can make good ethical sense to tell a person that she ought to love and respect herself.[46] This ethical sense does not disappear if that person becomes a patient in psychotherapy and it is the therapist who exhorts her. Psychotherapeutic praxis is here concerned with fostering the Demoralized Woman's potential for growth and self-restoration.

What are the virtues such praxis aims to enable? Self-respect is the maturity of character by which one takes one's life seriously, i.e., by which persons think it crucially important that they live well and that it would be a mistake to settle for a life of wasted opportunity and potential. It also makes one capable of respecting others.[47] As a distinct character trait, self-respect is a deep commitment to one's critical interests or deep evaluations, i.e., to one's goals, values, and convictions, and to one's growth and development. Self-respecting persons are characteristically true to their judgment that their interests are worth taking seriously. They have, as we say, the courage of the convictions that they have made their own. They are also committed to having their values be worthy of them and are thus committed to themselves as being worth the effort required to rise to the challenge of embracing worthwhile values. If a person has not taken herself to be worthy of rising to this challenge, then she will not be in harmony with herself. Self-respect is a reflective, rational commitment to oneself as valuable and worthy of values that one can respect. It is through this commitment that critical interests come to have a stable emotional and intellectual hold on oneself. Russell argues that self-respect is not one character trait among many. Rather, it is a global trait of the whole psyche that can flourish, succeed, and hit the mark, or it can wither, languish, and fall short. We should understand it holistically as informing all of the virtues and we see its success in virtuous persons.[48]

Self-respect mirrors self-love as a holistic, global character trait. Christine Swanton develops a similar idea in her account of self-love as a profile of all the virtues, i.e., even those that are not essentially self-regarding. Self-love is an expressive, psychological phenomenon that evinces a solid bonding with oneself rather than a mere recognition of one's status as rational and autonomous. Self-respect comes with proper self-love, which can be criticized if it lacks love and respect for others. The vitality, strength, and potency expressed by self-love enables one to express other-regarding generosity and concern that is undistorted by "the resentment of the threatened, vulnerable, hostile and envious." Self-love can be fundamentally distorted by a self-contempt that evinces various modes of inferiority complex.[49]

Swanton sees the "root cause" of deficient self-love as a failure to resolve a conflict reflecting two features endemic to our human condition: (1) a need to grow and express one's vitality and personal strength, and (2) the fact that this basic need is usually subject to the often unconscious baleful effects of environmental or congenital vicissitudes. These effects result in distortions in the way we see ourselves and the world. They reflect a conflict between our desires for strength and confidence "and our self-conception as inadequate to satisfy those desires."[50] In holistic, depth-motivational terms, Swanton sees self-love as part of what it means to be well-disposed in regard to all of the virtues. Note that she does not deny "that in some contexts we can talk about the virtue of self-love, for example, in a context where an agent is striving to overcome a wide range of deficiencies in this area."[51] Various claims can be made about the best ways of resolving these deficiencies, "including right living to improve one's own self-love ... behavioral reinforcements, and therapeutic catharsis and insight."[52] Swanton does not explore these issues and says nothing to prejudice them. Psychotherapy is conceivably one way of working to resolve deficiencies in self-love. If the therapeutic goal is a better mode of self-actualization, then acquiring the virtue of self-love in a good enough way can be seen as an ethical overlap.

The Demoralized Woman lacks a loving bond with herself by which she knows, feels, and lives by her identity-conferring values and commitments. It is through such living that she could express her strength and vitality. Her lack of this bond has nothing to do with self-contempt. It is rather a depleted sense of what a worthwhile life that is uniquely hers would be. Strong values and commitments are the adhesives by which a positive bond with oneself is held in place, and by which an ethical identity can coalesce.

The way the Demoralized Woman treats others is not the problem. In that regard, she is not immoral. Hers is an essentially self-regarding problem: there is something deficient about the way she sees and treats herself. More to the point, we hold her responsible for redressing this deficiency through efforts that only she should make.

But speaking of self-regarding ethical responsibility may seem anachronistic. It is hard to miss Foucault's point here: while the care of the self was a central tenet of ancient Greek and Hellenistic conceptions of ethics and the good life, it fell out of focus in moral philosophy after the eighteenth century.[53] During "the long summer of Hellenistic and Roman thought," the notion of caring for the self was thought essential to one's flourishing and the cultivation of virtue. Foucault presents this notion as being a prerequisite to knowledge. During antiquity, he claims, the question of "how to access the truth" was inseparable from the idea that one had to engage in certain transformational practices that would enable it. Thus the various modes of Stoic meditation were means of transforming the self to make one's access to self-knowledge possible. We must first work on and transform ourselves before we can truly know ourselves. Caring for the self is a self-regarding obligation. It identifies the question "What shall we do in order to live properly?" with the question "What shall we do so that the self becomes and remains what it ought to be?"[54]

The exhortation to care for oneself was sufficiently widespread in antiquity that it became "a truly general cultural phenomenon."[55] Foucault traces close relationships between the care of the self and Stoic perspectives on the cultivation of virtue.[56] In broad terms, the care of the self can be seen as reflecting a virtue ethical commitment to cultivating stable character traits that enable one to relate better to oneself and to others. For his part, Foucault was less than impressed with contemporary efforts to "reconstitute an ethic of the self" and he begged off a detailed discussion of whether psychoanalysis might be up to the task. Indeed, even though it may have been an exigent and "politically indispensable task," Foucault was unconvinced that it was even possible to reconstitute an ethic of the self.[57] I am not so sure.

There are also questions about Foucault's construal of the Stoic spiritual exercises. Hadot concurs with Foucault that they are practices by which "One seeks to be one's own master, to possess oneself, and find one's happiness in freedom and inner independence."[58] But Hadot reminds us that "this movement of interiorization rises … [in Hellenistic ethics] to a higher psychic level … which consists in becoming aware of oneself as a part of nature, and a portion of universal reason."[59] He claims that Foucault's practices of the self are focused excessively on the individual at the expense of this universalist dimension and thus amount to a "culture of the self which is *too* aesthetic."[60] I do not relate the responsible care of the self to either an aesthetics of existence or a cosmic transformation. I relate it instead to responsibility, and virtues of self-respect and self-love. Working toward the fulfillment of self-regarding responsibilities in some cases of psychotherapy can strengthen the patient's ability to assume obligations to others.

Notions of self-regarding responsibilities might have a deontological provenance. They were not uncommon in Kant's time and had a place in his own moral theory.[61] One might understand responsibility for self-regarding care as one of Kant's imperfect duties of virtue but for the fact that those duties are not concerned with one's temporal, sensate happiness, or well-being. Happiness, for Kant, does not conduce to the harmonious universality that he saw as necessary for ethics. Acts of respect for the moral law can be universalized such that the rational wills of all have the same object. But since each person has their own prudential notions of happiness, "the wills of all do not have one and the same object."[62] Thus, trying to make a moral end out of happiness would create "the extreme opposite of harmony."[63] This reflects the heteronomy of prudential reasoning. The empirical inclinations that motivate plans for happiness are for Kant inconstant and unpredictable. This makes happiness a "fluctuating idea" and "not an ideal of reason but of imagination."[64] The relevant imperfect duty to oneself would regard what Kant termed our natural perfection, i.e., our "powers of spirit" (or reason), "powers of soul" (or understanding, memory, imagination, and taste), and our powers of bodily strength and skill. Making efforts to improve ourselves in these areas is meritorious rather than strictly required. In other words, we are not held to blame because we remain less than naturally perfect.[65] Kant's imperfect duties to oneself are the architectonic principles for a life that flows from our rational moral agency. They are a corrective to the anomic and heteronomous aspects of prudential reasoning.[66] As such, their indifference to our temporal happiness makes them irrelevant to concerns about the restoration of a therapeutic self-regard.[67]

The notion of obligations to oneself is regarded as puzzling in some moral discourse, W.D. Ross being a leading exception. He saw self-improvement as a prima facie duty to oneself with respect to developing one's virtue or intelligence. Like his five other types of prima facie duties, the obligation to self-improve is intuitively evident to the moral sensibilities of "thoughtful and well-educated people."[68] No such duty was evident to Bernard Williams. He saw self-regarding duties as a duplicitous representation of one's pursuit of happiness. These duties enable one to take some "time off" from the potentially all-consuming demands of meeting obligations to others. We should not have to speak of such duties in order to reserve time for non-moral personal projects, the importance of which is not properly captured by the language of duty. Moral obligations should not dominate our lives altogether. Williams saw the notion of duties to oneself as pernicious and fraudulent.[69]

Mill was concerned that duties to oneself constrain us to promote our own happiness and that they could be publicly enforced, i.e., society could compel us to do things that it thinks will increase our happiness. Mill thought this would be counter-productive given his belief that individuals were the best judges of how to promote their own happiness.[70] Baier thinks that morality is born of interpersonal relations and requires interaction between persons. The purpose of morality is to move us to a consideration of the well-being of others. If morality moves us to consider our own well-being, it is in the cardinal service of attending to the well-being of others, e.g., a parent's indirect duty to stay reasonably healthy in order to care for his child or a pilot's indirect duty to stay sober while flying a plane. These are duties toward others that have normative implications for how one treats oneself. Otherwise, the notion of duties to oneself is "absurd."[71] Contractarians view self-regarding obligations as oxymoronic. Thus one is not immoral but imprudent in deliberately violating one's self-respect or allowing it to remain in a state of atrophy.[72] One might argue that a duty from which one can release oneself is no duty at all.[73]

Although some, perhaps many people "still think ... that there is something immoral about suicide or letting one's talents go to waste, even if no one else is harmed in the process,"[74] the regnant notions in contemporary philosophy are that self-regarding responsibilities are either fraudulent, unacceptably paternalistic, or at odds with the essentially social nature of morality.[75] I disagree. A responsibility is the state of being responsible. It is also the opportunity to (or ability to) act independently and take decisions without authorization. In a more limited sense, a responsibility is something which one is required to do as part of a job, role, or legal (or moral) obligation. A responsibility can also mean the proper sphere or extent of one's activities, as when we say: "it is his province to take care of himself." One's province is an area in which one has special knowledge and interest. We often think of responsibilities to others but there is also a sense in which we can envision responsibilities to ourselves. To say that one is responsible for oneself can mean one is accountable to oneself as well as to others.

To be responsible means having an obligation to do something, or having control over someone, or having to care for someone. It also means being the cause of something and so able to be blamed or credited for it, i.e., to be held accountable. A common understanding is that obligations denote commitments from which you cannot free yourself at will and are thus related usually to some external authority, i.e., other persons to whom you are obligated. Obligations thus relate to responsibilities we have to others; only they can release you at will from your obligations to them. Hence the puzzlement over the notion that one can have obligations to oneself. If you impose the obligation on yourself, then you are also the one who can free yourself at will from the obligation imposed. But being responsible also means personal accountability, or the ability to act without guidance or superior authority. It is thus not exhausted by the idea of obligation and we commit no semantic mistake in speaking of someone who holds himself responsible where others would not.

We can still speak meaningfully of ethical ideals or honorable and worthy aims to which we *should strive to realize in living a life that is most suitable for ourselves*. Virtues are partly but significantly concerned with one's personal ideals, self-image, and conception of life goals.[76] Virtuous ideals to which we should aspire can also encompass how we ought to treat ourselves. This tradition is echoed in Swanton's contemporary theory, which accommodates not only a virtue of self-improvement but also self-love as a profile of all the virtues. These aspirational virtues can facilitate greater self-realization. As such, their cultivation in psychotherapy, can, in some cases, be a crucial means to therapeutic ends. We can thus have a morality of other-regarding obligations and a virtue ethics of self and other-regarding aspirations, as when we aspire to provide our children with the best education and a superior upbringing to enhance their opportunities for personal flourishing.

Ronald Dworkin has reintroduced the notion of a self-regarding ethical responsibility that grounds other-regarding moral ones. This line of thought is echoed in his attempt to recapture an ethic of self-affirmation from which responsibilities to others are derived. We each have, he claims, "a sovereign ethical responsibility to make something of value of our own lives ... and our various responsibilities and obligations to others flow from that personal responsibility."[77] Recognizing our status as persons means that we affirm ourselves as worthy of respect by thinking it important that we live well and treat our lives "as having that kind of importance."[78] Self-respect means that I accept responsibility for caring about my life and recognize that it would be a mistake to waste it.

Dworkin cites our "common [ethical] convictions," that we have a "personal responsibility" to seek the right values for our lives and own up to ourselves for what we have made of them.[79] We share, I suggest, the common ethical conviction that a person betrays himself if he could not care less about his life and renders it a wasted opportunity. We also share the clinical conviction that some mental disorders can decimate self-regard and opportunities for living well. We speak of therapeutic recovery when a patient can reassume responsibility for his self-regard and begin to care for himself. I discuss responsibility to oneself further in chapter six.

At this point, I want to flag a province of accountability to oneself that I regard as fundamental to a psychiatric healing project. It is important to note that the Demoralized Woman's psychotherapy would not fit in Charland's category of moral treatment. The goal is not to transform her sense of herself so that she treats others in a morally acceptable way. Rather, the goal is to enable her to treat and care for herself in order to cultivate a satisfactory life. A psychotherapy dealing with these issues can be articulated primarily in self-regarding ethical terms. In the sense of "ethics" defined above, it is a treatment that aims at a transformation of the patient's relation to herself. We might think of it as a dialogical process that motivates her to formulate a self-loving engagement with deep evaluations and critical interests.

The development of self-respect and self-love are ethical goals to which the Demoralized Woman ought to aspire. These integrative qualities are the personal foundation on which engagement with critical interests or deep evaluations is developed. This engagement bespeaks an authentic way of living. The question is whether self-respect and self-love are plausible psychotherapeutic goals for this woman. I believe they are and I will connect these integrative qualities to one conception of mental health in the next section. A related question relevant to this section is whether there is a mode of psychotherapy that is apposite for this kind of problem. A psychodynamic approach could explore the woman's past for repressed traumas that are connected to bad relationships. Those relationships might have exacerbated the effects of a biologically based depression. Given what we know of her childhood, a psychodynamic therapist might see her demoralization in relational, as opposed to biochemical terms. He might offer the interpretation that her parents did not enable her to internalize a positive image of herself as a worthwhile person, whereas I might say that she lacks the strong internal resources to encourage herself to face the challenge of developing the critical interests that would express her self-regarding love and respect. Her childhood offers clues as to why she thinks that she does not merit this kind of self-engagement.

Assume that this interpretation was formulated through a ruthlessly honest dialogue between therapist and patient. Assume further that this dialogue was not a matter of fitting the patient to psychodynamic theory. The therapist strove instead to use psychodynamic theory in an open-textured way, i.e., to develop a particular, appropriately contextualized theory for this patient. We might detect a Kohutian influence in that both therapist and patient saw value in the patient's striving for a healthier self in which an "ambitious push" of creative tensions is experienced with some degree of confidence and "guided by reliable ideals that make the realization of skills and talents possible."[80] However valuable this interpretation might be, the patient is still left with the challenge of moving away from these aspects of her past into a remoralized future.

It is not initially clear what role, if any, that psychodynamic therapy could have in this case absent past traumas or conflicted relationships that affected her development. Suppose none of those parent–child dynamics were present and the woman's depression was purely biochemical. We might see the depression as having left her with a diminished sense of who she is. It has instilled repeated patterns of negative self-regard that distort the way she sees and interacts with her life-world. The exigent concern is what she chooses to make of herself as she moves into her future. Is there another mode of psychotherapy that would be apposite to confronting this challenge? An existential psychotherapy might seem a likely candidate. Authenticity is a well-established theme of existential philosophy, as is the responsibility to choose one's self-defining projects

At some point in the process, the patient must assume the responsibility for giving up her resistance to accepting the interpretation that she has worked out with the therapist. In this case, the Demoralized Woman should assume responsibility for giving up the idea that she is unworthy of cultivating the deep evaluations that are emblematic of an authentic self. Further, she must apply the understanding that she is worth this effort outside of the psychotherapeutic encounter. She must start doing the work of psychotherapy without the therapist and for herself.

The limits of the therapist/patient alliance should be clear. The psychotherapist will not "cure" the woman of her demoralization; he will not somehow invest or transfuse her with a set of critical interests and a concomitant sense of self-respect. This is the woman's task and her own ethical responsibility. Whether she meets this challenge in an excellent or good enough way will depend on her. Whether she accepts the initial belief that she is worthy of facing this challenge will depend in part on the psychotherapist. This is not a belief about which she can be indoctrinated. There is a primordial sense in which she must make her own leap of having faith in herself. She must come to see for herself that she is worthy of self-respect. In ethical terms, she should choose to believe in herself because she wants to owe this choice to herself and not because it is what she thinks that she owes the therapist. In making this choice authentically, she severs her dependence on the therapist for believing in herself. A good therapist can be instrumental in leading a patient to the edge of this choice, but no therapist can ensure that this leap will be made.

The psychotherapeutic praxes for dealing with demoralization can be articulated in virtue ethical terms. With reference to the cases that inform my account, these praxes consist of efforts by the therapist to inspire and challenge the patient to assume a goal-directed motivation and responsibility. The goal is the restoration of ethical identity and self-worth. The praxes also consist of efforts by the patient to cultivate the virtues of self-respect and self-love from which a conception of ethical integrity can develop. There are new developments in psychotherapeutic praxis that aim to assist patients in attaining well-being through creative engagement in a more meaningful life, e.g., Quality of Life Therapy, Well-Being Therapy, and Positive Psychotherapy. Each of these approaches reflects the positive psychology movement's concern for how people might be enabled to create lives of good quality for themselves. This movement emphasizes the development of positive human qualities and character strengths as a means of facilitating mental health and happiness over the prevention or treatment of negative qualities that lead to misery and mental disorder. It also emphasizes the social embeddedness of persons and the idea that they can be self-initiating agents for change in their own and others' lives. The development of character strengths—or virtues such as hope, curiosity, and creativity—is seen as crucial. I will return to these strengths as virtues in a psychiatric healing project. From the standpoint of positive psychology, enhancing our understanding of character strengths better enables us to promote well-being.[81]

## 4.6 Ethical and Moral Values in Conceptions of Positive Mental Health

I will concentrate the final part of my triadic analysis on how conceptions of positive mental health are laden with generic ethical values. Other values will be noted where appropriate. Some values might be clinically significant to mental health but lack generic ethical relevance. It is no doubt a good thing for a patient diagnosed with schizophrenia to ignore the internal voices urging him to prepare for the apocalypse. It would be clinically desirable for a patient diagnosed with major depression to be symptom free for a year. But it is not obvious in either case that these patients have thereby restored their ethical identity. As we saw with the Demoralized Woman and Linda Logan, effective drug treatments will reduce symptoms but will not retrieve a lost self.

Drug treatments may, however, enable a patient to begin the work of self-restoration. These cases indicate that mental health is not the absence of symptoms that comprise a disorder. If mental health consists in part of an affirmative sense of self, and if Taylor is right that one cannot find one's self without finding one's ethical identity, then there are close connections between mental health and considerations of a good and satisfactory life that is right for me. This indicates a desirable and valued set of psychological traits that both reflect and contribute to ethical identity. These traits can overlap conceptually with virtues of character. I would argue that if they can be developed to the point at which they enable a person to meet the demands of the world in an excellent or good enough way, then they can become virtues.

Virtues are revealed in therapeutic goals that stress the desirable and stable traits of character that mentally healthy persons have and that patients who want to restore lost selves ought to strive for. Hence the idea that mental health amounts to a virtuous state. Again, a plurality of multi-track dispositional states is endorsed in the literature. They range from "a sound personality structure characterized by growth, development, self-actualization, integration, autonomy, environmental mastery, ability to cope with stress, reality orientation [and] adaptation" to authenticity, altruism, honesty, and responsibility.[82] I will focus on what I regard as the ethical values that are implicit in the cultivation of a good life. In sum, my argument is that the realization of certain virtues, e.g., self-love, self-respect, and empathic concern and respect for others, are plausible psychotherapeutic goals for some patients given the problems they present. Their cultivation and attainment as sufficiently stable states amounts to positive mental health. The cultivation of other virtues enables the patient to realize these goals as fine inner states from which he will act. These virtues are instrumental to the healing project and include hopefulness, perseverance, courage, healing curiosity, respect for the healing project, and virtues of focus, dialogue, and constraint integration. The challenge is to formulate a psychotherapeutic approach that is suitably tailored to these patients and to a constructive exploration of their problems.

Martin proposes an "integrated moral-therapeutic perspective" that, while not equating mental health and moral virtue, affirms that they are "significantly interwoven in their meaning and reference."[83] Martin's integrated approach develops three themes that bridge morality and mental health. First, sound morality tends to overlap with mental health; it is realistic in its demands and aspirations, and tends to promote some degree of well-being and self-fulfillment. Second, while persons do not have complete control over their health, they do bear significant responsibility for taking prudent measures to care for their health within limits set by their resources, opportunities, and other obligations. It follows for Martin that sickness does not automatically excuse wrongdoing. We need to take seriously our "responsibilities to prevent disorders, to cope with them once they arise, and to avoid using them as excuses for wrongdoing. Those responsibilities must be understood contextually in assessing when and how far sickness excuses or mitigates responsibility."[84] Third, conceptions of positive mental health and modes of psychotherapy are laden with moral values. Defining mental health in negative terms as the absence of mental disorders presupposes moral values because the disorders invariably refer to standards of normal functioning that overlap with morally acceptable behavior. Think again about the Cluster B personality disorders. Positive definitions of mental health "as well-being, effective functioning, adaptive behavior, normalcy, growth, and maturity" can reveal moral values. Self-esteem, for example, can be seen to largely overlap with the virtue of self-respect "and self-control is both a moral and a therapeutic value."[85]

My approach is to acknowledge the conceptual distinction between mental health and moral virtue in narrow terms and pursue cases of their overlap largely in terms of Martin's integrated moral-therapeutic perspective. There is a plausible but narrow sense in which one can have, say, an obsessive compulsive disorder and yet be diligent in meeting one's other-regarding moral responsibilities. One may also have enough ethical self-regard to seek treatment. We see this in the case of the Demoralized Woman. Even though she continues to suffer from the attitudinal residue of her depression, she still sees herself as worth the effort of asking for help.

I will be presenting cases in which moral virtue and mental disorder co-exist. The former need not negate all vestiges of the latter. Thus mental disorder need not entail a lack of stable virtues, let alone pronounced vice. Conversely, a lack of stable virtues need not entail mental disorder. One might not meet the diagnostic criteria for a DSM mental disorder and yet be less than consistent in meeting one's other-regarding moral responsibilities. One's character can be weak and undependable without the presence of depression or schizophrenia. One might be wanting in moral strength, courage, and will without attaining the pervasive extremes of the Cluster B personality disorders. These are questions of judgment and perceptions of clinical degree.

The fact that some mental disorders do not entail conceptions of moral vice should not obscure the fact that some do. For instance, given its diagnostic criteria, some notion of vice is a logical consequence of antisocial personality disorder. Yet obsessive compulsive or anxiety disorders present no such logical entailment. Hence the conceptual overlap between mental disorder and vice in the Cluster B personality disorders. If a desirable treatment outcome in such cases is enhanced mental health, then that notion of mental health entails that the patient will evince appropriate ethical and moral response. Further, we need not, indeed should not, speak exclusively of vice when considering the conceptual and material overlap of generic ethical and clinical values.

In simple terms, we want successful treatment to replace deficits with gains in psychological assets, but these assets may not just spring back to life once symptoms are relieved. If we look at what the disorders take away from the patient, we might see that there is not always a simple precedent state to which the patient should be restored. In fact, they may have never been adequately developed in the first place. A patient on antidepressants might experience considerable relief from the symptoms of depression but have little psychological resilience to face situational adversity and handle stress. She may lack the ability to build and strengthen a durable sense of self-worth. She may need to work on her character by developing a capacity for self-love.

Martin's analysis of the relationship between virtues and the psychological components of positive mental health is most instructive, especially given his incorporation of Marie Jahoda's 1958 work *Current Concepts of Positive Mental Health*.[86] Jahoda was a seminal forerunner of the shift toward positive psychology. She proposed six major categories of positive mental health concepts: (1) attitudes toward the self; (2) growth, development, and self-actualization; (3) integration; (4) perception of reality; (5) autonomy; and (6) environmental mastery. She then elaborated on the psychological meanings of each category.[87]

As per (1), one's self must be accessible to the kind of "realistic" and "objective" reflection that enables one to distinguish pretensions and wishes from actual abilities. One should have an attitude of general acceptance toward one's self and recognize shortcomings in relation to strengths. These need to be realistically evaluated in considering the possibilities and costs of changing one's self. Citing Erikson, she states that balanced self-acceptance in adults assumes a sense of identity and a positive self-regard by which one maintains "inner sameness and continuity (one's ego in the psychological sense)."[88]

As per (2) one should be motivated to utilize one's developmental abilities with an orientation toward the future. Self-actualization requires "investment in living," or "the range and quality of a person's concern with other people and the things of this world, the objects and activities that he considers significant."[89] It is an attitude of affirmative dedication to living a meaningful life. It is also, I suggest, an affirmative dedication to creating an authentic one and living by one's deep evaluations and critical interests.

As per (3), integration requires a balance of psychic forces, a unifying outlook on life, and the ability to handle stress.[90] As per (4), perception of reality means empathy for others and the ability to perceive one's situation absent the distortions of wishful thinking. One should be able to see things as they are, and not as one needs them to be. As per (5), autonomy means inner regulation and self-determination in decision-making. Jahoda also related autonomy to self-reliance and the ability to take care of oneself: "an individual must be able to stand on his own feet without making undue demands or impositions on others." She noted that this ability is valued highly and is compatible with almost all of the positive mental health concepts she discusses.[91] Interestingly enough, the notion that well-being involves care of the self has been revived by current proponents of positive psychology. "Self-care entails the recognition that a meaningful life is one that uses signature strengths in the fulfillment of important goals ... [and one's] highest aspirations."[92] Finally, as per (6), environmental mastery means the ability to love; adequacy in love, work, play, and interpersonal relationships; behavior appropriate to situations; adaptation and adjustment to one's environment; and the ability to solve problems.[93]

Jahoda made no attempt to systematically integrate her criteria and was aware of the difficulties her summary raised. The criteria often overlap and we have no clear idea of the relationship between them. We don't, for instance, know anything about the degree to which they might be independent. Nor does Jahoda indicate a method for identifying satisfactory indexes of the criteria, which would enable us to confirm the presence or absence of a given criterion and measure its degree of manifestation. Jahoda saw these as problems for the empirical researcher. Overall, her summary has been assessed as rife with ambiguities and different levels of specificity. It has also been criticized for ignoring the idea that societal values might be relevant contextual criteria as well as for disregarding the psychological impact of one's social situation. Jahoda conceded the difficulties of reaching a correct or even a consensual definition of positive mental health given the value-laden nature of the criteria.[94]

Although I propose positive mental health as a threshold state of well-being, I also take Martin's point that it has to be more than the ability to function without being disabled by mental disorders—otherwise, positive and negative definitions of mental health will be fused. I thus understand positive mental health as falling somewhere between complete and barely adequate well-being, i.e., sufficient in degree to make a positive difference in one's life. It can be nascent and subject to incremental development. I diverge from Martin in seeing a plurality of different virtues that can overlap with Jahoda's criteria.[95]

As I explicate these virtues in the next two chapters, I will only note them provisionally here. I see (1) attitudes toward the self as overlapping with virtues of self-love and self-respect, which I articulate as recovery virtues in a psychiatric healing project; (2) growth, development, and self-actualization as overlapping with any virtues cultivated in the work of self-improvement, e.g., the healing virtues of honesty, courage, creative flexibility, and perseverance; (3) integration as overlapping with the virtue of self-love; (4) perception of reality as overlapping with the epistemic virtues noted in chapter three; (5) autonomy as overlapping with any virtues involved in self-regulation and the use of signature strengths to fulfill important goals; and (6) environmental mastery as overlapping with a multitude of other-regarding moral virtues, as well as Swanton's problem-solving virtues of focus, dialogue, and constraint integration which I discuss in chapter five.

This conception of positive mental health illuminates the existential malaise of demoralization. I will note the traits most relevant to my case examples. The Demoralized Woman was lacking in five of the six categories of positive mental health. Her attitude toward herself lacked positive self-regard and an accessible identity. Her potential for growth, development, and self-actualization was in a state of entropy that inhibited investment in living. She exhibits negative mental health, by which I do not mean pathology "but some form of vegetating without either positive health or disease."[96] She lacks integration through a unifying outlook on life. Her self-determination to care for herself is stalled. While perception of reality enables her to acknowledge her situation, she lacks much in the way of environmental mastery.

The challenge for the empirical researcher is to work out indexes to discover the presence of mental health and measure its degrees of manifestation. It is interesting to consider the application of current methods of measuring positive mental health that were not available in 1958. These assessments indicate that the problems acknowledged by Jahoda are still with us. On the basis of his thirteen-factor scale, Keyes distinguishes between "flourishing," or optimal mental health, "moderate mental health," and a state of negative mental health absent mental disorder that he terms "languishing." Flourishing persons score high on one of two measures of hedonic well-being and at least six of eleven measures of positive functioning. Languishing persons score low on at least one measure of hedonic well-being and low on at least six measures of positive functioning. They are in a state of being stuck, empty, stagnant, and seriously deficient in positive functioning. Persons in moderate mental health do not fit either of these criteria.[97]

Where might the Demoralized Woman fall on this scale? We might agree that the Demoralized Woman is languishing given her pervasive sense of emptiness. She could thus be assessed on Keyes' scale as exhibiting minimal mental health, e.g., she could score very low on the second hedonic criterion of feeling happy and satisfied with life overall and very low on the flowing four positive functioning criteria: (3) self-acceptance and a positive attitude to her past; (5) insight into her own potential and development; (7) goals and beliefs that affirm a sense of purposeful direction in a meaningful life; and (11) self-direction guided by socially acceptable standards. Jahoda's notion of "vegetating" might in the Demoralized Woman's case merely approximate the more serious state of languishing. There is much room for divergent opinion here.

Either way, I take two implications from the Demoralized Woman's case and the analysis preceding it. First, if concepts of mental disorder are ethically value-laden, then concepts of positive mental health are no less so. Assessments of positive mental health will likely pose challenges to the validity and inter-rater reliability of the concepts that purport to define it. It will be challenging to mark clear boundaries between criteria for, and constituent features of, positive mental health. Second, there is a plausible overlap between the concepts of positive mental health, notions of ethical identity, and meeting the demands of the world by living in accordance with the virtues that inform it. Empirical indexes aside, assessments of positive mental health are holistic in considering the whole person and generically ethical in evaluating his way of life.

## 4.7 **Conclusion**

I have argued that ethical and moral values are especially relevant to three points of reference: (1) conceptions of mental disorder; (2) psychotherapeutic praxis; and (3) conceptions of positive mental health. I have tried to show how ethical and moral values can permeate all three. My next step will be to connect this triadic analysis to a pluralistic virtue ethics. I want to concentrate on the ethical responsibility to develop and strengthen one's capacity for better responding to the demands of the world. Meeting this responsibility can be understood as the patient's striving to cultivate certain epistemic and ethical virtues in the dialogical process of psychotherapy. I want to focus now on the ethical virtues that are relevant to the patient's striving for psychological and behavioral improvement. In cases that fit the triadic analysis outlined above, this striving is tantamount to generic ethical self-improvement.

## Notes

1. **Ronald B. Miller**, *Facing Human Suffering: Psychology and Psychotherapy as Moral Engagement* (Washington, DC: American Psychological Association, 2004), 102–103.
2. Cf. **Alan C. Tjeltveit**, *Ethics and Values in Psychotherapy* (London: Routledge, 1999), 231.
3. **Ronald Dworkin**, *Sovereign Virtue: The Theory and Practice of Equality* (Cambridge, MA: Harvard University Press, 2000), 485 (note 1), 241, 242, 245, 253, 259, 270–271. See also Ronald Dworkin, *Life's Dominion: An Argument about Abortion, Euthanasia, and Individual Freedom* (New York: Vintage Books, 1994), 200–208.
4. **Tom L. Beauchamp** and **James F. Childress**, *Principles of Biomedical Ethics*, 6th ed. (Oxford: Oxford University Press, 2009), 3, 47–48.
5. **Ronald Dworkin**, *Justice for Hedgehogs* (Cambridge, MA: The Belknap Press of Harvard University Press, 2011), 14, 260.
6. **Aristotle**, *Nichomachean Ethics*, trans. Terrence Irwin (Cambridge: Hackett Publishing Company, 1985), 1166a5–1166b20, 1167b5.
7. **Julia Annas**, *The Morality of Happiness* (Oxford: Oxford University Press, 1993), 254.
8. **Annas**, *The Morality of Happiness*, 259.
9. **Louis Charland**, "Character: Moral Treatment and the Personality Disorders," in *The Philosophy of Psychiatry: A Companion*, ed. Jennifer Radden (Oxford: Oxford University Press, 2004), 71–73; see also 64–77; Louis Charland, "Moral Nature of the DSM-IV Cluster B Personality Disorders," *Journal of Personality Disorders* 20 (2006): 116–125; Charland refers to the fourth edition of DSM: American Psychiatric Association, *Diagnostic and Statistical Manual of Mental Disorders*, 4th ed. (Washington, DC: American Psychiatric Publishing, 1994), 649–661. The terminology for diagnosing Cluster B Personality Disorders has not changed substantially in DSM-5: American Psychiatric Association, *Diagnostic and Statistical Manual of Mental Disorders*, 5th ed. (Washington, DC: American Psychiatric Publishing, 2013), 659, 663, 667, 669 respectively.
10. **Charland**, "Character: Moral Treatment and the Personality Disorders," 73.
11. **American Psychiatric Association**, *Diagnostic and Statistical Manual of Mental Disorders*, 5th ed., 659–672, 461–480.
12. Cf. **American Psychiatric Association**, *Diagnostic and Statistical Manual of Mental Disorders*, 5th ed., 461.

13. Cf. **American Psychiatric Association**, *Diagnostic and Statistical Manual of Mental Disorders*, 5th ed., 161–163.
14. **American Psychiatric Association**, *Diagnostic and Statistical Manual of Mental Disorders*, 5th ed., 481–589.
15. **Walter Glannon**, "Responsibility, Alcoholism, and Liver Transplantation," *Journal of Medicine and Philosophy* 23 (1998): 31–40.
16. **Charland**, "Character: Moral Treatment and the Personality Disorders," 73.
17. **Charland**, "Character: Moral Treatment and the Personality Disorders," 73.
18. **Carl Elliott**, "Caring About Risks: Are Severely Depressed Patients Competent to Consent to Research?" *Archives of General Psychiatry* 54 (1997): 113–116.
19. **Charland**, "Character: Moral Treatment and the Personality Disorders," 71, 73.
20. **Charland**, "Character: Moral Treatment and the Personality Disorders," 73.
21. **Charland**, "Character: Moral Treatment and the Personality Disorders," 74; David Healy, *The Suspended Revolution: Psychiatry and Psychotherapy Re-examined* (London: Faber and Faber, 1990), 28–33, 200–204, 214–215.
22. **Charland**, "Character: Moral Treatment and the Personality Disorders," 74.
23. **Healy**, *The Suspended Revolution*, 28–33, 200–204, 214–215.
24. **Sigmund Freud**, "On the Beginning of Treatment," in *The Standard Edition of the Complete Works of Sigmund Freud*, Vol. 12 (London: Hogarth Press, 1953–1974), 135.
25. **T.M. Luhrman**, *Of Two Minds: An Anthropologist Looks at American Psychiatry* (New York: Vintage Books, 2000), 147, 152, 199.
26. **David Healy** has written about such patients. Too lengthy a depressive demoralization "may overstretch the capacity to bounce back." This demoralized psychological state has an existence that is predicated on but independent of the underlying brain disturbance. Once this state becomes fixed, "no amount of *pharmacological* [italics mine] treatment will bring about an improvement. We have no antidemoralization agents." See Healy, *The Suspended Revolution*, 146, 195.
27. **Lionel Trilling**, *Sincerity and Authenticity* (Cambridge, MA: Harvard University Press, 1971), 101; Gustave Flaubert, *Madame Bovary*, trans. Lydia Davis (New York: Viking Books, 2010).
28. **Healy** offers another interpretation for some treatment-resistant patients that does not involve a flawed personality. He observes that some of the "most seriously resistant depressed patients are those who have high standards for themselves." These standards have led them to above-average achievements when well. Treatment resistance stems not from a flawed personality but rather from their impatience and inability to "tolerate any fall-off in their level of performance and ... a slow pace of recovery. This intolerance and impatience inevitably leads to setbacks and demoralization." See *The Suspended Revolution*, 195. The woman in my example can be said to have a flawed personality—in this case, a lack of self-esteem and respect that has childhood origins. Even without such a pre-existing flaw, Healy concedes that an overlengthy subjection "to the subtle disturbances of depression ... without some assistance, is quite liable to seriously compromise one's ability to be authentic." See *The Suspended Revolution*, 197.
29. Cf. **Trilling**, *Sincerity and Authenticity*, 101.

30. **Charles Taylor**, *Sources of the Self: The Making of Modern Identity* (Cambridge, MA: Harvard University Press, 1989), 59.
31. **Charles Taylor**, "What is Human Agency?" in *Human Agency and Language: Philosophical Papers 1* (Cambridge: Cambridge University Press, 1985), 38–39, 35.
32. **Charles Taylor**, "The Moral Topography of the Self," in *Hermeneutics and Psychological Theory: Interpretive Perspectives on Personality, Psychotherapy, and Pathology*, eds. Stanley B. Messer, Louis A. Sass, and Robert L. Woolfolk (New Brunswick: Rutgers University Press, 1988), 298, 300.
33. **Taylor**, "Self-Interpreting Animals," in *Human Agency and Language: Philosophical Papers 1* (Cambridge: Cambridge University Press, 1985), 67–68.
34. **Taylor**, "What is Human Agency?" 40–41.
35. **Taylor**, "What is Human Agency?" 34–35.
36. **Taylor**, "What is Human Agency?" 34–35.
37. **Taylor**, "The Moral Topography of the Self," 300.
38. **John Chambers Christopher**, "Hermeneutics and the Moral Dimension of Psychotherapy," in *Culture, Psychotherapy, and Counseling: Critical and Integrative Perspectives*, ed. Lisa Tsoi Hoshmand (Thousand Oaks, CA: Sage Publications Inc., 2006), 187.
39. **Morris N. Eagle**, *Recent Developments in Psychoanalysis: A Critical Evaluation* (New York: McGraw-Hill, 1984), 72–73.
40. **Taylor**, "The Moral Topography of the Self," 300; Christopher, "Hermeneutics and the Moral Dimension of Psychotherapy," 187.
41. Cf. **James L. Griffith**, "Existential Inquiry: Psychotherapy for Crises of Demoralization," *The European Journal of Psychiatry* 27, 1 (2013): 42–47
42. **Linda Logan**, "Selfless," *The New York Times Magazine* April 28 (2013): 56–58.
43. **Logan**, "Selfless," 58–60.
44. **Ronald Dworkin**, *Justice for Hedgehogs*, 203–205.
45. **Swanton**, *Virtue Ethics: A Pluralistic View* (Oxford: Oxford University Press, 2003), 99–127. See also Daniel Russell, "Aristotle on the Moral Relevance of Self-Respect," in *Virtue Ethics Old and New*, ed. Stephen M. Gardiner (Ithaca: Cornell University Press, 2005), 101–121. Russell argues that it makes good *moral* (italics mine) sense to tell people that they ought to respect themselves. After Dworkin, I would speak of good ethical sense. Either way, Russell notes that the notion of self-respect as having moral significance in its own right, i.e., independent of other-regarding concerns, is contentious. Russell thinks that it is morally significant in its own right and hopes to make this thesis "much harder to deny" (103).
46. Cf. **Russell**, "Aristotle on the Moral Relevance of Self-Respect," 103.
47. **Russell**, "Aristotle on the Moral Relevance of Self-Respect," 119. Russell refers to Aristotle's argument that only those who love themselves are capable of loving others. See Aristotle, *The Nichomachean Ethics*, 1166a5–1166b20, 1167b5.
48. **Russell**, "Aristotle on the Moral Relevance of Self-Respect," 103–105, 119–120.
49. **Swanton**, *Virtue Ethics*, 134–135, 136. See also note 42 at 143.

50. **Swanton**, *Virtue Ethics*, 137.
51. **Swanton**, *Virtue Ethics*, 145.
52. **Swanton**, *Virtue Ethics*, 185 (note 15).
53. **Michel Foucault**, *The Hermeneutics of the Subject: Lectures at the College de France 1981–1982*, ed. Frederic Gros, trans. Graham Burchell (New York: Picador, 2005); Michel Foucault, *The Care of the Self: The History of Sexuality Volume 3*, trans. Robert Hurley (New York: Vintage Books, 1988), 37–68. This point is also stressed in Jens Timmermann, "Kantian Duties to the Self, Explained and Defended," *Philosophy* 81 (2006): 524.
54. **Foucault**, *The Care of the Self*, 14, 87, 178.
55. **Foucault** qualifies the generality of this cultural phenomenon. While its most sophisticated formulations were the province of the elite, the care of the self spread "quite widely" outside of aristocratic circles. Popular and "unpolished" versions filtered down to even "the most disadvantaged classes." See Foucault, *The Care of the Self*, 9, 112–115.
56. **Foucault**, *The Hermeneutics of the Subject*, 315–329.
57. **Foucault**, *The Hermeneutics of the Subject*, 251–252.
58. **Pierre Hadot**, *Philosophy as a Way of Life*, ed. Arnold I. Davidson, trans. Michael Chase (Oxford: Blackwell Publishing, 1995), 211.
59. **Hadot**, *Philosophy as a Way of Life*, 211.
60. **Hadot**, *Philosophy as a Way of Life*, 206–207, 211.
61. **Russ Schafer Landau**, *The Fundamentals of Ethics* (Oxford: Oxford University Press, 2010), 146; Timmermann, "Kantian Duties to the Self," 505–530.
62. **Immanuel Kant**, *Critique of Practical Reason*, trans. Lewis W. Beck (Indianapolis: Bobbs-Merrill, 1956), 27.
63. **Kant**, *Critique of Practical Reason*, 27.
64. **Immanuel Kant**, *Practical Philosophy*, trans. and ed. Mary Gregor (Cambridge: Cambridge University Press, 1996), 54.
65. **Alan Wood**, "Duties to Oneself, Duties of Respect to Others," in *The Blackwell Guide to Kant's Ethics*, ed. Thomas E. Hill (Oxford: Blackwell Publishing, 2009), 243.
66. **Robert S. Taylor**, "Kant's Personal Autonomy," *Political Theory* 33 (2005): 614.
67. **Timmermann**, "Kantian Duties to the Self," 507; Lara Denis, "Kant's Ethics and Duties to Oneself," *Pacific Philosophical Quarterly* 78 (1997): 333.
68. **W.D. Ross**, *The Right and the Good* (Oxford: Oxford University Press, 1930), 278, 283.
69. **Bernard Williams**, *Ethics and the Limits of Philosophy* (Cambridge, MA: Harvard University Press, 1985), 51, 181–182; Denis, "Kant's Ethics and Duties to Oneself," 321.
70. **John Stuart Mill**, *On Liberty*, ed. H.B. Acton (London: J.M. Dent and Sons, 1972), IV, 6. In his "Kantian Duties to the Self," Timmerman argues at 520–522 that "there is no sound argumentative route from moral duties to the self to totalitarian laws or paternalism."
71. **Kurt Baier**, *The Moral Point of View: A Rational Basis of Ethics* (Ithaca, NY: Cornell University Press, 1958), 215, 231; Lara Denis, *Moral Self-Regard: Duties to Oneself in*

*Kant's Moral Theory* (London: Routledge, 2001), 3–6; Timmermann, "Kantian Duties to the Self," 506.

72. **Landau**, *Fundamentals of Ethics*, 183.
73. **Denis**, *Moral Self-Regard*, 2–3. In his "Kantian Duties to the Self," Timmermann offers the following rebuttal at 516: "For it is hardly obvious that you *can* release yourself from any obligation that you impose on to yourself. *If* there are duties to the self, you cannot … Whoever argues against duties to the self on the grounds that the self could always release itself presupposes the very thesis that the argument purports to establish: that there are no duties to the self."
74. **Landau**, *The Fundamentals of Ethics*, 147.
75. **Denis**, *Moral Self-Regard*, 2–6. *The Cambridge Dictionary of Philosophy* defines "morality" in other-regarding terms, viz., "an informal public system applying to all rational persons, governing behavior that affects others, having the lessening of evil or harm as its goal, and including what are commonly known as the moral rules, moral ideals, and moral virtues." See Bernard Gert, "Morality," in *The Cambridge Dictionary of Philosophy*, ed. Robert Audi. 2nd ed. (Cambridge: Cambridge University Press, 1999), 586.
76. **Jorge L.A. Garcia**, "Virtue Ethics," in *The Cambridge Dictionary of Philosophy*, ed. Robert Audi. 2nd ed. (Cambridge: Cambridge University Press, 1999), 960, 961.
77. **Dworkin**, *Justice for Hedgehogs*, 13. He acknowledges the controversial nature of this judgment at 196. "You might ask: responsibility to whom? It is misleading to answer: responsibility to ourselves. People to whom responsibilities are owed can normally release those who are responsible, *but we cannot release ourselves from our responsibility to live well* [italics mine]. We must instead acknowledge an idea that I believe we almost all accept in the way we live but that is rarely explicitly formulated or acknowledged. We are charged to live well by the bare fact of our existence as self-conscious creatures with lives to lead. We are charged in the way we are charged by the value of anything entrusted to our care."
78. **Dworkin**, *Justice for Hedgehogs*, 205.
79. **Dworkin**, *Justice for Hedgehogs*, 206, 208, 213.
80. Cf. **Allen M. Siegal**, *Heinz Kohut and the Psychology of the Self* (New York: Routledge, 1996), 110; cf. Heinz Kohut, *The Restoration of the Self* (Chicago: University of Chicago Press, 2009), 53–54.
81. **P. Alex Linley, Stephen Joseph, John Maltby, Susan Harrington,** and **Alex M. Wood**, "Positive Psychology Applications"; Ed Diener, "Positive Psychology: Past, Present, and Future"; Shane J. Lopez and Mathew W. Gallagher, "A Case for Positive Psychology"; and James E. Maddux, "Self-Efficacy: The Power of Believing You Can," in *The Oxford Handbook of Positive Psychology*, eds. Shane J. Lopez and C.R. Snyder. 2nd ed. (Oxford: Oxford University Press, 2009), at 35, 37–38, 8–9, 3–5, and 341, respectively.
82. **Hans H. Strupp** and **Suzanne W. Hadley**, "A Tripartite Model of Mental Health and Therapeutic Outcomes With Special Reference to Negative Effects in Psychotherapy," American Psychologist 32 (1977): 190; Tjeltveit, *Ethics and Values in Psychotherapy*, 220–221.
83. **Mike W. Martin**, *From Morality to Mental Health: Virtue and Vice in a Therapeutic Culture* (Oxford: Oxford University Press, 2006), vii, 17.

84. **Martin**, *From Morality to Mental Health*, 7–8.
85. **Martin**, *From Morality to Mental Health*, 8.
86. **Martin**, *From Morality to Mental Health*, 29–36; Marie Jahoda, *Current Concepts of Positive Mental Health* (New York: Basic Books, 1958).
87. **Jahoda**, *Current Concepts of Positive Mental Health*, 22–80.
88. **Erik H. Erikson**, "Growth and Crises of the Healthy Personality," in Symposium on the Healthy Personality, ed. Milton J.E. Senn (New York: Josiah Macey Jr. Foundation, 1950), 143; Jahoda, *Current Concepts of Positive Mental Health*, 29.
89. **Jahoda**, *Current Concepts of Mental Health*, 30–35.
90. **Jahoda**, *Current Concepts of Positive Mental Health*, 35–43.
91. **Jahoda**, *Current Concepts of Positive Mental Health*, 45–52, 80.
92. **Michael M. Handesman**, **Samuel Knapp**, and **Michael C. Gottlieb**, "Positive Ethics: Themes and Variations," in *The Oxford Handbook of Positive Psychology*, eds. Shane J. Lopez and C.R. Snyder. 2nd ed. (Oxford: Oxford University Press, 2009), 107–108.
93. **Jahoda**, *Current Concepts of Positive Mental Health*, 49–64.
94. **Morris S. Schwartz** and **Charlotte Green Schwartz**, "Mental Health: The Concept," in *International Encyclopedia of the Social Sciences*, ed. David L. Sills, Vol. 1 (New York: Macmillan, 1968), 216.
95. **Martin**, *From Morality to Mental Health*, 29. Martin rewords Jahoda's criterial concepts as: (1) self-esteem; (2) psychological integration; (3) personal autonomy; (4) self-actualization; (5) social coping; and (6) realistic cognition. He sees the following virtues as overlapping with these criteria: (1) self-respect; (2) integrity; (3) moral autonomy; (4) authenticity; (5) responsibility; and (6) truthfulness.
96. **Jahoda**, *Current Concepts of Positive Mental Health*, 74. The concept of "negative health" did not originate with Jahoda. She cites Dorothy C. Conrad, "Toward a More Productive Concept of Mental Health," *Mental Hygiene* 36 (1952): 456–473.
97. **Corey M.L. Keyes**, "Toward a Science of Mental Health," in *The Oxford Handbook of Positive Psychology*, eds. Shane J. Lopez and C.R. Snyder. 2nd ed. (Oxford: Oxford University Press, 2009), 90–91. Keyes' scale has two diagnostic criteria: hedonia and positive functioning. Hedonia requires a high level of at least one of symptoms (1) and (2). Positive functioning requires high levels of six or more of symptom scales (3) to (13). The following is an abbreviated description of Keyes' symptom scales: (1) Regularly cheerful; (2) Feels happy or satisfied with life overall; (3) Holds positive attitudes toward oneself and past life and accepts varied aspects of self; (4) Has a positive attitude toward others and acknowledges their differences and complexities; (5) Shows insight into own potential and is open to new and challenging experiences; (6) Believes that people and society have positive growth potential; (7) Holds goals and beliefs that affirm a sense of meaningful, purposeful direction in life; (8) Feels that one's life is useful to society and valued by others; (9) Exhibits capability to manage complex environments to suit needs; (10) Interested in social life; (11) Exhibits self-direction guided by socially accepted internal standards; (12) Has satisfying, trusting, empathic relationships with others; and (13) Has a sense of belonging to a community.

Chapter 5

# Psychotherapy and the Virtuous Patient

## 5.1 Introduction

The standard approach to generic ethics in psychotherapy is to focus primarily on the conduct of the therapist. This approach is prioritized in the current edition of the *Oxford Textbook of Psychotherapy*: "Thus, when we talk about ethics in psychotherapy, we are talking about how therapists should behave in clinical practice with patients, and what the therapist ought to do in difficult interpersonal situations with patients and colleagues."[1] There is a growing acknowledgement that psychotherapy and generic ethics are interrelated in other ways that cut deeply into our sense of what a talking cure ought to be about and how it ought to be conducted.

Psychotherapeutic claims and concepts have been examined for their relevance to perennial issues in generic ethics such as moral responsibility, normative egoism, and principles of nonmaleficence, benevolence and autonomy. The other-regarding moral convictions of therapists and patients have been examined for their contribution to psychotherapeutic practice.[2] Societal norms and the culture in which psychotherapy is practiced have been seen as having a significant influence on the implicit moral values of the therapeutic dialogue.[3] There is also an emerging recognition that these issues raise interesting questions about the role of virtue in psychotherapy. This should not surprise us. While normative "boundary" ethics revolves around what the therapist ought, or ought not, to do, virtue ethics can revolve around the kind of person the therapist ought to be. Hence the role-specific virtues proposed for psychotherapists, e.g., empathic respect, benign and tolerant curiosity, emotional honesty, openness and humility, and self-control.[4]

Recent work by Jennifer Radden and John Sadler has articulated the role-specific virtues that psychiatrists should cultivate to meet the moral demands of providing care to patients with severe mental disorders. In *The Virtuous Psychiatrist: Character Ethics in Psychiatric Practice*[5] they make an engaging and, I think, convincing case that the provision of care can be a virtue ethical endeavor for the psychiatrist who aims to heal by treatment that is respectful of the patient's sense of self. Radden notes two distinct rationales for psychiatrists to cultivate relevant virtues. First, certain virtues are called for by the professional code of ethics in the mental health care setting in which psychiatrists practice, e.g., exercising respect for a patient's vulnerability to exploitation by not accepting gifts. These are role-specific virtues demanded of the psychiatrist regardless of clinical outcome. Second, the cultivation of certain traits "will be useful to therapeutic effectiveness," i.e., they might be "required for and/or markedly enhance the effectiveness of treatment."[6] If so, then psychiatrists should cultivate those traits given their duty to promote therapeutic benefit. Thus, these traits are considered distinguishable role-specific virtues whose possession by the psychiatrist are thought to enhance clinical outcome.

Radden emphasizes the significance of therapeutic reasons for being virtuous in psychiatry. The psychiatrist "uses her persona in forming, maintaining, and fostering the relationship or alliance with the patient out of which healing derives."[7] One can thus apply virtue ethical theory to clinical practice and argue for therapist virtues that are vitally relevant to living up to professional standards and to working effectively through the problems that arise in psychotherapy.[8] In this chapter, I show how an application of virtue ethical theory can support an argument for the relevance of patient-centered virtues to the working through.

## 5.2 **The Virtuous Patient**

Those who practice psychodynamic therapy have been known to stress its values in moral terms. Responsibility and honesty are crucial. Therapists can grant the premise that the patient is not responsible for the circumstances that fomented a conflict and led to maladaptive behavior. But psychodynamic practice involves helping a patient to first take responsibility for the maladaptive behavior that evolved from those circumstances, and second to take responsibility for changing it. Patients often need to be persuaded that the resulting maladaptive behaviors can be brought under their conscious control. The therapist aims to foster a relationship with the patient in which the latter can assume "a firm moral commitment" to attempting to see himself clearly with his limitations and fallibility intact. Therapists often speak of the "courage" that this effort to face painful truths about oneself entails. In this ethos, the ideal patient is the one who comes to understand her behavior "as honestly as possible" while admitting the impossibility of perfect self-understanding.[9]

The ethos of a therapeutic dialogue can also revolve around the sort of person the patient should be. In their first footnote, Radden and Sadler state the following: "Emphasis on the character of the practitioner is not intended to diminish the importance and efforts of … the patient. A more complete analysis … would acknowledge … other moral virtues—persistence, honesty, courage, hopefulness, flexibility, and trustfulness, for instance—of the 'good patient.' "[10] If the therapist's virtues are part of what makes the practice of psychotherapy possible, then there might be virtues that suitable patients can develop in their striving for therapeutic goals.

I suggest that virtues can be relevant to patients in two ways. First, persons who deal with various mental disorders or problems in living might aim to overcome them by attaining certain virtues as therapeutic goals. Second, the process of resolving such problems through psychotherapy might itself require the development and application of certain virtues. Thus the working through required of the patient might, in some cases, involve the cultivation of certain virtues that facilitate problem resolution.

I want to articulate some of the virtues that patients who are serious about psychotherapy can cultivate to meet the generic ethical challenges that these cases present. I argue that there are nascent virtues which the patient can bring to the psychotherapeutic encounter that, when cultivated with the therapist, can facilitate a beneficial outcome, e.g., perseverance and self-love. I claim that these traits may function as virtuous implicatures of character and indicate an ethical/moral capacity for virtuous response. The evaluative language by which they are defined can be related to Swanton's pluralistic conception of the virtues that is constrained, but not determined by, an adequate "background theory of healthy human growth and development." Hence the acute importance to the virtuous life of striving for "psychological improvement." I will relate some of these patient virtues to Swanton's conception of virtues of practice.[11]

If a patient has cultivated these virtues to some degree outside of psychotherapy, then he is responsible for exercising them within it. If the patient has yet to cultivate these virtues, but has the requisite personality traits from which they can be developed, then a key element of the therapeutic alliance would be the patient's willingness to cultivate them. Some patients might be easier than others in this regard. The easiest patient would be one who lives within an ethical/moral outlook and has sufficiently developed her character such that rudimentary virtues are in place. A less easy patient would be one whose virtues are incipient and require development. She has a capacity for virtuous response and would be responsible for exercising and strengthening the relevant virtues to address the problem that brought her to psychotherapy. The therapist would assist her to that end via the psychotherapeutic process. A difficult patient is one whose problem revolves around some degree of arrested personality that hinders character growth and her capacity for virtuous response. The most difficult patients would be those who live on the periphery or even outside a moral outlook and have a seriously diminished capacity for virtuous response, e.g., those with a diagnosis of a Cluster B personality disorder under DSM-5, specifically borderline personality and antisocial personality disorder. One aspect of the psychotherapeutic goal for these difficult patients is the development of this very capacity. I explore the relevance of mentalization-based psychotherapy to this goal in chapter seven.

## 5.3 **Virtue-Laden Psychotherapy Cases**

I am hardly the first to claim that some psychotherapy cases are ethically value-laden. My analysis builds on a rich and growing literature that elucidates the ethical space of the talking cures. I have noted that psychotherapy is connected intimately with self-improvement insofar as many patients wrestle with the gap between the persons they would like to be and the persons they are.[12]

The earlier analyses of Margolis and London laid much groundwork for the claim that ethical values guide the transformative process of psychotherapy.[13] London argued that "much of the material" that psychotherapists deal with can be neither used nor understood without reference to moral values. Those values may influence the practice of therapy, the conception of a patient's needs, and the definition of terms such as "health," "illness," and "normality."[14] Margolis averred that since psychotherapy is concerned with effecting changes in a patient's actions and motivations, a concern that usually falls within the moral domain, it "clearly presupposes a set of values in the name of which the alteration of the lives of patients is undertaken."[15] Like Jahoda,[16] Margolis saw some therapeutic values as being formulated within "that part of the moral tradition that concerns happiness and well-being."[17] Additionally, Matthews has claimed that these values may cohere in a "moral vision" of a "fully satisfactory life."[18] Recent analysis augments the notion that this set of values can amount to an implicit conception of a flourishing life.[19] Psychotherapy would thus involve a conception of what a satisfactory life should be like, a way of interpreting the patient's disorder or problem in living as a deviation from that conception, and a way of treating patients that aims to show them how to achieve that conception in their own lives.[20]

Despite Freud's position that his talking cure did not need anything approaching a moral *Weltanschauung* of its own, practicing psychoanalysts have long acknowledged the ethically value-laden nature of their work. Roazen used case illustrations from his practice to illustrate his insistence that it is impossible to exclude "the problem of moral values" from psychoanalytic thought.[21] Ramzy argued that the "everyday work" of analysts involves them unavoidably in matters pertaining to moral values and the formation of value judgements on the patient's ways of relating to self and other.[22] Bieber felt that the analyst's goal of benefitting patients and facilitating their "mental" improvement was itself "the expression of a positive moral value and direction."[23]

Other notable analyses include Woolfolk and Richardson, Fowers, Guignon, and Lomas. Woolfolk argues that psychotherapy is "an activity involving the development, elucidation, and application of practical knowledge and acumen through dialogue—a form of pedagogy encompassing fact and value, analogous to what in other times has been called the cultivation of character or the development of practical wisdom."[24] Thus, to engage with a person's pattern of emotional responses to the world is also to engage with her value system, and as such psychotherapies that analyze and modify emotional responses "will be deeply involved in moral-evaluative material."[25]

Richardson, Fowers, and Guignon argue that a "hermeneutic-dialogical view of psychotherapy" can best reveal the "essentially moral issues" with which it often deals. A person might seek psychotherapy because he "lacks a wider conception of life and the good life that would define his fulfillment."[26] Guignon sees "addressing questions about what constitutes the good life and how we can be at home in the world" as the central task of contemporary psychotherapy.[27] Like Guignon, Charles Taylor affirms these as moral questions for which morality includes "questions about how I am going to live my life … which touch on the issue of what kind of life is worth living … or of what constitutes a rich, meaningful life—as against one concerned with secondary matters or trivia."[28] Lomas made an eloquent plea "for the moral element of living to be fully recognized" by psychotherapists and patients alike. Therapists cannot confront the "whole being" of their patients without asking how they might help that person lead a better life and what that better life might be. Given his belief that "there are ways of living that are better than others," Lomas felt that it was better for his patients not to be "crippled" by unrealistic fears, "consumed" by hate, or engaged in persistent lying. Their daily encounters with patients force therapists "to enter personal dilemmas of a moral nature," thus making them "continuously embroiled in questions of morality" and the kind of life that is worth living.[29]

I find the psychotherapy cases that are best elucidated in virtue ethical terms to have the three parts of my triadic structure: (1) the problem for which psychotherapy is sought; (2) the desirable outcome or goal of the psychotherapy; and (3) the joint praxis of therapist and patient that aims to realize that outcome. Here is how I approach the triadic structure of these cases. If (1) the problem can be elucidated in self- or other-regarding ethical terms and (2) the goals of treatment involve any or all of the following: ethically desirable changes in (a) tendencies of affective/emotional response, (b) a better understanding of how one should treat oneself and/or others, and (c) better patterns of behavior, then (3) the efforts the committed patient makes to resolve the problem can involve the affective, cognitive, and practical facets of generic ethical self-improvement through the cultivation of certain virtues.[30]

The triad starts with an ostensible mental disorder or a problem in living that is best illustrated by another-regarding, morally objectionable character fault for which the patient can be sensibly held capable of and responsible for changing. Matthews contends that *some* of the conditions that we call "mental disorders" can be thought of as unchosen moral disorders in the sense that they comprise a divergence from a moral conception of a satisfactory life. Persons feel, think, and behave in ways that significantly affect their chances of achieving a satisfactory life.[31] Charland has analyzed the Cluster B Personality Disorders of DSM-4 as paradigmatic examples such as character faults.[32] Hence the disorder or problem for which psychotherapy is sought becomes the first part of the triad when it can be elucidated in ethical terms.

The second part of the triad is the goal of treatment. This can be a positive state of mental health that transcends symptom relief, which is attained by changing a patient's emotional, cognitive, and behavioral dispositions in ways that significantly increase their chances of flourishing. This can involve at least a threshold state of being virtuous if the morally objectionable character faults are to be superseded by morally desirable character strengths. The goal would be to replace the character faults with settled cognitive, emotional, and behavioral dispositions that with sufficient effort will become stable character traits over time. Two modes of moral response that can be desirable goals of psychotherapy are appropriately greater measures of self-love and respect for self and others. The case I will present also posits the virtue of anger management as an ethically desirable goal of psychotherapy. Hence the desired outcome or goal of treatment becomes the second part of the triad when it can be elucidated in self- and other-regarding virtue ethical terms.

We can then move to the third part of the triad, which is a form of what Charland would call "moral treatment" that essentially involves a concerted effort by the therapist and patient to replace character faults with character strengths or virtues. Treatment would assist the patient to make the requisite choices that would lead to the "correction" of the unchosen moral disorder. This would involve informing the patient of what a morally satisfactory life might be like and how the desirable virtues would contribute to it. This approach to treatment is like a mode of education that requires the active involvement of the patient.[33] At some point, the patient has to accept responsibility for working with, on, and for herself. The working through can involve cultivating affective, cognitive, and behavioral inclinations in the effort to effect morally desirable changes in the way the patient treats other people. It can also involve strenuous efforts at improving oneself by cultivating an appropriate measure of self-love. I think the patient's efforts can also involve Swanton's three virtues of practice, to which I return below. Hence the treatment becomes the third part of the triad when it can be elucidated in self- and other-regarding virtue ethical terms.

## 5.4 An Apposite Theory of Virtue Ethics

I turn now to a brief account of Swanton's theory of virtue ethics. Swanton offers a pluralistic theory of the virtues, which revolves around the following axial points. We face the challenge of appropriately meeting "the demands of the world."[34] Virtues enable us to do this. A personality trait becomes a virtue for Swanton if it is developed to the point of being a disposition to respond (e.g., through fine inner states of respecting, loving, creating, etc.) in a good enough or excellent way to items or "targets" in the field of a virtue. Items can be people, objects, situations, inner states, or actions. As targets, they are what virtues aim at, e.g., the well-being of others is the target of beneficence. The field of a virtue consists of those items that constitute the virtue's spheres of concern. The demands of the world include demands of the self, e.g., the demand for self-development. Virtue is a threshold concept for Swanton. One person can be virtuous to some degree while another can be even more virtuous. Whether less than perfect virtue reaches the threshold for virtue is a matter of judgement that involves assessments about the extent to which the exercise of the putative virtue meets the demands of the world.[35]

Virtues have a plurality of bases and modes of moral responsiveness. The bases of moral responsiveness are the kinds of morally significant features that items have. There are four such bases that lie in the nature of items that virtuous persons respond to: value, status, good (or benefit), and bonds. The modes are the manner of pertinent response to the four bases. They encompass various ways of responding well to items in the field of a virtue, e.g., promoting, honoring, appreciating, respecting, being receptive to, and loving items that have value or status, or are good, or to which we are bonded.[36] Thus we do more than promote value or goodness. We also respect persons in terms of different kinds of status, express and act upon bonds of love, create and appreciate things of high quality, and are receptive to the value of things.[37]

Modes of moral responsiveness like self and universal love, respect, creativity, and expression are "central" to all specific virtues and are evinced in the nature of the responder. A virtuous moral response must express fine inner states that have amongst them a background motivation to act from virtue. Thus benevolence, generosity, and other virtues aimed at the good of others express fine inner states of self and are constrained by respect for the other's status as client, patient, student, friend, spouse, or child. Swanton argues that the features that turn traits into virtues are the same features that determine virtuous responses to items in the field of a virtue. Virtues thus have a "profile," which Swanton defines as "that constellation of modes of moral responsiveness ... which comprise the virtuous disposition."[38] The modes of moral response that profile all virtues can, in some contexts, be specific virtues themselves. We can "talk about the virtue of self-love, for example, in a context where an agent is striving to overcome a wide range of deficiencies in this area."[39] As I will argue below, psychotherapy is one such context.

Swanton distinguishes between acting from virtue and a virtuous act. The former means that one's actions express the fine inner states that I associate with positive mental health, e.g., the emotional dispositions, practical wisdom, and motivations that comprise the virtue to a sufficient degree. An act from virtue is dependent on the state(s) from which the agent acts. Although actions from virtue tend to be right actions, they can sometimes miss the target due to misfortune. By contrast, whether an act is virtuous is independent of the motives or inner states from which the agent acts. An act is virtuous if, and only if, it hits the target, or realizes the proper goal, of the virtue. An act might do this without expressing the fine inner states that would make it an act from virtue.[40] Thus, Swanton's account of right action involves a pluralistic notion of the right. A virtuous act hits the target of a virtue so a right act might be a generous one that may diversely promote good, promote value, or show love for certain persons appropriate to their status or the bonds we have with them.[41]

Since virtue is a threshold concept, the plurality of standards for attaining it are "to some extent" relative to the person's own capacities. Persons are beings who develop and mature; they grow both physically and psychologically. Hence Swanton's claim that an adequate conception of virtue ethics inherits the complex task of understanding "psychic health" and requires a background conception of healthy human growth "and the vicissitudes that interfere with it." Given the importance she ascribes to striving for psychological improvement and self-realization, her analysis emphasizes psychological components of virtue. But Swanton is careful to avoid conflation. The virtues do not reduce to health. Rather, they are constrained by it. Hence her constraint on virtue: a correct conception of the virtues must at least be partly shaped, or constrained by, an adequate theory of healthy growth and development which in part constitutes our flourishing. This constraint does not entail that the point of every virtue is to maximize or even conduce to the health of the virtuous. It does suggest that our notions of virtuous modes of moral response "should be appropriate to both human development and to ideals of human health."[42]

Swanton rejects a "strong" form of an ethics of self-realization. She is suitably pessimistic about anyone attaining "full health" and emphasizes that personal growth is but one demand among many that the world makes on us. Since virtues respond to more than exigencies of self-realization, they do not conduce by definition to self-realization. Still, since virtues are traits that often benefit those who attain them, Swanton's constraint on virtue allows for a close connection between virtuous lives, healthy growth, and personal flourishing. She appeals to psychological findings to confirm this connection. "Chronic anger and hostility form the basis not only of much vice, but also of human ill health: *ill health that can be averted by the cultivation of virtue* [italics mine]."[43] Indeed, Swanton allows for "virtues associated with the regulation of anger" and regards her constraint on virtue as offering an understanding of psychological health as a state that necessitates the living of lives that are virtuous in many ways.[44]

Pursuing goals of psychological improvement, says Swanton, is extremely important to the virtuous life. She argues that in working to overcome problems that obstruct one's ability to grow, one works to express greater self-love through attaining a better bond with oneself. This bond enables one to express personal strength in undistorted ways that incorporate "respect for self and other." I think that some of the problems for which psychotherapy is sought can be plausibly seen to obstruct the development of this bond. I contend that they can often be seen "in terms of various kinds of failure of self-love."[45]

Consider again the cases of psychotherapy to which the triadic analysis applies. A theory of virtue ethics that best accommodates them should, I suggest, be pluralistic, moderately, as opposed to impossibly demanding, and acknowledge a virtue associated with self-improvement. Swanton's theory reflects these features. Her theory is pluralistic in its insistence that no one standard, i.e., that of the ideally healthy or splendidly well-adjusted person, should set the requirements for virtue. Standards of virtue should, to some extent, be contextual in their acknowledgement of psychological conflict and relative to a person's own capacities.[46]

Her theory is moderately demanding in its recognition that persons leading ordinary lives are usually imperfect and may lack the strength to imitate the acts of the supremely virtuous. It is also moderately demanding in its rejection of the idea that the attainment of virtue requires that right action will flow unimpeded and absent psychological conflict from a mature agent.[47] Hers is not a thick perfectionist account that turns on the standards set by the fully or supremely virtuous. This reflects the fact that the world is marred by the frequent occurrence of conflict, catastrophe, scarcity, and evil, as well as the difficulty of attaining full virtue. Rather, her notion of virtue is not excessively demanding. Virtuous responses must meet the threshold for virtue. Beyond that, they can range from being good enough to excellent to supererogatory. Consequently, virtuous responses can be "expressive of attempts in the agent to gain greater strength."[48] Finally, Swanton's theory acknowledges a virtue associated with self-improvement. Patients in psychotherapy may want to overcome paralyzing obsessions, defuse excessive guilt, or control inappropriate hostility. I think Swanton's theory can acknowledge that persons who deal with various mental disorders or problems in living might aim to better themselves by cultivating certain virtues.[49]

On my reading, Swanton's theory can also acknowledge that a patient's efforts to work through difficulties in psychotherapy might themselves require the development of her three virtues of practice. These are virtues of focus, virtues associated with the integration of constraints to a problem's solution, and dialogical virtues. Swanton argues that the aim of virtues of practice is to get things right by acting virtuously overall in solving problems.[50] In this context, and with some modifications, we can think of virtues of practice as dispositions of character that enable a patient to make the most of psychotherapy and facilitate attempts to resolve the problems that led him to seek it. If the triadic analysis applies, then they can be seen as instrumental to the working through of ethical self-improvement and will vary in their state of development.

First, to make the most of psychotherapy as a process of constructing solutions to problems, patients need virtues of focus so plights can be discerned and addressed. Second, given Swanton's analysis that problem resolution proceeds via integrating constraints (i.e., dealing effectively with the impediments to its solution), patients need a number of moral, epistemic, and creative virtues to inform their reflection. Third, given the need to integrate constraints having due regard to the perspectives of the psychotherapist, patients need "virtues of dialogue."[51] While some patients might bring highly developed virtues of practice to psychotherapy, they might be merely nascent in others and require much cultivation for the working through to be successful. The working through can involve acquiring virtues of practice in the effort to effect morally desirable changes in the way the patient treats others. It can also involve strenuous efforts at improving oneself by strengthening one's character and cultivating an appropriate measure of self-love.

## 5.5 Seneca's Angry Man

The following case illustrates psychotherapy as "a dynamic process of feedback, learning and modification" by which a patient learns to exercise three virtues of practice to better bond with himself and develop a more satisfying, less limited response to the world.[52] The patient was a thirty-five-year-old male who complained of episodic depressions, chronic self-loathing, and continual problems with anger management. Like Seneca's Angry Man, he was "constantly swollen" with a simmering antipathy.[53]

His anger was directed at himself as well as others. He was twice divorced, both ex-wives having left him for violent behavior and excessive drinking. He believed that he was "fated" to be punished for his past mistakes of which he was deeply ashamed. He felt singled out by the world and persecuted. He was obsessively preoccupied with thoughts of hitting people or being attacked by strangers. Equally obsessive was his extreme sensitivity to perceived slights and deprecations. He personified the world as being out to antagonize him. Misplacing his keys was viewed as a personal affront by a hostile world that was pushing him to the brink. His characteristic response was to kick in the door. He once punched his computer screen because he lost his internet connection. He thus alternated between periods of depression and hostility. Both traits had a corrosive effect on himself and others. He sought psychotherapy to both relieve his symptoms and to explore his sense that his self-loathing and volatility were putting him out of touch with the person he felt that he should be. He told the therapist that he was tired of going through life with the mark of Cain on his forehead.

The initial psychotherapy was broadly psychodynamic. The patient found it difficult to discuss his childhood and family life, especially when the therapist challenged him to be more forthcoming. This added to his anxiety and on three occasions he almost terminated psychotherapy but resolved each time to continue. The dialogues revealed the patient's past as an only child caught up in the emotional maelstrom of his parents' marriage. He had vivid memories of his father slapping and choking his mother. Sudden fulminations were the norm. His father would erupt without warning, punching his fist through the walls of their tiny bungalow or throwing whatever came to hand at whomever was near enough to be hit. The patient developed a nervous and timid disposition for which his father ridiculed him. He was beaten often with a leather strap after which he would be shut in his room for hours. He grew up terrified of and enraged at his father.[54]

The therapist offered the following account: the patient learned to anticipate emotional and physical violence at a very early age. Since "attacks" were usually impending in his home, he lived in a persistently anxious state of "fight or flight." Hence his proclivity to respond explosively to fractious or challenging situations. The patient also came to identify with his aggressor to the point of acquiring his father's intimidating and violent personality. There were mixed motives here: he would be more like the man whose love he sought, but he would also be the man of whom even his father would be afraid. He dealt with his own fear by making others wary of provoking him and eventually became abusive himself. He felt excoriating guilt at having become the man who abused him.

Anger, guilt, fear, a view of the world as hostile, a view of others as persecutory, and a repetitive compulsion to attack himself with self-disparaging thoughts are thus core aspects of Seneca's Angry Man. These core aspects can be rendered thick or thin depending on the level of theoretical refinement that is brought to their delineation. Overly thin accounts can belabor the obvious. Seneca's Angry Man does not need to be told by his therapist that he "carries a lot of guilt and hostility." Thicker accounts elucidate these aspects with theory:

> You were emotionally and physically abused as a child by your father. You lacked an empathically supportive holding environment and came to see the world as threatening. You identified with your abuser and learned at a very young age to be hostile in your life-world. You were terrified of your father and ashamed that you could not stand up to him. You became resentful and took this out on others whom you perceived to be antagonistic. You thought that by becoming angry, your father would identify you with himself and stop attacking you. You also thought that the best defense in a predatory world was an angry offensive toward others.

One can imagine variations on these psychodynamic themes with different survivors of childhood abuse. It is trite to point out that theoretical interpretation is a creative endeavor that moves beyond mere discovery; that reflective observers influence what they observe, and that any science reflects this. But do these interpretations fit the facts? There is growing empirical evidence that early childhood abuse victims compulsively perpetrate similar abuse as adults.[55] There will be clinical cases that beckon psychodynamic interpretations and cases that do not. I posit Seneca's Angry Man as one that does. By contrast, imagine a war veteran who comes from a loving family and had a happy childhood but who deals with post-traumatic stress disorder as a result of his experience in combat. I posit this as a case that does not.

More to the point, psychodynamic, existential, or cognitive behavioral elucidation can be informed by a therapist's careful attempt to make theory fit the core aspects of patients. It would be immoderately skeptical to assume that every theoretical refinement of the patient's core aspects is a fabricated distortion of some pristine reality that should be left to elucidate itself. There are bound to be some very basic, true, and definitive things we can say about the patient, about who he is and how he lives; about how he regards himself and others.

I have also noted that psychotherapy does not stop with the accurate delineation of core aspects. The harder questions involve interpretations about how the core aspects originated and the psychological mechanisms by which the patient maintains them. How did Seneca's Angry Man get that way? Why does he persist in being *that* way when he senses that it obstructs the cultivation of a *better* way to be? What exactly is that better way and how ought he to act so as to cultivate it? Even harder are the normative questions about why and how a patient ought to change his core aspects. Should they be modified to a degree or should the patient aim to change them altogether and develop new ones? Justified true beliefs about the core aspects of the patient are seen by many as the building blocks on which interpretations, remedial insights, and treatment goals should be based. But we might say that the real work of psychotherapy begins after the core aspects have been accurately identified. These questions are less amenable to confirmation as justified true beliefs but they can be central to psychotherapy. On my account, meaning reorganization follows from and reflects the patient's core understanding of self and world. It does not create that understanding.

In this case, the patient eventually felt he had acquired an accurate perspective on the development of his attitudes and behavior and he reluctantly began to accept responsibility for changing both. Although his depressions were less frequent, he learned that insight alone does not guarantee change. He still had difficulty controlling his anger and continued to experience what he believed were subtle slights and provocations from those around him. He could not shake the belief that people were trying to punish him. After eighteen months, the patient accepted his therapist's suggestion to begin cognitive behavioral therapy in a further effort to modify his negative attitudes and manage his anger.

## 5.6 **From Theory to Practice: Patient-Related Virtues in Psychotherapy**

Let's apply the triadic analysis. (1) We have a problem that can be elucidated in self- and other-regarding ethical terms. In self-regarding terms, the patient lacks a sense of personal worth. His self-contempt obstructs his ability to love and respect himself, appropriate measures of which are crucial to feelings and behavior that reflect care and respect for others. In other-regarding terms, his anger is emotionally and occasionally physically harmful. These ethical terms can be reflected in an "official" diagnosis of mental disorder. There could be clinical deliberation using the DSM about whether the patient's volatility should be distinguished from the aggressive behavior that can occur in either antisocial or borderline personality disorder. If a diagnosis of one of these disorders is made, then we revisit the Cluster B personality disorders that can be construed as character faults that the patient can be reasonably held responsible for changing. If the patient's volatility is so distinguished, then he might be diagnosed with intermittent explosive disorder, one of the DSM's impulse control disorders not elsewhere specified.[56] (2) We have psychotherapeutic goals that can be elucidated in virtue ethical terms. The goals are greater self-love, respect for others, and anger management. The treatment goals involve ethically desirable changes in dispositions of emotional response, and in a cognitive understanding of how one should treat oneself and others that is expressed in better behavior. Thus, impulsive feelings and displays of anger ought to be replaced by stable degrees of measured emotional calm and behavioral restraint, as well as an improved understanding of why managing one's anger is a better way to live. The goal is for the patient to modify his feelings, cognitions, and behavior in ethically desirable ways. (3) The efforts the patient makes to work through his problems will involve the affective, cognitive, and practical facets of generic ethical self-improvement. This working through is a concerted effort to replace character faults with character strengths or virtues.

Now let's apply ideas from Swanton's virtue ethics. Her notion of "hypersubjective vice" arguably captures much of this patient's problem. His childhood traumas set the conditions for a failure in self-love. His angry way of responding to the world was expressive of this failure and resulted in a twisted sense of himself as despised by others.[57] Swanton might say that his distorted affective and cognitive dispositions typify a conception of egocentricity that owes much to Adler and Horney: his childhood left him with "a peculiarly sharp sense of life's hostility" which he subconsciously exaggerated. His interest in the "bitterness" of life was predominant. The patient remained in a juvenile phase reminiscent of a spoilt child. Understandable wishes or needs, such as finding his keys or efficiently using his computer, turned into claims or demands that he made on the world. The non-fulfillment of these demands caused resentment and much more than "normal frustration." It was felt as an offence about which he was entitled to feel indignant. "The desire to escape a self seen as defective or contemptible … [can] cause difficulty in the acknowledgement of necessities, restrictions, losses, or deprivations."[58] I am reminded again of Seneca's Angry Man whose "every sense of grievance grew into self-torture." The patient thus fueled his hostility by either suspecting what was untrue or by exaggerating what was unimportant.[59]

I think this case places virtue ethics in a therapeutic context. We can understand the patient's striving to overcome personal deficiencies as an exercise in working toward self-love and empathic concern and respect for others, and establishing modes of moral responsiveness that comprise a more virtuous disposition. These are two of the "recovery virtues" that I elaborate further in chapter six. Given the wide range of distortions wrought by his internalized anger, self-love was a virtue he sought to attain.[60] We can see that these distortions affected his receptivity to the demands of the world. To paraphrase Iris Murdoch, his mind was constantly active in fabricating an anxious, self-preoccupied, and often falsifying veil of hostility that obfuscated his moral vision.[61] Swanton defines self-love as an essentially bond-centered, psychological phenomenon that reflects a Kantian distinction between coming close to and keeping an appropriate distance from oneself. Coming close involves bonding with oneself to express one's "strength, vitality, and energy" in undistorted ways that should "make room for both self-respect and respect for others."[62]

Keeping a balanced distance from oneself involves self-respect, i.e., a recognition that, out of regard for oneself as a person, one does not act as if one lacks worth.[63] This equilibrium can be tilted toward egocentricity by internalized self-hate. The Angry Man, notes Seneca, is hurled headlong by his "inner tumult" and loses his balance. As if on a "stormy sea," he sees nothing clearly.[64] This egocentricity is invasive to the self through its suffocating effect. It distorts the expression of one's vitality by leaving little room to breathe easily with, or be accepting of, oneself. One loses distance from oneself if one is blinded by a narrow preoccupation with one's own "ego problems." In this case, the patient went through much of his life choking on his anger. In seeking therapy, he began, however dimly, to see beyond his falsifying veil of hostility. He sought to put some distance between himself and his anger and to acquire a better bond with himself. Swanton sees perseverance as a "virtue" that "requires self-love if a healthy bonding with one's projects is to be possible."[65] I think this case illustrates an alternate reading that would not be at odds with Swanton's theory: where this healthy bond is decidedly lacking, striving for appropriate measures of self-love can require perseverance.

Although Swanton claims that self-control is an "admirable" trait that will not always count as an ethical virtue, I think this case epitomizes a striving for the virtuous self-control of anger. In reconceiving his persecutory view of the world, the patient slowly became more open to and trusting of others. In wanting to be that kind of person, he came to express a finer inner state, i.e., a background motivation to act from the virtues of self-love, respect for others, and anger regulation.[66] I do not intend this case to illustrate a Jamesian conversion to supreme healthy mindedness. The patient had drunk too deeply from the cup of anger to ever forget its taste, but through therapy he had realized a finer internal state that calmed its affective edge.[67] His proclivity to anger slowly became less forceful and he learned eventually to manage his reactions to quotidian frustrations fairly well. Further, he came to feel closer to the more open and empathic person he thought he should be. If psychotherapy was not going to completely eradicate his anger, it was aimed at enabling him to "at least ... rein it in and check its violence."[68]

I noted previously Swanton's claim that the process of resolving problems requires the application of her three virtues of practice. I think these virtues are relevant to this patient's striving for self- and other-regarding ethical improvement. Like perseverance, these are some of the "healing virtues" that I discuss in chapter six. First, this patient needed virtues of focus so plights could be discerned and addressed. A shared focus with the therapist motivated his involvement and provided an operational context for "dialogical virtues" of relevant information. Where that information is "difficult or embarrassing," virtues of focus involve "not just acumen, discipline, [and] sensitivity," but may also involve "courage and persistence." This patient brought propitious character traits to psychotherapy. He did not have "wisdom, experience, and localized expertise"[69] in resolving psychological problems, but he gradually acknowledged that his therapy would involve ongoing work. This required initial dispositions to honesty and perseverance. These traits gave the therapist much to work with but they also enabled the patient to work on, with, and for himself.

We can say the patient began therapy with incipient traits that could be strengthened and developed as virtues of focus. He revealed a fledgling disposition to sustain a shared, concentrated effort to unravel the thorns in his psyche. This disposition grew in strength as the psychotherapy progressed. He faced his difficulties in disclosing his past with laudable measures of courage and persistence. His initial reluctance to confide was eventually supplanted by a steadfast fixity on providing unvarnished revelations about "shameful" behavior that evinced his growing commitment to valid information. In Swanton's terms, we can say that he worked through a dialogical process of feedback, learning, and modification by which virtues of focus could be cultivated and strengthened in effecting a good enough solution to his problems in living.[70]

Second, we can apply Swanton's analysis that problem resolution proceeds via integrating constraints, i.e., dealing effectively with the impediments to the problem's solution. Constraints can include relevant values, material resource levels, time, energy, and existing practices which a solution must accommodate. Hence some of the patient's constraints were external, e.g., he was limited to two-weekly sessions and had to occasionally cancel them for work-related travel. He was also faced with the challenge of integrating the following internal constraints: (1) initial confusion about the origins of his condition and his motivations for perpetuating it; (2) behavioral embeddedness, i.e., the extent to which his angry reactions and self-loathing had become "wired" into his personality; (3) initial discomfort in re-examining his traumatic past and accepting responsibility for having sustained his violent behavior; and (4) initial discomfort in accepting the psychotherapist's challenge to assume responsibility for changing the frame of mind that informed his behavior. An effective psychotherapy must accommodate these constraints and enable the therapist and patient to gradually work through them. We might view psychotherapy as the process by which the patient progressively specified and re-specified the constraint structure of his problem, moving from a problem that initially appeared intractable to one that was transformed to "take on a more tractable air."[71]

Swanton claims that "insight, depth of understanding, creativity, and commitment to valid information" are "central" to the virtues required for integrating constraints. Other virtues include dispositions to assemble and acknowledge relevant data, to examine and evaluate assertions made during the process of resolving the problem, to trust and acknowledge expertise, and "to change one's beliefs on the strength of evidence" and admit mistakes. In these ways, the patient developed "the imaginative and analytic virtues required to facilitate constraint integration."[72] His disclosures facilitated the testing of his outlook through the scrutiny of the therapist. His insight into his anger grew along with his creativity in dealing more effectively with it. Hence his eventual understanding that psychodynamic dialogue would only take him so far and his propitious involvement in cognitive behavioral therapy. The latter mode of treatment "re-specified" his persecutory attitudes as negative schemas and his destructive reactions as amenable to modification.

The way the patient integrated constraints need not have been fully excellent. Remember, he vacillated about remaining in therapy, was initially not forthcoming and candid about his childhood and marital misconduct, and succumbed to intense guilt when his efforts to control his anger failed. He thus had to develop resolve to remain in therapy, had to work on being completely honest with the therapist, and had to work even harder to accommodate setbacks in his efforts at anger management. Yet the patient strove to overcome his weaknesses and meet the targets of the virtues of practice in a right, reasonable, and good enough way.

Third, given the need to integrate constraints having due regard to the perspective of the psychotherapist, this patient needed "virtues of dialogue" to overcome his limitations and participate adequately in therapy. The strong therapeutic alliance in this case enabled the cultivation of these virtues. Psychotherapy was thus an ongoing conversation in which both parties contributed thoughts on how the patient had acquired his attitudes and reactive behavior patterns and how he should go about the task of removing the traumatic past from his present.[73]

It is interesting to note that some of the patient dispositions that are thought to facilitate psychotherapeutic benefit might be seen as implicitly describing virtues of practice. Three researchers come to mind. I am thinking first of Hanna and Puhakka's notion of a patient's "resolute perception," which they define as "the steady and deliberate observation of or attending to" an intimidating, painful, or stultifying experience. This involves an "openness" to that experience and a "readiness to honestly examine it, evaluate it, and, if need be to change it with therapeutic intent." A therapeutic intention means that the resoluteness aims at promoting the patient's well-being, which is "variously described as personal growth, adaptive behavior, [or] authenticity."[74] I am also thinking of Arthur C. Bohart's work, in which he notes several variables that can be correlated with personality traits that have been shown to enhance the probability of patients "doing well in insight-oriented psychotherapy," such as psychological mindedness, ability to participate in interpersonal dialogue, openness and receptive listening, creative flexibility, perseverance, and courage. His model of the activities of productive patient thinking in psychotherapy has some intriguing parallels with Swanton's three virtues of practice that I think merit further research and reflection.[75]

## 5.7 **Counter-Arguments and Qualifications**

Virtue ethics is often seen to pivot on supremely virtuous exemplars, i.e., persons who have attained a high degree of excellence in acting consistently from virtue. The inner states from which they act are supposedly fine and stable to the point of making their virtuous actions consummately adroit. My own sense is that Swanton rightfully avoids making virtue ethics too ideal for any flawed person's good. This moderately demanding, pluralistic approach may still attract criticism for being too expansive and for accommodating pedestrian efforts.

In addition, we need a better sense of whether, and if so how, psychotherapy might influence the ethical motivation that patients in these cases must have. Presumably, patients who do well in the triadic structure cases must begin therapy with some degree of ethical motivation. But suppose they do not? Either way, how might a psychotherapist enable and influence it? How should this exercise in educative ethics work? The cases on which I focus would rule out the impassively "abstinent" therapist of traditional psychoanalysis. They would also exclude patients who would resist psychotherapeutic process with a "flight into health," i.e., those who resist the burdens of working through difficult experiences by claiming that they have attained prompt relief of the symptoms that brought them to therapy.[76] We should also consider whether a therapeutic alliance in these cases requires a confluence of ethical values between therapist and patient.

In the case at hand, psychotherapy enabled the patient to make a start at overcoming his self- and other-regarding character flaws. In particular, it enabled him to develop and apply virtues of practice in a sustained effort to cultivate self-love, respect for others, and virtuous anger management. Given Swanton's "threshold view in which the standards for virtue are relative to context,"[77] I think this case epitomizes how psychotherapy can be a virtue ethical endeavor for the patient.

One might agree with Mike W. Martin that my analysis epitomizes instead an insufficient sensitivity to the perspectival differences between those who observe psychotherapy and those who conduct it.[78] Martin does not argue that morally explicit language appropriate to third-party observers has no place in psychotherapy. He does argue that it should be modified by a therapeutic lens, or "filtered through the prism of therapy." He then makes the finer point that "positive moral language" can be relevant to the promotion of therapeutic goals, "as when therapists convey hope about the future, praise patients for their courage and for accepting responsibility, and urge patients to love and respect themselves." He notes, I think correctly, that "nuance and context" do much to determine when such language is appropriate and that therapists are trained to be especially sensitive to "how patients can misinterpret even positive moral language." We agree that the questions of whether and when the language of virtues is therapeutically beneficial require empirical study.[79] We also agree that the healing role will modify and restrict how therapists might use morally explicit language.

Martin's concern covers the morally explicit but negative language of blame. Some explicit uses of blaming will be inappropriate during therapy. Martin asks us to imagine a psychotherapist who makes the following statement to a patient:

> You have several very serious character faults or vices. You lack the virtues of self-control, self-respect, empathy, and respect for other people. You feel guilt and shame because you actually are guilty and shameful in your conduct. We need to work together to help you become a morally better person. One of my contributions will be to educate you about morally appropriate ways of thinking, feeling, and behaving. Working together, we can improve your character.

Although this might be a suitable statement for a third-person observer, Martin claims that it might be unsuitable for a psychotherapist. His concern is that such statements could be both therapeutically and morally self-defeating. Therapists need to respect patients' autonomy and maintain caring, supportive relationships with them. This requires psychotherapists to be largely nonjudgmental and to avoid "the language of vices and faults, which can push psychodynamic buttons that interfere with the relationship."[80]

I have no quarrel with Martin's caution that "much depends on nuance and context" as to whether, when, and how moral language should be used by psychotherapists. Even in triadic structure cases that I think are best elucidated in virtue ethical terms, the use of that language by psychotherapists can be more or less sensitive; the elucidations better or worse. Consequently, I do not think that such language is only appropriate for third-party observers and I do envision cases where it is appropriate for psychotherapists to use it in fairly straightforward terms.

In noting the limitations of my analysis, I distinguish between those patients who begin therapy with some degree of insight and ethical motivation, and those who do not. Seneca's Angry Man is one of the former. It is an easier case because he knew that the feelings, thoughts, and abusive behavior that plagued him were morally objectionable and he wanted to change for the better. He was ashamed of his past mistakes and sought therapy because he wanted to get closer to the more empathic person he thought he should be. The patient gradually accepted his responsibility for having perpetuated his faults, as well as his responsibility for overcoming them. In such a case, the psychotherapist might use explicit moral language in the following way:

> You have come to me for help. You tell me that you can't control your temper, do not respect yourself, and take advantage of others. You feel shame and guilt about treating yourself and others in a morally reprehensible way. We've both acknowledged the problems that brought you here. You've found fault with your character. That's a crucial step. Some people with your problems never honestly face themselves and own up to their responsibility for changing. But you also have a sense that you can and should become a better person than you feel you currently are. We need to work together to help you improve your character and become that person. You are worth that effort, and I believe you understand that. But you're not going to become that better person unless you stop putting so much effort into loathing yourself and then taking it out on others. You can think of our therapy as an exercise in acquiring virtues of self-control, self-respect, empathy, and respect for other people.

I do not see these remarks as either therapeutically or morally self-defeating. Indeed, I think it would be self-defeating on both counts for the psychotherapist to avoid acknowledging the patient's account of what led him to seek help. Since part of the problem is the patient's difficulty in getting beyond his self-condemnation, I can only assume that Martin agrees that it would again be self-defeating on both counts to reinforce it. This patient does not need his nose rubbed in his character flaws. The point is to facilitate the patient's efforts to better understand those flaws so that he stops rubbing his own nose in them. The patient may not improve unless he does. Nor do I see this response as detrimental to the maintenance of a caring, supportive relationship that is respectful of the patient's autonomy. The psychotherapist encourages the patient to accept responsibility for change through moral self-improvement. He does not assign the patient a past-oriented responsibility for acquiring the problems that led him to therapy.

Martin astutely raises a case in which a violent patient can be assigned that past-oriented responsibility. He claims that even in this case, the therapist's role is to avoid blaming the patient in order to help him. If we make the case harder by supposing that the patient does not acknowledge this responsibility, and denies that his character is flawed, then there is one sense of blame that I do not think can, or should, be avoided. We need to pay careful attention to what we do when we blame someone. Blame is the state of being responsible for a fault or error. To blame means primarily to hold responsible, or to assign responsibility for a fault or wrong. It can also mean to censure, to express strong or severe disapproval, to criticize harshly and condemn (*American Heritage Dictionary of the English Language, Collins English Dictionary, Concise Oxford English Dictionary*, s.v. "Blame" and "Censure"). The harder case arguably requires an effort by the psychotherapist to help the patient understand and accept *his* responsibility for the wrongful violent behavior. Part of that effort will conceivably involve the psychotherapist pointing out that the patient, and no one else, is responsible for it. In that primary sense, the psychotherapist blames the patient, but I am not convinced that this assignment of responsibility requires condemnatory expressions of severe disapproval and harsh criticism. This is a familiar idea if we consider the moral education of children. Parents are well aware that assigning responsibility to their children for faults or wrongs is an unavoidable facet of raising them. Good parents are able to do this without excessive, harsh, and severe expressions of disapproval. Moderation in this regard is arguably a parental virtue. It can also be a role-specific virtue for psychotherapists.

To blame in the primary sense might be helpful where to blame censoriously would probably not be. The point is to enable the patient to acknowledge and understand his character flaws. He is not likely to improve unless he does, but rolling him in the mud would not be the best way to help him get clean. I would also think it crucial to the goals of psychotherapy that the therapist supportively encourage the patient to acknowledge responsibility for his behavior and for making the transformative efforts required to improve it. That may well involve occasions when the patient has to be told what he does not want to hear. In this case, the psychotherapist might use explicit moral language in the following way:

> You must understand that you are responsible for your violent behavior. It is not morally defensible and that is something you should care about. You should also understand that you are the one person who can change yourself for the better—no one else can do that for you. Improving your character will take some work that I can help

> you with, and you will have to share my belief that you are worth the effort. You will need to develop some different aspects of your character to see this work through, but I believe you have that potential. I would like us to start working together by exploring the thoughts and feelings that inform your behavior. Once we understand why you act like this, we can think creatively about strategies for change. You can also think of our therapy as an exercise in acquiring virtues of self-control, self-respect, empathy, and respect for other people.

In assigning responsibility for the wrongful behavior, the psychotherapist clearly blames the patient without expressing severe disapproval, harsh criticism, or condemnation. In so doing, he honestly acknowledges the presenting problem. But this is as it should be. Psychotherapy is supposed to work against the patient's denial, not for it. This acknowledgement is a necessary first step in an exploration of the patient's motivations. If this assignment of responsibility pushes "psychodynamic buttons," then we might have a transference issue that has to be worked through. Indeed, there might be cases in which psychotherapy cannot proceed unless those buttons are pushed. If a non-censorious assignment of responsibility is more reality than the patient can bear, then both he and the psychotherapist have their work cut out for them. I concede that these harder cases are not for the faint of heart.

An acknowledgement of the value-laden nature of psychotherapy indicates a modified understanding of what psychotherapists are supposed to do and how they are supposed to do it. I think there is much work to be done in exploring the overlap between psychotherapist and ethical/moral educator. If I am right about this, then I think that developing a conception of the best practices for using generic ethical language in psychotherapy is a pressing concern.

## 5.8 **Responsibility with Temperate Affective Blame**

The best practices for using the moral language of blame will likely reflect the practical wisdom and sensitivity of the therapists who use it. They would need to be especially sensitive to how patients might react to negative moral language and willing to moderate their remarks accordingly. I think that experienced therapists can moderate the language of blame and, in some cases, ought to use it with their patients to promote therapeutic goals. I argue that positive regard and respect for the patient need not prohibit making them feel guilt or remorse for morally objectionable behavior for which they can be held responsible, as long as those emotions can motivate the moral self-improvement at which therapy aims. I concede at the outset that the emotional sting of blame can be therapeutically defeating if it is immoderately expressed by the therapist or felt too acutely by the patient. But that is only to concede that emotional sting comes in degrees, some of which could be constructively handled by a patient and some of which could not. It might be averred to the contrary that a therapist's deliberate inducement of emotional sting is never justified in a healing encounter. One such argument has been made forcefully by Hanna Pickard. I want to respond first to her analysis before further developing my own.

Pickard's analysis aims to resolve a vexing clinical conundrum in both conceptual and practical terms. Therapists recognize first that patients with the DSM's Cluster B personality disorders behave in ways that cause harm to others, e.g., a willingness to exploit others (narcissistic personality disorder), extreme and inappropriate anger, recklessness, and impulsivity toward others (borderline personality disorder), and disregard for others and violation of their rights (antisocial personality disorder). Therapists recognize second that effective treatment for these patients (hereinafter PD patients) requires encouraging them to take responsibility for their morally objectionable behavior and learn to act appropriately if they are to improve and recover. Hence the conundrum: how is it possible to hold PD patients responsible for such behavior without inappropriately blaming them for it?[81]

The key point is Pickard's distinction between "two sorts of blame," which she terms "detached" and "affective." It is affective blame, as opposed to detached blame, that is deleterious to effective treatment. Affective blame is a reactive attitude that induces "sting," whereby the person blamed feels bad, e.g., "judged, shamed, berated, attacked, or hurt." Pickard claims without qualification that "effective treatment is not possible" if the PD patient is made to feel any of the latter.[82] Affective blame consists in a range of emotions and feelings, e.g., "hate, anger, and resentment ... disapproval, dislike, disappointment, indignation, and contempt." Its expression can be manifest in "punishing ... berating, attacking, humiliating, writing off, rejecting, shunning, abandoning, and criticizing." Affective blame can also be irrational, in that a person can be blamed in the absence of a judgment or belief that they are blameworthy.[83]

Detached blame consists in a "judgment or belief of blameworthiness." Most importantly, it expresses that judgment of blameworthiness without negative emotional affect. Detached blame does not have the characteristic sting that makes affective blame so disturbing to the person blamed. It can be accompanied by a revision of attitudes to the person blamed, the imposition of negative consequences, or just demands for accountability. Detachment can be maintained by the blamer even when she revises her interpersonal attitudes and intentions toward the blamed. According to Pickard, "one can rationally and politely decide to stop socializing with an acquaintance who routinely offends because one judges them blameworthy and no longer wishes to see them, without either party minding very much."[84]

As best I can make out, it is a non-reactive, "non-stinging sort of attitude" that would unify instances of detached blame. Clinicians are thus able to hold patients "responsible, indeed blameworthy, for harm, without blaming them, because blame comes in [these] two forms." Affective blame is detrimental to effective treatment. Detached blame can encourage responsibility and may thus be essential to effective treatment. "Responsibility without blame is responsibility without affective blame: without a sense of entitlement to any negative reactive attitudes and emotions one might experience," no matter what the patient has done. Detached blame can be appropriate in treatment where affective blame is not.[85]

## 5.9 Temperate Affective Blame and Moral Emotions in Psychotherapy

Although Pickard notes that the emotional features of affective blame can be irrational, she does concede that they can be amenable to some degree of control. Blamers can reflect and try to contain or moderate the degree of their emotions and behavioral expressions.[86] This suggests that affective blame can be a moderate expression of an emotionally informed judgment. Blamers could aim to regulate their emotional arousal to a mean between excess and deficiency. I call this "temperate affective blame."

The sting felt by the person who is blamed also comes in degrees, i.e., it is not a one-size-fits-all experience. If temperate affective blame can induce apposite degrees of sting, then perhaps it should have a limited place in therapy for some PD patients. Here are my reasons for thinking this. Like Pickard, I view effective treatment as, in part, augmenting the PD patient's existing capacity for agency and motivated change.[87] Therapeutic goals for PD patients are thus partly normative and can include motivating them to make positive changes in their moral character and forge positive bonds with others.[88] Some of the negative, self-conscious emotions associated with blame's sting (e.g., guilt, regret, contrition, and remorse) have been shown to be motivating influences to those normative ends. Far from always discouraging persons or paralyzing them with an unshakeable sense of condemnation, these negative emotions can inspire reparative action. As such, they can be understood as moral emotions because they influence the link between moral standards and moral behavior. Moral emotions can foster a moral life lived to the benefit of self and others by providing the motivational impetus to do good and avoid doing bad. If induced by a blamer, they can evoke self-reflection and self-evaluation in the blamed.[89]

Guilt is a negatively valenced self-conscious moral emotion that would fall under the sting induced by affective blame. It is focused on bad behavior (I *did* that bad thing) rather than a bad "core" self (*I* did that bad thing). Hence the prevailing distinction by Helen Block Lewis between guilt and shame. Where Lewis defines shame as a negative evaluation of the global self, she defines guilt as a negative evaluation of specific behavior.[90] Tangney, Stuewig, and Mashek have noted empirical evidence to support this differential emphasis on self versus behavior, although we can question whether shame's focus on the self has to be global. Presumably, one can feel ashamed for aspects of oneself that are reflected in one's behavior without feeling that one's entire self is bad. They have also noted empirical studies that support the claim that guilt appears to be an adaptive moral emotion that benefits persons and their relationships in various ways. Once in the throes of guilt, people are more likely to consider the consequences of their behavior, which leads to tension, remorse, and regret. Even so, they are more likely to recognize and be concerned about the effects of their behavior on others and to confess, apologize, or attempt to undo the consequences of their actions.[91] More to the point, Tangney, Stuewig, and Mashek cite empirical evidence that "guilt appears to motivate reparative action, foster other-oriented empathy, and promote constructive strategies for coping with anger."[92] These are very plausible therapeutic goals for PD patients.

If guilt motivates a patient's empathic and reparative capacities, then temperate affective blame may not compromise the therapeutic alliance and may promote therapeutic goals. Psychopaths aside, many PD patients are not completely lacking in capacity for moral awareness and behavior. PD patients can, to some degree, feel the sting of blame, although some may want to deny or suppress it. They also have, to some degree, abilities to take responsibility for and control their actions, to empathize with others, and to appreciate and honor moral commitments. These are the capacities, however disturbed, that therapy aims to develop and strengthen.

Therapists would not aim to promote denial when treating such patients, any more than parents would want their children to deny their moral emotions. Presumably, therapists would work to help such patients confront the sting of blame and to regulate their emotional reactivity to a mean between excess and deficiency. But therapists do that anyway. Those patients who are prone to excessive and inappropriate self-blame present different challenges to goals of emotional regulation. Here again, therapists do not work to render such patients immune to the sting of their moral emotions. Rather, they work to help such patients moderate excessive sting.

To paraphrase Pickard in service to my own account, a reduction in an overly acute capacity to feel sting is not, and should not be, an extinction. When we consider how therapists work to help PD patients regulate their emotional over-reactivity, it is hardly a stretch to assume that they can work the other way to enable patients to develop apposite degrees of morally emotional response to "things most of us would identify as moral transgressions."[93] There is no calculus we can employ here, no algorithm for generating appropriate degrees of sting. Nor does there have to be. Like parents who work to raise their children to be appropriately responsive to their moral emotions, therapists have to rely on their observation of and empathy with the patient to assist them in striking the responsive mean.

Consider the patient who is made to feel guilty by his therapist's ascription of temperate affective blame. He will feel judged, criticized, and disapproved of. But these could be apposite dimensions of "sting" if they reflect a focus on the patient's behavior. The patient need not feel hated, contemptible, or incapable of moral self-improvement. Put another way, the patient need not feel that he has been censoriously condemned as both an irrevocably bad person and a lost therapeutic cause. Even shame, i.e., an evaluation of the self that hinges on a sense of disappointment in (or despair about) aspects of one's moral character, might be morally constructive if those aspects are within one's ability to improve. One way to ease the sting of being shamed "would be to prove to ourselves that the failure is not irreparable."[94]

We should proceed cautiously here. There is also empirical evidence that shame is a much less adaptive moral emotion than guilt. Shame is induced in the same type of situations that typically induce guilt and is just as likely to be felt in the presence of others. The guilt experience is focused more on the guilty person's effect on others, whereas the shame experience is focused more on the self. The former is thus other-oriented where the latter is egocentric. Most accounts emphasize the totalizing nature of the shame experience; it is a focused, negative evaluation of the entire or global self. Empirical evidence connects shame with behaviors that are plausibly symptomatic of some PD patients. Shame has a disruptive effect on one's "ability to form empathic connections to others," and seems to strengthen an egocentric capacity to focus on one's own distress. Shame is also correlated extensively with anger, perpetration of psychological abuse, "the propensity to blame factors beyond the self for one's misfortunes," low self-esteem, depression, and anxiety. It would be a daunting challenge indeed to "transform a self that is defective at its core."[95] There are, I believe, instances of shame that amount to a total condemnation of one's self—a feeling that one is essentially, irremediably bad or contemptible. Shame can indeed be a paralyzing emotion.

Tangney, Stuewig, and Mashek concede that we may not be able to generalize the differential link of shame and guilt across all populations with respect to all behaviors.[96] I also think there are quotidian experiences of shame that are temporary stings and nowhere near as extremely felt. These need not be any less morally adaptive than feelings of guilt. Like guilt, the sting of shame comes in degrees. In terms of the blamed person's lived experience, shame and guilt can overlap, i.e., one can feel ashamed about that aspect of oneself that engages in the behavior one feels guilty about. It is not as if the bad behavior is lacking in relation to one's self. Nor is it the case that bad behavior is a complete summation of that self, as if one's self is defined by nothing more than one's moral lapses. Of course, some PD patients may feel that way, but that is precisely the kind of self-induced emotional exaggeration that therapists help them to work against.

Most people who confess to feeling ashamed about lying, for example, are indicating their self-assessment about a morally salient capacity that they value and have the ability to transform. Feeling ashamed can indicate that one has failed on occasion to be the more consistently truthful person that one should be and, through one's efforts, that one can be. One has some degree of control over the state of one's character, and to that degree is therefore responsible for it. Shame can thus illustrate a felt sense of disappointment in the shape of one's moral character. Far from indicating a globally contemptible self, some instances of shame can be managed by coming to understand the aspect of one's self that one finds offensive, and then forming beliefs about the degree to which that aspect might be changed for the better. Feeling ashamed about one's mendacious behavior can be expiated by venturing back into the world as a truth-teller. Global self-denigration is not the only response to feeling moral shame when one can improve the trait about which one feels ashamed.[97] Manion makes a philosophical point that implicates psychotherapy: "Since feeling ashamed about morally relevant aspects of ourselves can force us to recognize failed aspects of the self, working through feelings of shame might very well help us shape new, more positive ideals about who we can be in the future."[98]

Given its potential sting, patients might go to great lengths to suppress or deny shame, and this suppression can be the festering cause of ongoing conflict. "Hidden like this," says Robert Karen, "shame can stalk one's being, inflicting an unconscious self-loathing."[99] In such cases, shame can be understood by the therapist as an experience the patient must confront and work through. Indeed, acknowledging and confronting shame might be the first step in getting past it and the therapist must win over the hiding, shameful aspect of the patient's personality and gradually help it to heal. The psychotherapeutic experience suggests that a patient who is able to bring his shame out of hiding and speak of it to another person is able to take the first step that a healing process requires. "To stop running and experience the shame" can afford the patient "a chance to recognize that being in the wrong … does not … make her into a poisonously deformed and unlovable thing."[100]

A therapist may have to induce the sting of shame to initiate this process, but the point would be to focus on that aspect of the patient's self that is reflected in bad behavior. This is also an effort to counteract the notion that the patient's entire self is defined by that aspect. The empathic therapist can understand why the patient exhibits the bad behavior without being obliged to agree with it or suppress feelings of disapproval. Nor can the therapist understand the patient's capacity to responsibly shape her character for the better without being obliged to encourage, motivate, and express her belief in the patient's ability to do so. Peter Lomas, a psychotherapist who did not shy away from confronting "the moral failings" of his patients, noted that while shame and guilt can be theoretically distinguished, they are interwoven and difficult to separate experientially.[101] They can also be "paralyzing and discouraging," but are not necessarily so. Lomas observed that a patient's ownership of these emotions could be central to the psychotherapeutic experience in that, by exposing themselves to shame, some patients can "engender a wish to change" that may be "a potential source of growth and a help to a therapist … The shamed person has to repair himself in order to be, in some way or in some degree, a different person—one who no longer does such [shameful] things."[102]

Like Lomas, I believe that this initiative towards moral self-improvement should be encouraged in therapy. Pickard concedes in other writings that, with reference to the friends and family of PD patients, there may be occasions where affective blame is not only natural but also helpful in the long term to the person blamed. Deciding when affective blame is, and when it is not, a positive motivating force is part of having real, genuine relationships.[103] Insofar as a therapeutic relationship can be real and genuine, I think there can be occasions when clinicians should consider whether, and if so, the extent to which affective blame can be helpful.

## 5.10 **Conclusion**

Two assumptions merit further scrutiny. These are, first, the assumption that PD patients have the ability to appreciate negative emotions such as guilt or remorse as motivating factors in their moral growth and, second, the idea that shame can be a motivating moral emotion. Shame has been defined as an egocentric feeling that one's self is bad and defective at its core (*I'm* bad to the bone). This would be the censorious condemnation of one's self that temperate affective blame is meant to avoid. Finally, if therapists resort to blame, then it should be particularized to the patient with six qualifications. (1) The objectionable behavior must be within the patient's control such that she has some ability to change it. (2) Blame must not amount to a global condemnation of the patient's character and potential for change. It must be ascribed with an acknowledgement that the patient is capable of self-improvement and the encouragement to pursue it. (3) Blame must be ascribed in conjunction with empathy. It should not be ascribed if the emotions that inform the blame have overcome the therapist's empathy for the patient's suffering and distress. (4) Blame should be reserved mainly for patients who avoid or deny their responsibility for behavior that is harmful to others. (5) Blame should be conjoined with an invitation for the patient to reflect upon their behavior. (6) Clinical practice in accordance with these caveats requires the therapist's most careful attention. Therapists should remember that they might be inaccurate in their attribution of deliberate behavior that is harmful to others—that they should not make this attribution without critical reflection on their sense of entitlement to their negative reactions, the patient's perspective and potential for adverse reaction, the therapeutic relationship, and any relevant cultural influences. I agree with Nancy Potter's claim that therapists have a responsibility "to develop a just vision whereby they bring to bear the considerations of accountability and blameworthiness and the conditions of judgment that preserve fairness and accuracy in all their complexity and cultural context."[104] Any such therapeutic relationships will be embedded in the larger context of a psychotherapeutic healing project, the facets of which I now want to explore.

## Notes

1. **Gwen Adshead**, "Ethics in Psychotherapy," in *The Oxford Textbook of Psychotherapy*, eds. Glen O. Gabbard, Judith S. Beck, and Jeremy Holmes (New York: Oxford University Press USA, 2007), 477.
2. **Ernest Wallwork**, *Psychoanalysis and Ethics* (New Haven: Yale University Press, 1991), 2; Alan C. Tjeltveit, *Ethics and Values in Psychotherapy* (London: Routledge, 1999), 1–17. See also W.W. Meisner, *The Ethical Dimensions of Psychoanalysis: A Dialogue* (Albany: State University of New York Press, 2003).
3. **Phillip Cashman**, *Constructing the Self, Constructing America: A Cultural History of Psychotherapy* (Cambridge, MA: Da Capo Press, 1995).
4. Cf. **Adshead**, "Ethics in Psychotherapy," 484. See also Ernest Wallwork, "Ethics in Psychoanalysis," in *The American Psychiatric Publishing Textbook on Psychoanalysis*, eds. Glen O. Gabbard, Bonnie E. Litowitz, and Paul Williams (Washington, DC: American Psychiatric Publishing, 2012), 357–360.
5. **Jennifer Radden** and **John Z. Sadler**, *The Virtuous Psychiatrist: Character Ethics in Psychiatric Practice* (Oxford: Oxford University Press, 2010).
6. **Jennifer Radden**, "Virtue Ethics as Professional Ethics: The Case of Psychiatry," in *Working Virtue: Virtue Ethics and Contemporary Moral Problems*, eds. Rebecca L. Walter and P.J. Ivanhoe (Oxford: Oxford University Press, 2007), 115, 116, 117.
7. **Radden**, "Virtue Ethics as Professional Ethics," 117.

8. **Elliot D. Cohen** and **Gale Spieler Cohen**, *The Virtuous Therapist: Ethical Practice of Counseling and Psychotherapy* (Pacific Grove, CA: Brooks Cole, 1998).
9. **T.M. Luhrmann**, *Of Two Minds: An Anthropologist Looks at American Psychiatry* (New York: Vintage Books, 2000), 115, 147, 198, 199.
10. **Radden** and **Sadler**, *The Virtuous Psychiatrist*, 5.
11. **Christine Swanton**, *Virtue Ethics: A Pluralistic View* (Oxford: Oxford University Press, 2003), 15, 258–266.
12. **Alan C. Tjeltveit**, "The Good, the Bad, the Obligatory, and the Virtuous," *Journal of Psychotherapy Integration* 14 (2004): 158–159.
13. **John Margolis**, *Psychotherapy and Morality* (New York: Random House, 1966); **Perry London**, *The Modes and Morals of Psychotherapy*, 2nd ed. (New York: Hemisphere Publishing Corporation, 1986).
14. **London**, *The Modes and Morals of Psychotherapy*, 6.
15. **Margolis**, *Psychotherapy and Morality*, 21.
16. **Marie Jahoda**, *Current Concepts of Positive Mental Health* (New York: Basic Books, 1958).
17. **Margolis**, *Psychotherapy and Morality*, 26.
18. **Eric Matthews**, "Moral Vision and the Idea of Mental Illness," *Philosophy, Psychiatry, and Psychology* 6 (1999): 307–309.
19. **Robert L. Woolfolk** and **Dominic Murphy**, "Axiological Foundations of Psychotherapy," *Journal of Psychotherapy Integration* 14 (2004): 179.
20. **Matthews**, "Moral Vision and the Idea of Mental Illness," 309.
21. **Paul Roazen**, "The Impact of Psychoanalysis on Values," in *Moral Values and the Superego Concept in Psychoanalysis*, ed. Seymour C. Post (New York: International Universities Press, 1972), 202.
22. **Izak Ramzy**, "The Place of Values in Psychoanalytic Theory, Practice and Training," in *Moral Values and the Superego Concept in Psychoanalysis*, ed. Seymour C. Post (New York: International Universities Press, 1972), 218, 221–222.
23. **Irving Bieber**, "Psychoanalysis and Moral Values," in *Moral Values and the Superego Concept in Psychoanalysis*, ed. Seymour C. Post (New York: International Universities Press, 1972), 246.
24. **Robert L. Woolfolk**, *The Cure of Souls: Science, Values, and Psychotherapy* (San Francisco: Jossey-Bass Publishers, 1998), 5.
25. **Woolfolk**, *The Cure of Souls*, 117.
26. **Frank C. Richardson**, **Blaine J. Fowers**, and **Charles B. Guignon**, *Re-Envisioning Psychology: Moral Dimensions of Theory and Practice* (San Francisco: Josey-Bass Publishers, 1999), 266.
27. **Charles B. Guignon**, "Authenticity, Moral Values, and Psychotherapy," in *The Cambridge Companion to Heidegger*, ed. Charles B. Guignon. 2nd ed. (Cambridge: Cambridge University Press, 2006), 270.
28. **Charles Taylor**, *Sources of the Self: The Making of the Modern Identity* (Cambridge, MA: Harvard University Press, 1989), 14. See also Guignon, "Authenticity, Moral Values, and Psychotherapy," 217.

29. **Peter Lomas**, *Doing Good? Psychotherapy Out of Its Depth* (Oxford: Oxford University Press, 1999), 16, 19–20, 39.
30. **Brad K. Wilburn**, "Moral Self-Improvement," in *Moral Cultivation: Essays on the Development of Character and Virtue*, ed. Brad K. Wilburn (Plymouth, UK: Lexington Books, 2007), 69–84.
31. **Matthews**, "Moral Vision and the Idea of Mental Illness," 308–309.
32. **Louis Charland**, "Character: Moral Treatment and Personality Disorders," in *The Philosophy of Psychiatry: A Companion*, ed. Jennifer Radden (Oxford: Oxford University Press, 204), 64–77.
33. **Matthews**, "Moral Vision and the Idea of Mental Illness," 308.
34. **Swanton**, *Virtue Ethics*, 14.
35. **Swanton**, *Virtue Ethics*, 1, 14, 20–21, 29, 63, 65, 93, 235.
36. **Swanton**, *Virtue Ethics*, 2–5, 21–23, 101–102; Stephen M. Gardiner, "Review: Virtue Ethics: A Pluralistic View, by Christine Swanton," *Mind* 114 (2005): 211.
37. **Swanton**, *Virtue Ethics*, 3, 16, 93; Gardiner, "Review: Virtue Ethics," 211.
38. **Swanton**, *Virtue Ethics*, 2–3, 93.
39. **Swanton**, *Virtue Ethics*, 145.
40. **Swanton**, *Virtue Ethics*, 233, 238–239.
41. **Swanton**, *Virtue Ethics*, 1–4; Lisa Tessman, "Review of Virtue Ethics: A Pluralistic View," *The Philosophical Review* 114 (2005): 414–415.
42. **Swanton**, *Virtue Ethics*, 10, 13, 15, 61.
43. **Swanton**, *Virtue Ethics*, 65, 61.
44. **Swanton**, *Virtue Ethics*, 21, 61.
45. **Swanton**, *Virtue Ethics*, 11, 185, .
46. **Swanton**, *Virtue Ethics*, 3, 63.
47. **Swanton**, *Virtue Ethics*, 204; George Harris, "Review: Virtue Ethics: A Pluralistic View, by Christine Swanton." *Notre Dame Philosophical Reviews* 2004.01.02. Accessed May 4, 2010, http://ndpr.nd.edu/review.
48. **Swanton**, *Virtue Ethics*, 182, 210–211.
49. **Swanton**, *Virtue Ethics*, 205–206.
50. **Swanton**, *Virtue Ethics*, 252.
51. Cf. **Swanton**, *Virtue Ethics*, 253.
52. **Swanton**, *Virtue Ethics*, 250, 265.
53. **Seneca**, *Dialogues and Essays*, trans. John Davie (Oxford: Oxford University Press, 2007), 41; cf. Raymond DiGiuseppe and Raymond Chip Tafrate, *Understanding Anger Disorders* (New York: Oxford University Press USA, 2006), 192: "Despite the abundant rhetoric on the relationship of anger and depression, there is little empirical research to support this notion, compared to the large body of literature on the co-occurrence of anxiety and depression ... Nevertheless, a sufficient number of studies have demonstrated a moderate correlation between depression and anger to establish that some relationship exists between these constructs."

54. Seneca's angry man has many real-life counterparts. For an evocative account of this family dynamic, see Charles Bukowski's autobiographical novel *Ham on Rye* (1982). Bukowski's dedication reads: "for all the fathers."
55. **Ruth A. Lanius, Eric Vermetten,** and **Clare Pain**, eds., *The Impact of Early Life Trauma on Health and Disease: The Hidden Epidemic* (Cambridge: Cambridge University Press, 2010).
56. **American Psychiatric Association**, *Diagnostic and Statistical Manual of Mental Disorders*, 5th ed. (Washington, DC: American Psychiatric Publishing, 2013), 659–666, 466–469.
57. **Swanton**, *Virtue Ethics*, 184–185.
58. **Swanton**, *Virtue Ethics*, 190; cf. Alfred Adler, *Understanding Human Nature*, trans. W.B. Wolfe (London: Allen and Unwin, 1932); cf. Karen Horney, *Neurosis and Human Growth: The Struggle Toward Self Realization* (New York: Norton, 1970).
59. **Seneca**, *Dialogues*, 32, 41, 28
60. Cf. **Swanton**, *Virtue Ethics*, 136, 145.
61. **Iris Murdoch**, *The Sovereignty of the Good* (London: Routledge, 1970), 84; cf. Swanton, *Virtue Ethics*, 113.
62. **Swanton**, *Virtue Ethics*, 145, 134–135.
63. **Swanton**, *Virtue Ethics*, 143.
64. **Seneca**, *Dialogues*, 28, 39, 41.
65. **Swanton**, *Virtue Ethics*, 21, 100, 113.
66. **Swanton**, *Virtue Ethics*, 21, 25, 28–29.
67. Cf. **William James**, *The Varieties of Religious Experience* (New York: Image Books, 1978), 193.
68. **Seneca**, *Dialogues*, 18.
69. **Swanton**, *Virtue Ethics*, 260, 258.
70. Cf. **Swanton**, *Virtue Ethics*, 260–261, 265.
71. Cf. **Swanton**, *Virtue Ethics*, 252, 254–255.
72. Cf. **Swanton**, *Virtue Ethics*, 261–262.
73. Cf. **Swanton**, *Virtue Ethics*, 253, 258, 264.
74. **Fred J. Hanna** and **K. Puhakka**, "When Psychotherapy Works: Pinpointing an Element of Change," *Psychotherapy* 28 (1991): 599.
75. **Arthur C. Bohart**, "Insight and the Active Client," in *Insight in Psychotherapy*, eds. Louis G. Castonguay and Clara E. Hill (Washington, DC: American Psychological Association, 2002), 258–263, 265–266, 268.
76. **I.B. Weiner** and **R.F. Bornstein**, *Principles of Psychotherapy: Promoting Evidence-Based Psychodynamic Practice* (Hoboken, NJ: John Wiley and Sons, 2009), 200.
77. **Swanton**, *Virtue Ethics*, 25.
78. This argument has been made by Mike W. Martin. I am grateful for his thought-provoking commentary "Psychotherapy as Cultivating Character," *Philosophy, Psychiatry, & Psychology* 19 (2012): 37–39. See also my response "Psychotherapy through the Prism of Moral Language," *Philosophy, Psychiatry, & Psychology* 19 (2012): 45–48.

79. **Martin**, "Psychotherapy as Cultivating Character," 38–39.
80. **Martin**, "Psychotherapy as Cultivating Character," 38–39.
81. **Hanna Pickard**, "Responsibility without Blame: Empathy and the Effective Treatment of Personality Disorder," *Philosophy, Psychiatry, & Psychology* 18 (2011): 210. Pickard refers to the text revision of DSM-4: American Psychiatric Association, *Diagnostic and Statistical Manual of Mental Disorders*, 4th ed., Text Revision (Washington, DC: American Psychiatric Publishing, 2000).
82. **Pickard**, "Responsibility without Blame," 216.
83. **Pickard**, "Responsibility without Blame," 218.
84. **Pickard**, "Responsibility without Blame," 218.
85. **Pickard**, "Responsibility without Blame," 218–219.
86. **Pickard**, "Responsibility without Blame," 219.
87. **Pickard**, "Responsibility without Blame," 213.
88. Cf. **Jennifer C. Manion**, "The Moral Relevance of Shame," *American Philosophical Quarterly* 39 (2002): 81.
89. **June Price Tangney**, **Jeff Stuewig**, and **Debra J. Mashek**, "Moral Emotions and Moral Behavior," *Annual Review of Psychology* 58 (2007): 345–347.
90. **Helen Block Lewis**, *Shame and Guilt in Neurosis* (New York: International University Press, 1971).
91. **Tangney, Stuewig,** and **Mashek**, "Moral Emotions and Moral Behavior," 349–350.
92. **Tangney, Stuewig,** and **Mashek**, "Moral Emotions and Moral Behavior," 352.
93. Cf. **Manion**, "The Moral Relevance of Shame," 75; Cf. Pickard, "Responsibility Without Blame," 213.
94. **Tangney, Stuewig,** and **Mashek**, "Moral Emotions and Moral Behavior," 76–81.
95. **Tangney, Stuewig,** and **Mashek**, "Moral Emotions and Moral Behavior," 350–353.
96. **Tangney, Stuewig,** and **Mashek**, "Moral Emotions and Moral Behavior," 354.
97. **Manion**, "The Moral Relevance of Shame," 75–77, 79–80.
98. **Manion**, "The Moral Relevance of Shame," 84.
99. **Robert Karen**, "Shame," *The Atlantic Monthly* February (1992): 2.
100. **Karen**, "Shame," 15.
101. **Peter Lomas**, *Doing Good?* 111–113.
102. **Lomas**, *Doing Good?* 111, 107.
103. **Hannah Pickard**, "Responsibility without Blame: Philosophical Reflections on Clinical Practice," in *The Oxford Handbook of Philosophy and Psychiatry*, eds. K.W.M. Fulford, Martin Davies, Richard G.T. Gipps, George Graham, John Z. Sadler, Giovanni Stanghellini, and Tim Thornton (Oxford: Oxford University Press, 2013), 1150.
104. **Nancy Nyquist Potter**, "Oh Blame, Where Is Thy Sting?" *Philosophy, Psychiatry, & Psychology* 18 (2011): 226–227.

Chapter 6

# The Responsibilities of Patients in a Psychotherapeutic Healing Project

## 6.1 Introduction

A psychotherapeutic healing project[1] is a normative covenant by which therapist and patient make mutual commitments to each other that are shaped by fidelities, expectations, principles, and the cultivation of virtues, some of which are contextual to the project.[2] This relational matrix ideally begins with a therapeutic alliance, i.e., a negotiated relationship between therapist and patient in which each agrees to work together to help the patient with his or her problems.[3] Both aim to merge their efforts to promote the patient's well-being. It evolves into a more independent effort by which the patient develops a therapeutic alliance with himself and assumes greater responsibility for his own care. As the patient becomes less dependent on the therapist, the healing project becomes the former's project of self-regarding care.

The interacting personalities of therapist and patient contribute essentially to the therapeutic alliance. Through negotiation, they achieve an understanding of the goals and methods of treatment that is mutually satisfying and meaningful. This is a two-way process that requires the virtuous engagement and empathy of both participants. The therapist's fidelity, respect, and tactfulness are clearly important factors. Equally important is the therapist's consistent position "that the patient will be meaningfully involved in the therapeutic process and will accept and observe his own responsibilities both within and outside of the therapy … in a mature and constructive manner."[4] This is not to deny Weisman's claim that responsible agency can also be a goal of treatment.

> The day-to-day reckoning of sickness is determined by the way it prevents healthy concordant conduct. The least part of the healing function of medicine is to restore only physical competence, without necessarily reinstating purposeful behavior; the largest—and most laudable—part is to help replenish and encourage the sense of being responsible.[5]

Responsibility is a normative component of the patient's progression toward healthy, adaptive functioning and a restoration of self.[6] It can be understood in both moral and ethical terms.

I will concentrate on 1) the ethical and moral responsibilities that patients can have in a psychotherapeutic healing project (hereinafter healing project) and (2) the virtues that I think patients should cultivate to meet them. Since mental disorder affects volitional, communicative, affective, and cognitive aspects of personhood, I understand recovery and the healing project that brings it about as having moral and ethical significance.[7] Beyond symptom relief, it involves efforts to restore the integrative constituents of a unified self that mental disorder can diminish, and even decimate. Since this can involve rebuilding one's character, i.e., the mental and ethical/moral qualities that are distinctive to a person with a vision of a satisfying life, these efforts can be virtuous ones. I posit the constituents of self-unity to include ethical virtues of self-love and self-respect that the patient becomes responsible for cultivating. I will expound the following principal idea: if the patient in a therapeutic alliance is a "normative project" for the therapist, then that patient is no less a normative project for him or herself.[8] Ideally, the patient gradually assumes responsibility for a project of self-regarding care. I argue that this involves the cultivation of healing virtues that work towards establishing the recovery virtues of self-respect, self-love, empathic concern, and respect for others. I will focus on six healing virtues: honesty, imaginative flexibility, perseverance, hopefulness, healing curiosity, and respect for the healing project.[9]

I distinguish the patient's responsibilities in the healing project between those that 6.3a regard others and those that 6.3b are self-regarding to the patient. This distinction is not a clean dichotomy as there is some overlap between each. Even so, I think there is a notable contrast that merits examination. As per 6.3a, other-regarding moral responsibilities are obligations that pertain to what we owe others in the way of duties and to the kind of responsible conduct that we can expect from them. To say, as per 6.3b, that one is ethically responsible to oneself can mean that one holds oneself answerable to intra- (as well as inter-) personal critical perspectives on one's identity-conferring values, choices, and conduct.[10] We can thus speak of striving to meet responsibilities to others and to ourselves in an excellent or good enough way.

I relate other- and self-regarding responsibilities to certain morally and ethically desirable character traits of the patient. I do not posit a notable distinction between other- and self-regarding virtues, if only because some of the virtues that the patient should cultivate are conjoined to how the patient should relate to the therapist as well as to herself. Like Froding, I think we should recognize that most virtues have other- and self-regarding facets and that a person who aspires to virtue must cultivate it in both spheres. I suggest, however, that given the aims of the healing project, some patient virtues can be described contextually as largely or predominantly self-regarding,[11] especially if their attainment constitutes recovery. In this sense, the sufficient attainment of self-love and self-respect enables the patient to recover a greater degree of self-unity.

I thus distinguish between 6.4a healing and 6.4b recovery virtues. I explicate first some healing virtues that make overlapping contributions to the patient's other- and self-regarding responsibilities, i.e., to developing both the therapeutic alliance and the patient's more independent project of self-regarding care. Healing virtues are conducive to the patient's recovery because they inform the working collaboration between therapist and patient. They can also inform the patient's independent efforts to manage her own care. These virtues are instrumental in bringing about recovery. I then discuss the virtues of self-respect and self-love that are eventually realized through the healing project and sustained through the patient's project of self-regarding care. These are the recovery virtues, the attainment of which indicates that some degree of self-unity has been realized. These virtues are the goals of the healing project and are largely self-regarding in terms of well-being and responsibility. A patient's well-being can also involve the way she treats others. I posit recovery virtues of empathic concern and respect for others as largely other-regarding and especially relevant to recovery from the personality disorders I discuss in chapter seven. In sum, the healing virtues enable the patient to attain and strengthen the recovery virtues that consolidate her well-being.

## 6.2 **The Responsible Patient**

One of the primary concerns of medical ethics has been the definition of physicians' responsibilities to their patients. This is supplemented with discussions in the clinical literature about the responsibilities that patients have to their physicians, to themselves, and to society. These discussions are often focused on the patient's responsibilities to comply with treatment programs and healthy lifestyles.[12] Hence the American Medical Association's statements that patients have a responsibility to cooperate with an agreed-upon treatment plan and should be committed to health-enhancing behavior.[13] To claim that the patient has responsibilities in a therapeutic alliance means that the patient and physician are working to realize the goals of treatment. If the healing process in this alliance is truly collaborative, then both parties are working.[14] Thus the patient has work that she is responsible for doing.

Given that we see psychiatric disorders as often depriving patients of full responsibility, the patient's accountability must be commensurate with her capacity for assuming it. Strengthening that capacity would be an ongoing facet of the healing project. While the concept of the working patient has generally been absent "from the discourse of medical ethics," psychiatry is one of two medical fields in which that concept is familiar, the other being rehabilitative medicine.[15] The working patient concept has its clearest psychiatric expression as a praxis in psychotherapy. Cognitive behavioral therapy is explicit in its prescriptions for the patient's work. Patients are to learn specific skills in their ongoing involvement with formulating treatment plans, conducting homework exercises, and deciding on therapeutic goals. The effort to think through their negative schemas is designed, in effect, to enable patients to become their own therapists.[16]

The notion that psychiatrists can expect patients to be responsible in a therapeutic alliance raises the concomitant idea that they can hold patients responsible. This in turn raises questions about how responsibility is reinforced and the consequences to the patient of not living up to it. It can be argued that absent such consequences, any talk of patient responsibilities is "moral window dressing."[17] A concern is that holding patients responsible can devolve into blaming them for their illness, or for less than acceptable efforts to deal with it. Addressing this concern requires close attention to what we mean by blaming someone. It also requires us to clarify both the sense in which patients should be held responsible and the ways by which that accountability will be reinforced. The treating psychiatrist may have to help the patient understand and accept his responsibility for contributing to the alliance. There may also be cases where the psychiatrist has to inform the patient that he has not met this responsibility and is so accountable. Blame can thus be expressed without censure. Moderation in these contexts is arguably a virtue of psychiatrists.[18] The focus, I think, should be on prospective responsibility for contributing to the alliance.[19]

The notion of a patient's responsibility also requires a flexible sense of accountability that reflects the fluctuating and profound impact that some mental disorders can have on global functioning. Suppose that the therapist is working with a patient who has a chronic, remitting, and recurring bipolar disorder. During times of crisis, as when a severe manic episode renders the patient incapable of insight into her illness, or when a severe depressive one eviscerates her sense of self-regard, it would be morally obtuse to exhort the patient to step up to the plate and resume efforts to recover. The alliance with the therapist should be able to accommodate the vicissitudes of a major mental illness.[20]

## 6.3 Moral and Ethical Patient Responsibilities

As per 6.3a, I discuss how responsible participation involves meeting the moral commitments a patient makes to her therapist. As per 6.3b, I posit the patient's responsibility to herself as crucial to the work of sustaining recovery. It is the sense in which one is predominantly responsible for restoring and maintaining personal unity by cultivating self-love and self-respect. The latter notion can involve more than a reverent acknowledgement of one's moral status and worth. It can also include "having, and living by, personal standards or ideals that one sees, whether objective or not, as an important part of oneself."[21] This account of self-respect is akin to ethical integrity, or living by the conviction that our values, desires, and projects are uniquely right for our own lives and the best response to our situation.[22] I argue below that self-unity reflects threshold degrees of both a consolidated psychological subjectivity and the coherence of ethical integrity. It is a personal cohesion attained through the virtue of self-love, or the positive, psychological bonding with oneself that is devoid of self-contempt.[23] Intuitively plausible cases of self-regarding responsibility seem to be ones in which a patient lacks the unity of self-love, e.g., when a depressed patient's "interests, projects, and plans seem worthless" even to *herself*.[24] Self-regarding responsibility pertains to holding oneself accountable for striving to attain an affirmative bond with oneself through a commitment to such identity-conferring values and projects.

### 6.3.1 Other-Regarding Moral Responsibilities

The patient commits to psychotherapy and undertakes to do his part in contributing to the treatment process. He assumes responsibility for attending the sessions, paying the therapist's fees, and especially for dialogical participation, i.e., disclosing psychic material and working with the therapist to process and even interpret it. On Meissner's account, bilateral negotiation is a core component of the process by which psychotherapist and patient achieve mutually satisfying and meaningful interpretations.[25] There is a moral onus on truthfulness here as the disclosures must be candid ones. This can be a daunting challenge for the patient who is uncomfortable confronting aspects of himself that he would rather avoid. Given our customary attitudes about self-disclosure, this requirement to be unreservedly candid is out of the ordinary.

### 6.3.2 Self-Regarding Ethical Responsibilities

There is also a logically coherent sense in which we can envision ethically significant responsibilities to ourselves. A common understanding is that responsibilities are related to an external authority and denote commitments from which you cannot free yourself at will, i.e., other persons to whom you are obligated. Responsibilities thus relate to obligations that we have to others. Only they can release you at will from your obligations to them. Hence the puzzlement over the notion that one can have responsibilities to oneself. If you impose the obligation on yourself, then you are also the one who can free yourself at will from the obligation imposed.

Hill Jr. argues that the disanalogies between promises to others and promises to oneself do not show that the latter are logically impossible or ethically insignificant. His "puzzling" and "controversial" examples suggest that the "ultimate ground" of plausible obligations to oneself is self-respect, and not a quasi-contractual relation with oneself, a general need to bolster one's motivations, or an ethical/moral requirement to promote one's own welfare. Some promises to oneself might promote one's welfare, but one could promise oneself to strengthen one's resolve and motivation to pursue altruistic as well as self-interested goals.[26]

Falk has analyzed the leading reasons why the standard position that no personal ought can be a moral one has such strong purchase. At the very least, where the reasons for acting are social rather than personal, other-regarding oughts feel "more binding, more relentless, and more properly called 'moral' for this reason," and the way we commonly use moral language makes this strictly and trivially true. But this usage does not show that a personal ought cannot be like an other-regarding moral ought in calling for serious commitment and precedence in our conscientious, action-guiding considerations. Granted, there will be cases where personal oughts are less thoroughly committing than other-regarding moral oughts. The latter can have reasons in their favor that establish their precedence. Thus I should temporarily suspend my focused efforts at writing a novel to support a loved one on her sickbed. But personal oughts need not always take second place. Concerns for one's health or self-respect might reasonably oblige a person to put herself first. Even if one takes the position that self-regarding personal oughts are not fully moral in form, it must still be conceded that there is more to being a "right-living person" than only observing one's other-regarding responsibilities. Neglecting a self-regarding commitment would still be quite like a moral failing by being the evasion of a commitment that is supported by valid reasons.[27]

Arguably, there are cases, however rare, in which self-regarding oughts are, like social ones, fully prescriptive in form, i.e., they are "validly action-guiding and committing through and through."[28] Self-regard can be fractured by mental disorder or cases of demoralization. Persons who are separated from their own good as an end can have reasonable grounds for seeking it even when sufficient inclination is absent. One's own good hinges on "possession of oneself as a mind." One cannot earnestly desire to have one's life reduced to a "shaky mess" by losing hold of oneself. One needs controlled self-determination and the ability to cope with adversity. One may find that the responsible preservation of oneself as a "capable ego" is something that "one ought to care for even when one is too driven or despondent to be inclined to care for it."[29] One's own good will then becomes something that one ought to seek and stand up for more than one is wont to or can readily bring oneself to; and to do the things which one's own good requires can then become a thorough self-regarding commitment. A commitment to cultivating one's own good rests on a person's "inmost concern" to preserve himself intact as a functioning self; as someone who is mentally in possession of himself and his world, and able to look at himself and what he is doing without denial.[30] Losing that concern can indicate self-destructive pathology. Reason-guided, responsible, ought-abiding living exists "for the sake of sane and well-ordered individual being" as well as "the regulation of the social order."[31] One can argue with Falk that such living exists "in the first place" for the sake of individual well-being insofar as acting "as someone willing to seek direction from the counsel of cogent reasons" turns initially on one's personal "stake in the kind of self-preservation which requires that one should be able to bear before oneself the survey of one's own actions."[32] If valid ought judgements are based on choice-supporting reasons, then there is arguably no logical limit to what might be a valid ought. Where the care of others might be a valid ought for one, the proper care of oneself might be a valid ought for another.[33]

Patients ought to be responsible to and for themselves. The assumption of this responsibility will to some extent be relative to the patient's capacities and should be exercised in at least a good enough way. Absent external constraints or deficits in mental or physical capacity, there is a clear sense in which we expect persons to take up the responsibility of caring for themselves. Indeed, Frankfurt avers that the presumption that one should responsibly care for oneself through a propensity to self-love is ubiquitous in our culture.[34] Much as we expect children to gradually assume responsibility for controlling their bodily activities—"from the regulation of excretory functions to speech and the purposive use of the limbs"[35]—we expect persons with the requisite capacity to assume some control over the dispositional qualities for which they can reasonably be held responsible. In short, we expect these persons to assume responsibility for both their actions and the kind of people they choose to become. Where the assumption of responsibility for controlling bodily functions is viewed as "an early and significant developmental achievement, which is a source of childhood self-esteem as well as a precondition for socialization,"[36] we can view the assumption of responsibility for one's actions and character as a later but no less significant response to "the demands of the world"[37] and "the challenge of living well."[38]

Indeed, we expect people to hold themselves to this responsibility. There are other-regarding moral aspects to this. We expect others to assume this responsibility in no small part because it would be a burden on us to have to assume it for them. We should also want to avoid burdening others with assuming it for us. If one has a responsibility to oneself to strive to make one's life go well, then this is conceivably true of others and will affect what is morally expected of them. But there is also a self-regarding ethical aspect. We each have, Dworkin claims, "a sovereign ethical responsibility to make something of value of our own lives ... and our various responsibilities and obligations to others flow from that personal responsibility."[39] Recognizing our status as persons means that we affirm ourselves as worthy of respect by thinking it important that we live well and treat our lives "as having that kind of importance."[40]

We owe it to ourselves to strive to live well by being well. We owe ourselves a positive and integrated sense of self that is based on appropriate measures of self-respect and self-love. Indeed, we take persons to be badly at odds with themselves if they lack this self-regarding bond and neglect, disrespect, or dislike themselves even if others are not disadvantaged thereby.[41] There are, notes Falk, "sick drives towards self-effacement and self-denial."[42] Frankfurt claims that persons who are wantonly indifferent or severely depressed, who do not care at all for themselves, "are so discordant with our fundamental expectations concerning human nature that we generally regard them as pathological."[43] Despite his insistence that self-love is deeply entrenched in our nature, we can question his assumption that self-love is less susceptible than other-regarding love to being inhibited, blocked, or diminished.[44] Mental disorders can put people badly at odds with themselves by (1) subverting this self-regarding bond, e.g., depressed persons may have a negative sense of self or (2) subverting the very sense that one has a coherent self, e.g., schizophrenic patients might lack any cohesive notion of who they are. There is much room for variations between these two extremes.

On my account, self-neglect can be ethically irresponsible and calls for self-accountability, if not self-reproach. I would hold mentally capable persons responsible to themselves for a measure of self-care that supports degrees of physical and mental health that are better than adequate and less than supremely excellent. I would also hold them responsible for not being evasive about identity-conferring commitments that they are convinced they really ought to live by.[45] Indeed, I think these commitments can have a significant overlap with one's mental well-being. Thus I would add the idea that such persons should not be evasive about the vague and troubling sense of not living as one should when they lack them. Where a self-regarding sense of ethical well-being overlaps with one's positive mental health, a severe demoralization can diminish it.

Dworkin has noted that self-regarding responsibility had a broader provenance in the ancient Greek ethics of what he terms "self-affirmation," i.e., the idea that each person has a life to live that they should want to live well. He reads Plato's and Aristotle's ethics as impelling us to seek "the fulfillment of a successful life conceived as a whole."[46] Virtue ethics has long recognized the normative relevance of both self- and other-regarding concerns and is thus well-poised to acknowledge that the scope of our responsibilities encompasses ourselves and others. The good of self-love "generates a strong obligation to look after oneself" that is "essential for living a fulfilled life."[47] We can thus speak meaningfully of being responsible for our own well-being in ways which others cannot assume for us. We affirm ourselves as worthy of respect by thinking it important that we live well. Dworkin cites our "common [ethical] convictions" that we have a "personal responsibility" to "seek the right values for our lives" and own up to ourselves for what we have made of them.[48] I posit a common clinical conviction that some mental disorders can decimate self-regarding bonds and opportunities for living well. We can speak of therapeutic recovery when a patient can start living outside of her mental illness and assume responsibility for living well by being well. The patient who holds herself responsible for managing her care has an intrapersonal disposition to engage in critical dialogue and own up to herself for what she makes of her therapeutic work.[49] One can thus have a self-regarding responsibility to cultivate and maintain self-unity and one should aim to do this in an excellent or good enough way. This normative project of personal care can be an ethical exercise in character development, i.e., it can involve strengthening a number of virtues in the initial context of a therapeutic alliance.

The alliance is a relationship within which and from which the patient grows. The healing project begins as the patient develops an alliance with the therapist. It becomes less dependent as the patient develops a stronger alliance with herself and works toward recovery on her own. This independent work becomes the patient's project of self-regarding care. It reflects efforts to manage treatment and restore self-unity that the patient is responsible for making on her own behalf. The patient's alliance with the therapist can thus evolve into the patient's alliance with herself. While there might be periods during which the patient relies heavily on the therapist's care and support, the alliance is not about fostering dependence. It aims instead at empowering the patient to assume an increasingly responsible role in caring for herself. She thus internalizes what she has learned in therapy and assumes responsibility for her continuing care.

This idea applies to psychotherapies that are widely divergent, e.g., psychodynamic and cognitive behavioral ones. The psychodynamic patient is encouraged to gradually assume responsibility for self-analysis and continue the working through on her own. The cognitive behavioral patient learns to recognize her negative schemata and apply the corrective ones by herself. The patient thus moves from being cared for by the psychiatrist to being cared for by herself. As we saw in chapter three, Meissner regards the patient's autonomous evaluation of interpretations and insights as a key responsibility in psychoanalysis. Openness to therapeutic influence must be balanced by increasing degrees of "circumspection, independence, and judgment" that contrasts with indoctrination or compliance to theory.[50] The patient who seeks help displays an initiative that psychotherapy aims to strengthen by having the patient assume increasing degrees of responsibility. Given a balanced trust in the therapist and a stable sense of intellectual autonomy, the patient is gradually more willing and able "to undertake, on his own recognizance ... the interpretation and application of his own therapeutic material."[51]

## 6.4 The Virtues by which Responsibilities are Met

I want to make connections between the patient's responsibilities and the cultivation of some domain-specific virtues by which they can be met, i.e., one develops and exercises certain virtues in meeting these responsibilities. I will relate these efforts to various aspects of positive mental health noted by Jahoda. I thus propose an overlap between the cultivation and maintenance of certain virtues and degrees of positive mental health. In so doing, I apply Martin's moral-therapeutic perspective to the specific domain of the healing project. Where Martin has his own scheme for this overlap, which the reader is well advised to consult, I often relate different aspects of positive mental health to different virtues.[52] Virtues can reflect the patient's contribution to the healing project in two ways: (1) the cultivation of virtues can inform the patient's therapeutic work and (2) virtues can be what patients strive to sustain in recovery.

I relate other- and self-regarding responsibility to morally and ethically desirable character traits of the patient. I distinguish here between 6.4a healing and 6.4b recovery virtues. This is a rough distinction since recovery can be seen as both a healing process and a therapeutic goal. As a process, one is recovering as one cultivates the healing virtues. We speak of this as the work of recovery.[53] As a goal to be attained, one has recovered when one has restored a stable and enduring self-unity by which a satisfying life is lived. Recovery virtues are what the healing virtues aim to bring about. I use the term "healing" to mean improving, alleviating, relieving, assuaging, easing, and lessening the patient's disorder. Healing reflects the transformative process of recovery, part of which involves exerting control and defining a stable self apart from the disorder.[54] The process of reconstructing an enduring, integrated sense of an active and responsible self provides a crucial source of improvement.[55]

Recovery is not synonymous with a return to a premorbid state. Davidson's notion of recovery is broad enough to include patients who recuperate fully from a mental disorder and those who continue to have the disorder but learn to live a life that is not completely defined by it, i.e., those who learn to live outside their disorder. If a patient has work to do in the healing project, then the patient is the subject and the illness becomes the object of the efforts to recover. Thus the patient is not defined entirely by the illness.[56] Recovery is brought about through the efforts a patient makes to reclaim responsibility for her life and assume increasing control over managing her care. It involves efforts to change one's attitudes, values, and goals to grow beyond mental disorder and live a satisfying life with new meaning and purpose.[57] These efforts can be virtuous ones insofar as they involve rebuilding one's character, i.e., the mental and ethical/moral qualities that are distinctive to a person with a vision of a satisfying life.

In chapter five, I discussed Swanton's three virtues of practice (i.e., virtues of focus, dialogue, and constraint integration) as healing virtues. In this chapter, I will explicate six new healing virtues that make overlapping contributions to the patient's other- and self-regarding responsibilities: honesty, imaginative flexibility, perseverance, hopefulness, healing curiosity, and respect for the healing project. They inform the collaboration between therapist and patient and the latter's independent efforts to manage her own care. These are the character traits by which an arduous healing process is initiated and sustained. They enable the patient to work toward recovery. One might say that patients are in the process of recovery to the extent that they work toward it. But patients can be in recovery without having recovered. These virtues are thus instrumental in bringing about recovery.

I then discuss the virtues of self-respect, self-love, empathic concern, and respect for others. These are the recovery virtues, the stable attainment of which indicates that some degree of self-unity has been realized. More to the point, these virtues need to be sustained if the patient is to continue living a recovered life, i.e., if the patient is to live well by being well. Recovery virtues are the therapeutic goals of the healing project. In sum, the healing virtues enable the patient to attain and strengthen the recovery virtues that express her well-being. Many healing projects are not smooth sailing. They present setbacks, adverse events, and disappointments. These are problems to be managed and hopefully resolved. The three virtues of practice focus discussed are also relevant here.

## 6.4.1 Healing Virtues

### 6.4.1.1 Honesty

Sincere truthfulness is a virtue that straddles the epistemic and ethical spaces of normative appraisal. It involves a commitment in therapy to forgo deception of others and oneself. It reflects a patient's motivation to face up to what he might otherwise want to avoid and to candid disclosures of same. It also reflects a motivation to forgo self-deceptive rationalizations. Eagle's devoted and truth-seeking attitude is a healing virtue that infuses the patient's work in psychotherapy.[58] It is intrepid, unflinching, and courageous, i.e., the patient must work up a measure of self-possession to face the vicissitudes of psychotherapy.

### 6.4.1.2 Imaginative Flexibility

Imaginative flexibility is an ability to envision options and possibilities, a willingness to change, and an ability to modify behavioral strategies and core aspects. As a configuration of personality traits, it covers a range of abilities to

> recognize and adapt to various situational demands; shift mindsets or behavioral repertoires when these strategies compromise personal or social functioning; maintain balance among important life domains; and [to] be aware, open, and committed to behaviors that are congruent with deeply held values. In many forms of psychopathology, these flexibility processes are absent.[59]

As a virtue, it is a good dispositional quality of character to respond to the demands of the world in a good enough or excellent way. If the demands of the world include the demand for self-improvement, then imaginative flexibility aims at the targets that this demand indicates, i.e., the desired changes to the patient's psyche and behavior that are improved ways of relating to oneself and to others. It can be especially relevant to patients with borderline, antisocial, or narcissistic personality disorders, many of whom are fixed and rigid in entrenched patterns of affective and cognitive response. Seeing beyond their embedded maladaptations is perhaps the first step in changing them for the better.

### 6.4.1.3 Perseverance

This is a virtue that requires one to bond with institutions, persons, or projects.[60] In a role-specific sense contextual to the healing project, it requires the patient to bond appropriately with the therapist and the collaborative treatment plan worked out in the alliance. It eventually enables the patient to bond with the more independent normative project of her self-regarding care. In broad terms, it enables the patient to firmly continue her efforts to work with the therapist and for herself in spite of difficulties and setbacks.

Maintaining perseverance can be a creative challenge. There is more at play than simply gritting one's teeth and forging ahead no matter what. Perseverance involves both protracted effort and the ability to endure adverse events by way of flexible response. Virtues of focus are crucial to this ability, as is a patient's positive appraisal of his problem-solving skills. A clear relationship has been established between consistent and beneficial coping skills and a positive problem-solving appraisal. The latter is a critical strength for coping with the demands of the world.[61] Setbacks in the healing project do not diminish the perseverant patient's motivation for sustaining it; they challenge and inspire his ability to revise his strategies for coping with them. Perseverant patients are resilient: they persistently evince capacity for flexible, creative, and positive adaptation during or following significant adversity or risk.[62]

The patient develops incremental degrees of tenacity in making repeated efforts towards recovery. These efforts can involve small steps by which commitment to the treatment plan is strengthened over time. A depressive relapse or the adverse side effects of medications can drain confidence in the plan and in one's ability to manage it. Perseverance is the trait by which the patient comes to offer strong resistance to this depletive effect. To the extent that she develops it, she refuses to be "used up" by her disorder. Consider the bipolar patient whose treatment plan consists of psychotherapy and drugs. She might have to endure protracted periods of experimentation before her drug regimen is sufficiently fine-tuned to alleviate her symptoms. She might have to acquire the coping skills that enable her to deal with unwanted side effects. There is also a daunting existential call to re-engage with herself and others. She will have to reconfigure her conception of what it means for her to live well as someone who is challenged by her disorder. Allusions to Camus' portrayal of Sisyphus are not instructive here. Where Sisyphus persevered without hope, the virtuous patient cannot.[63]

#### 6.4.1.4 Hopefulness

Hopefulness is a disposition to believe that one can find pathways to desired goals and summon the motivation to follow them. The ability to conceive multiple routes is crucial when a patient encounters barriers or setbacks to therapeutic goals. Some research has indicated that hopeful persons are effective at generating alternative routes to goals.[64] This capacity for flexible, creative, and positive adaptation during or following significant adversity or risk suggests an interrelation between perseverance and hope by which the latter might drive the former. A sense of agency is the motivational component in hopefulness. It is the self-referential belief in one's ability to initiate and sustain goal-directed efforts along a pathway. It is also crucial when patients encounter setbacks because it enables them to apply the necessary motivation to move along alternate routes to therapeutic goals. Hopeful patients see barriers to recovery as challenges to be resolved.[65]

Hope can be thick or thin. It can range from tentative beliefs in the mere possibility of recovery, to ever more confident expectations and even, perhaps, to a trust that one will recover. It can also encompass the intemperate, extravagant optimism associated with manic states. As a healing virtue, I posit the desires and expectations of hope as judicious.[66] This confidence and trust in oneself can become stronger the more the patient's self is unified. This virtue is closely connected to perseverance since it requires renewed commitment and continuing efforts. Davidson has stressed that "having hope and believing in the possibility of a renewed sense of self and purpose" is essential to recovery. Hope can direct effective efforts to improve one's condition when it is "translated into a desire and commitment to recover."[67]

The patient's hope is directed towards the therapist, the healing project, and himself. He hopes that the therapist can be helpful and comes to rely on, or trust in, that expectation. A commitment to the healing project will be stillborn without "hopefulness that the process has meaning and will eventuate in a good therapeutic outcome."[68] As the patient's sense of self-reliance is strengthened in the alliance with the psychiatrist, he develops greater ability to work towards recovery and gradually acquires the confident expectation that he can rely on managing his own care. Persistent hope indicates the first steps towards recovery. Consider how it can counter the enervating symptom of depression. There is considerable overlap between hope as a virtue and hope as a manifestation, however incipient, of mental health.[69]

There is substantive literature on how hope theory provides insight into the psychological recovery process, most notably Frank's view that hope is a common factor across the myriad techniques of different psychotherapies.[70] It can be argued that most psychotherapies provide patients with a mental "boost" that represents an increase in agency thinking, fostered by the patient's newly acquired belief that she can get well. A psychotherapy technique, then, provides a strategy for improving and maintaining well-being, e.g., insight in psychoanalysis or schema restructuring in cognitive therapy. These strategies are the patient's pathways to therapeutic goals.[71] Psychotherapy might be a praxis by which hopefulness can be cultivated and strengthened. A therapeutic alliance with a firmly hopeful patient is an auspicious beginning to a healing project. But what of patients whose lack of hopefulness is part of the presenting problem? How can they learn to cultivate it? This is arguably an important direction for future research in positive psychology. It might be the case that findings related to the development of positive coping strengths for physical disabilities can be extended to psychological ones. I raise this idea as a hypothesis for further investigation.

#### 6.4.1.5 Healing Curiosity

Used as synonyms, curiosity and interest refer to a positive motivational-emotional state that is associated with exploration through pursuit of challenging activities. Curiosity can be defined as the acknowledgement, pursuit, and intense desire to explore novel, challenging, and uncertain events and activities. It motivates persons to think and act in novel ways and to be immersed in, to investigate, and to learn about the interesting target of their attention. There is thus an "exploratory striving" component and a "mindful immersion" component to curiosity. As such, curiosity is an ideal candidate for enhancing well-being. In seeking out and investing effort in new and challenging activities, curious persons "expand their knowledge, skills, goal-directed efforts, and sense of self."[72] They also appear to increase their tolerance for the distressing states of self-awareness that can result from trying novel responses to challenges "and behaving in ways outside of one's comfort zone."[73] Although the putative link between curiosity and well-being requires much further study, I would aver the following: patients who are regularly curious and willing to embrace the novelty, uncertainty, and challenges of a psychiatric healing project are better able to sustain hope and perseverance in meeting them. Curiosity might facilitate a psychotherapeutic alliance by promoting engagement, responsiveness, and flexibility to the therapist's varied perspectives. These curiosity-relevant dispositions would be most desirable in the formative stages of the alliance.[74]

Halpern has written of how a psychiatrist's empathy can induce the return of a "healing curiosity" in a depressed patient. The patient takes "herself seriously and ... becomes curious about her convictions about the future."[75] As noted, mental illness can decimate the dispositions by which one cultivates self-unity and responds to the demands of the world. Patients can acquire the belief that they will forever live inside their illness, thus rendering them unable to see their future as tolerable. Patients can experience schizophrenia or major depression as a reified state that envelops their being and paralyzes any sense of existential momentum. Such patients lack the security and comfort "to feel a sense of ongoingness" into their future.[76] This can destroy a patient's confident belief in his capacity to live by identity-conferring goals and values that are cultivated over time. Healing curiosity enables the patient to better sympathize with himself. He can respect the challenges his illness presents as he develops a sense of perspective by which they can be faced and hopefully overcome. He thus becomes curious about how he might move through the "concretized state"[77] of his illness and live a life outside of it. Curious patients who focus on novelty and challenge are ones who test their views of self, others, and the world by increasing their knowledge and skills. This forward momentum toward valued goals can be seen as a pathway to the construction of a meaningful life. It simultaneously involves a positive, mindful engagement in a meaningful present and an equally positive orientation to the future by which one plans an approach to long-term goals.[78]

The healing effect of the psychiatrist's empathy is not limited to the "sense of being accompanied" but may also involve the facilitation of a sense of agency and self-efficiency in the patient.[79] Healing curiosity includes curiosity about the modes of healing themselves. The patient would thus take her treatment options seriously and become curious about how they might enable her to restore the unity of her person. Healing curiosity might be related to other virtues of the responsible patient like hopefulness, perseverance, and flexibility, i.e., if healing curiosity is not a specific virtue in its own right, it is arguably a dimension or facet of the latter three that can be expanded upon. These virtues can be especially relevant given the long-term, uncertain course and debilitating symptoms of some disorders. Patients may also have to cope with a variable and sometimes refractory range of response to their treatments. The clinical uses of curiosity merit greater empirical and theoretical attention. It would be particularly interesting to determine whether the facilitation of curiosity in psychotherapy could build "self-regulatory resources" to endure the "avoidance and disengagement" that often occur after episodes of extreme depression and anxiety. That facilitation might also be an effective route to confronting, processing, and making meaning out of difficult emotional material.[80]

Perseverance, hopefulness, and healing curiosity overlap with facets of some of Jahoda's conceptual criteria for positive mental health. Under the criteria of growth, development, and self-actualization, these healing virtues coincide with the motivational processes that sustain a future-oriented, forward momentum toward a richer life. The healing virtues are the traits by which the patient moves away from the stagnating immobilization of major mental disorders or problems in living, like demoralization. They are also the traits by which the patient cultivates renewed investment in life. Under the criterion of environmental mastery, the virtues of focus discussed in chapter five overlap with a capacity for engaging in a problem-solving process. As a facet of positive mental health, problem solving presupposes a conscious awareness of problems and an ongoing intention to deal with them. Jahoda distinguishes three dimensions of this process. There is, first, an awareness of the problem followed by reflection on the means that might resolve it, a choice of one or more of those means, and then the implementation of that choice. There is, second, the maintenance of an appropriate tone of feeling by which one sustains the positive incentive to work the problem through. The third dimension concerns the maintenance of a direct approach to the problem, absent evasion or denial.[81]

#### 6.4.1.6 Respect for the Healing Project

Healing curiosity might also be related to the virtue of respect for the healing project. Radden and Sadler note this as a psychiatrist's virtue that involves "respect for the person of the patient" and reverence "for the moral seriousness of the project itself."[82] They surmise that these attitudes will generate in the psychiatrist a degree of self-respect and faith in her healing abilities. Insofar as patient and psychiatrist work in alliance, these attitudes might generate in the patient a degree of self-respect and faith in his own healing abilities. This possibility has been raised by Radden and Sadler with reference to other virtues, e.g., the psychiatrist who maintains and conveys hope in the treatment project can engender it in the patient.[83] In sum, respect for the healing project can be construed as a virtue of both therapist and responsible patient.

Regarding the patient, respect for the healing project will intersect with the project of self-regarding care. It begins in the therapeutic alliance when the patient's efforts to resume control and responsibility for managing symptoms are supported, perhaps even managed, by the psychiatrist. It continues after the patient has assumed the primary responsibility for using therapeutic techniques and interventions to manage his own care.

### 6.4.2 Recovery Virtues

I argue that self-unity reflects threshold degrees of both a consolidated psychological subjectivity and the coherence of ethical integrity. It is a personal cohesion attained through the virtue self-love, or the positive, psychological bonding with oneself that is devoid of self-contempt. Self-unity means the patient's regard for his well-being has achieved some consolidation through self-love as tempered by self-respect. Threshold degrees of each contribute to an integrated sense of self. Pursuing goals of psychological improvement, says Swanton, is extremely important to the virtuous life. She argues that in working to overcome problems that obstruct one's ability to grow, one works to express greater self-love through attaining a better bond with oneself. This bond enables undistorted self-expression that incorporates "respect for self and other."[84]

#### 6.4.2.1 Self-Love and Self-Respect

Swanton defines self-love as an essentially bond-centered, psychological phenomenon that reflects the Kantian distinction between coming close to, and keeping an appropriate distance, from oneself. Coming close involves the positive bonding with oneself.[85] I define this affirmative bond as the self-embrace of having, and living by, identity-conferring standards, values, and projects that unify psychological well-being with personal coherence and ethical character.[86] Attending to one's well-being by working to restore and sustain self-unity is a loving trait. Keeping a balanced distance from oneself involves self-respect, i.e., a recognition that out of regard for oneself as a human being one does not act as if one is totally expendable. Self-respect is a reflective commitment to oneself as valuable and worthy of values that others can respect. Self-love is thus delimited or tempered by self-respect. Some of the problems for which psychiatric treatment is sought can be plausibly seen to obstruct the development of this affirmative bond, i.e., as failures to attain personal unity through self-love as delimited by self-respect. These failures are arguably what psychiatrists allude to when asking depressed patients if they feel worthless.[87] It is what the schizophrenic patient lacks when he speaks of feeling depersonalized.

Swanton's analysis of self-love is not without rich historical precedent. I would note the relevance of Aristotle and the contemporary work of Harry Frankfurt. Both Aristotle and Frankfurt distinguish between proper and improper, or decent and base self-love. Self-love for Aristotle involved being a friend to oneself. It was psychologically primary in that the ways we relate to friends are first the ways we relate to ourselves. The decent person relates to her friend as to herself since the friend is another self. Such people are "concerned with themselves and each other" since they all seek a good life that is lived according to the virtues. The base person is conflicted in that she has no friendly feelings for herself. Swanton's idea that self-love is an affirmative bond devoid of contempt echoes Aristotle's idea that a person who shuns vice and strives to be virtuous will have a friendly relation to herself as well as others.[88] She will extend the relevant aspects of her self-love to others and "care about their good for their own sakes."[89]

The base form of self-love is premised on an incorrect view of what the self should strive for, e.g., the largest share of sensual pleasures, honors, or money for the person himself. This is to gratify the non-rational part of the soul. Proper self-love is fundamental to a virtuous life guided by practical reason. It involves a striving to award oneself with what is best and finest through fine actions. If everyone strives to so award themselves, then each person will receive the greatest of goods, since that is virtue's character. It is in this way that Aristotle claimed that all of us must be self-lovers, i.e., by loving ourselves as having the capacity for practical reasoning by which we can lead virtuous lives. The self-lover will help himself and benefit others by living virtuously.[90]

Aristotle felt that if each person strives to achieve the most good by living virtuously, then they do not live at the expense of others because living virtuously "just is" doing things like acting out of concern for oneself and for others for their own sakes. Indecent persons evince their self-love in greedy or unjust actions where decent persons will evince it in acting virtuously, since the self they love is their developed ability for practical reasoning, and virtuous actions are the expression of properly developed practical reasoning. Thus developing the virtues was for Aristotle "an expression of self-love, for it will be an expression of the rational moral agency which a true self-lover identifies with." Where self-love for Swanton is a profile of all virtues, Aristotle saw it as the dispositional wellspring by which they were nourished.[91]

Frankfurt contrasts his notion of proper self-love with self-indulgence, whereby persons are mainly driven to satisfy their own strongest inclinations and desires. A primary motivation to pursue whatever persons happen to want most and to gratify impulses and desires can conflict with the "true interests" that are "genuinely important to them." Proper self-love requires a different kind of conscientious attention, as it is a deep and essential achievement of a successful life. It shares the four features of other-regarding love: it is (1) a concern for the flourishing or well-being of the person loved; (2) unavoidably personal; (3) an identification with the beloved, or the taking of the beloved's interests as one's own; and (4) determined by conditions that surpass our voluntary control. Frankfurt assumes that we are naturally moved to love ourselves and that this inclination is very difficult to overcome.[92] This assumption has been questioned with reference to persons whose presenting problem is their difficulty in being able to love themselves. There is arguably much more room for divided selves and their "uncertainties, hesitations, and doubts than Frankfurt's picture allows."[93] Other questions can be raised about Frankfurt's claim that people care about their own well-being "in a way that is exclusively non-instrumental" and valued "*only* for its own sake."[94] In terms of "genuine interests," many persons align with causes or identity-conferring projects that are larger than themselves such that their self-love has instrumental and intrinsic value. This kind of self-transcendence is arguably a significant part of what "our own good" actually is. As Lippitt notes, a crucial feature of Frankfurt's proper self-love is that it points outside the self.[95] A key theme in Frankfurt's thinking is that we infuse the world with importance by caring about things. "The totality of the various things that a person cares about—together with his ordering of how important to him they are—effectively specifies his answer to the question of how to live."[96] There is a necessary connection between proper self-love and "loving the things that one cares about, the things that give one's life meaning."[97] Hence Frankfurt's claim that a person "cannot love himself except insofar as he loves other things."[98] This reflects Swanton's idea that self-love is a bonding phenomenon if coming close to oneself is understood in part as the self-embrace of living by identity-conferring projects, which unify psychological well-being with personal coherence and ethical character. As a profile of the virtues, Swanton sees self-love as "indirectly involved" where the field of a virtue is one's projects or future possibilities. These fields correspond respectively to virtues of perseverance and hope. Bonding with one's projects through virtuous perseverance is only possible when it is infused with self-love, and when future possibilities are perceived misanthropically hope is stillborn and distorted.[99] Although self-love is a mode of generic ethical acknowledgement for Swanton, there is a sense in which it points outside the self to the fields of the virtues. These fields will contain the totality of the things a person cares about.

Recovery virtues can be seen as contextual to the healing project and constituting the goals at which it aims.[100] They are nascent in the healing virtues and gather strength as the patient works towards recovery. Self-love will gradually emerge through perseverance as a healthy bonding with the healing project becomes stronger. It will emerge through hope as the patient develops a positive rapport with her future possibilities.[101] Once a threshold level of self-unity is restored, the patient continues to cultivate recovery virtues by which it is sustained. The distinction between healing and recovery virtues is not a sharp bifurcation. In the work of self-improvement and restoration, the former can shade into and inform the latter.

#### 6.4.2.2 Empathic Concern and Respect for Others

Depending on the presenting problem, some recovery virtues will be predominantly other-regarding. As I will soon discuss, borderline personality and antisocial personality disorders involve significant disregard of others. Respect for others, or forbearance, involves calibrating one's ability to come appropriately close to, and maintain, deferential distance from another. Both disorders involve multifaceted deficits in the patient's abilities to understand or consciously recognize another person's perspective and experience (i.e., cognitive empathy) and to imaginatively share another's emotional state (i.e., affective empathy).[102] If empathy is understood in the limited sense of "feeling with" another, then it can be distinguished from sympathy, i.e., "feeling for" another. For instance, one might consciously recognize another's suffering by feeling with her, yet without caring or feeling concern for her. A sadist might empathize cognitively with his victim's pain and affectively delight in it. Someone else might empathize cognitively with the victim's pain but be indifferent to it.

I understand empathy in what Simmons terms its "fullest" form, which includes the cognitive and affective dimensions. One cannot, arguably, empathize affectively with another's suffering without feelings of concern for her or empathize affectively with her concerns for her well-being without caring for her well-being. To empathize fully with another's suffering means experiencing similar feelings of dislike or concern for her distress. To empathize fully with another's concerns for her well-being is sufficient to feel concern for her and incompatible with sadistic enjoyment or indifference. I both acknowledge that she has those concerns and experience them from her perspective, i.e., I see and feel those concerns as she does. If I empathize fully with her goals and purposes, then I experience them as worthwhile and mattering too and will share in her desire to fulfill them.[103] "Insofar as sympathy is just feeling concern for others over aspects of their welfare which they too feel concern over, it seems to be nothing more than empathizing with others' feelings of concern. It makes sense to refer to such sympathy as empathetic concern or caring."[104] If being a fully moral person includes having right and fine inner affective states, then empathic concern for others is an essential facet of being a fully moral person for those who have the capacity to feel it. In its fullest form, empathy is "typically essential for sympathy."[105]

Healing curiosity can aim at the development of this fuller sense of empathy as a recovery virtue. Halpern's ideas about how physicians develop empathy can also be relevant to patients. Arguably, one way to strengthen empathic capacity is to help such patients develop and sustain an "engaged curiosity" about the experience of others that is "grounded in an affective experience of connecting—wanting to relate to another person as another self, as a center of meaning and initiative."[106] While patients cannot directly will themselves to empathize, cultivating curiosity is a way to develop empathy. Learning to listen to the verbal and nonverbal communications of others with attentive openness is a crucial first step in facilitating the emergence of empathic response. Reviewing approaches to teaching empathy in medical schools, Halpern notes that "patients who feel that their doctors pay careful attention are more likely to talk about their situations, and listening to patients tell their stories in their own words helps engender empathy." While I share Halpern's reservation about reducing empathy to "mechanistic mirroring," the idea that patients can learn to internalize their therapist's attunement and develop their own capacity for directing it toward others is worth considering. One might learn to empathize, at least in part, by being empathized with.[107] I examine the praxis of mentalization-based therapy as a means to developing empathy in chapter seven.

## 6.5 Recovery Virtues and Positive Mental Health

The recovery virtues also overlap with some of Jahoda's conceptual criteria for positive mental health. Under the criterion of attitudes toward the self, the recovery virtues relate to feelings about the self and a sense of identity. Both virtues coincide with how a person feels about himself and imply the self-acceptance of strengths and shortcomings. They coincide in turn with a sense of identity. A positive sense of self-regard helps to integrate aspects of the self through a global, essentially benevolent view of the whole self, as when we say of someone: he knows who he is and does not feel basic doubts about his identity. This can be contrasted with the sense of self-disintegration experienced by those with major depression, schizophrenia, or demoralization.[108]

Under the criterion of growth, development, and self-actualization, the recovery virtues relate to ongoing and sufficiently stable motivational processes and to investment in living. The forward momentum of a meaningful orientation toward the future does not stop with hopefulness. Or rather, hopefulness does not stop with recovery. Living by one's deep evaluations and critical interests is not a static state. The self-unity of the recovery virtues and the values and interests by which that unity is defined overlaps with an affirmative dedication to living well by being well, the range and quality of one's engagement with others, the objects and interests that one considers significant, and participation in a richer, differentiated life.[109]

Under the criterion of integration, the recovery virtues coincide with a unifying perspective by which one feels that there is purpose and meaning to one's life. That feeling enables a striving to extend one's vision of a good life into the future. Like Taylor's deep evaluations, this perspective might take effort to articulate, but it affords a sense of one's place in a coherent scheme of things. A unifying outlook on life enhances and guides a strong investment in it.[110] This, in turn, along with the motivational facets noted above, integrates meaning in one's life to involve ideas of self-identity, a worldview, interactions with others, and a fit between identity and worldview, as well as a comprehension of what one is trying to achieve and sustain. We can define meaning in life as "the extent to which people comprehend, make sense of, or see significance in their lives," along with the degree to which they see themselves as having a purpose, mission, or set of overarching aims.[111] Baumeister identifies four components of meaning in life that have a conceptual kinship with Taylor's notion of moral identity: feeling a sense of purpose, having a basis for self-worth, a clarified scheme of values by which one judges right and wrong, and a sense of efficacy (Taylor would refer to "agency").[112] There is some evidence that treating psychological distress enables persons to rebuild meaningful lives. A research agenda for positive psychology should include studies that aim to determine whether enabling persons to rebuild meaningful lives is a means of treating psychological distress. Rigorously conducted trials that compare meaning-centered interventions with validated treatments could assist in determining the potential of concentrating on meaning as a therapeutic aid.[113]

A successful course of therapy that reflects the application of healing and recovery virtues should enable post-traumatic growth. Remember Linda Logan: while she regained some facets of her pre-depression self, she also developed in novel ways to become a different person. Post-traumatic growth is modeled on the following four requirements: (1) a precipitating and significant disruption to one's sense of self or worldview; (2) the task of reconstructing a meaningful and coherent view of one's self and world; and (3) the awareness that one has changed for the better by (4) responding to these challenges.[114] Mental disorders and problems in living like demoralization can present these four requirements. For growth to occur, the disruption to one's identity and worldview must constitute a loss that seriously taxes one's psychological resources for dealing with it. One must work through and reconcile what the loss means to one's life, acknowledge that the reconstructed worldview and sense of self is an improvement, and attribute that positive change to having worked through the trauma. Growth results from purposive action, from working through a trauma and pursuing newly set goals for living well by being well. It will not result from merely reappraising a situation, or being the passive recipient of therapeutic guidance and help.[115] Clearly, psychotherapy is one context in which this working through can occur. The recovery virtues are especially relevant here, as post-traumatic growth involves "significant, sustained positive changes in major commitments and life goals" as well as changes in self-awareness. It is not just a matter of adopting a "new philosophy of life." It is a matter of "engaging in and sustaining behavior directed toward achieving new goals."[116] On my account, it is the affirmative, self-loving bond of having, and living by, identity-conferring standards, values, and projects that unify psychological well-being with personal coherence and ethical character.

We see again that some of these ideas are not limited to psychotherapeutic healing projects. Indeed, they resonate especially well with research into positive growth following physical disability. Hopefulness, a focus on developing one's real or potential character strengths, and the sustained effort of working toward desired states aligned with future happiness are seen as crucial. Still, we should be mindful of the limitations of my account. So far as I am aware, longitudinal studies that track the development of character strengths before and after physical or psychological crises are not currently available. Like many in the positive psychology movement, I believe that some patients not only appreciate, but also effect a recovery by developing certain character strengths or virtues in the process. I also believe that healers who work with physical or psychological disabilities should aim to devise therapeutic interventions that might increase such character strengths.[117]

I should stress the provisional nature of the catalogue of virtues that I see as relevant to the healing project. Any one of these virtues can be further refined. The epistemic virtues discussed in chapter three are no less germane insofar as some patients aspire to better know or holistically understand themselves through psychotherapeutic exploration, e.g., the co-creation in psychodynamic therapy of a patient's narrative that both "seems true" and opens up "new possibilities for living a better life."[118] I also stress the overlapping, interdependent nature of these virtues in praxis. Hopefulness and perseverance arguably thrive together. Through mutual synergy, I see the problem-solving virtues of focus as going hand in hand with imaginative flexibility.

I do not propose an isolationist approach by which virtues relating to epistemic and generic ethical fields are distinguished by sharp and final divides. Like Swanton, I see the various fields of the virtues as integrated in the practical truth of right action at which virtue aims. She posits inextricable and often contested connections between the fields of the virtues, which integrate them in the broad normative sense of responding to the demands of the world with practical wisdom. Persons who possess sufficient degrees of practical wisdom in numerous fields of virtue are necessary for their integration. As such, to portray a single trait as a virtue can involve consideration of its relevance to the different fields in which it is applicable, e.g., epistemic and generically ethical ones. Thus open-mindedness can have both epistemic and generically ethical fields of application. Swanton argues further that "at a deep level of analysis virtue is aimed at practical truth and not merely at 'moral' or 'epistemic' truth."[119]

## 6.6 Authenticity as a Virtuous Way of Living

In some cases, the psychotherapeutic healing project will be tantamount to what Healy terms the patient's "call to authenticity."[120] I do not see this search as relevant to every case of psychotherapy, although it might be implied in many to various degrees. Some implications will be stronger than others. Seneca's Angry Man was arguably aspiring to a life that would reflect his truer, less distorted self, but I think there are cases in which the search for authenticity is not just suggested but directly expressed. Authenticity can be defined in terms of a uniquely realized personal identity or the psychological facets of a true self. Hence the standard notion that authenticity is about being who you really are. Although these definitions capture relevant aspects of authenticity,

I propose a broader account with a larger social context. I define authenticity as the mode or style of living that can emerge from the above-noted virtues. It is both an ethical ideal and the quality of an ongoing engagement in one's life. Where Radden and Sadler posit integrity and authenticity as separate metavirtues,[121] I regard ethical integrity and authenticity as overlapping terms for what Dworkin and Taylor would call a mode or style of living. "We discover what we have it in us to be," says Taylor, "by becoming that mode of life, by giving expression in our speech and action to what is original in us."[122]

Authenticity is usually understood to involve being true to oneself in one's manner of living. Dworkin writes of ethical integrity, which is living by the conviction that my life, in its central features, is an appropriate one for me such that no other life I might live would be a better response to my situation.[123] It is this notion of ethical integrity that overlaps with authenticity, which Dworkin later defined as a person's "responsibility to act consistently with the character and projects he identifies for himself."[124] Authenticity is expressing yourself in life by "seeking a way to live" that you can endorse as right for you and your circumstances.[125] It implies some degree of self-unity insofar as one is bonded with one's core values and projects and has some positive, coherent sense of self as that to which one is true. I regard authenticity as reflecting a creative balance between self-love (i.e., the affirmative bonding with one's deep evaluations, critical interests, and identity-conferring commitments by which one attains a positive self-regard) and self-respect (i.e., a reflective commitment to oneself as valuable and worthy of living well by values that can be respected by others). Their mutually balanced realization in a way of living comprises authenticity.

I propose authenticity as an engaged and avowed way of life. It is responsive to the challenge of living well in accordance with our strong evaluations and critical interests. These involve in no small part one's ethical ideals about the person one aspires to be and the life that one fashions as best expressing that identity. Formulating and living by strong evaluations and critical interests requires the cultivation of certain virtues—notably self-respect and self-love. I present authenticity as more than an ethical ideal. If attained, it is a mode of living expressive of the self that emerges from the cultivation of these virtues. We can relate Taylor's strong evaluations to Dworkin's critical interests. Taylor defines strong evaluations as the goods to which one cannot help but have recourse in determining the purposes of one's *own* life.[126] Taylor also refers to these "goods" as our "deepest evaluations," our ownmost, identity-defining sense of what is important to us; what is "worthy or higher, or more integrated, or more fulfilling."[127] Our deepest evaluations comprise a moral topography; a space of aspiration and assessment that orients us to life by demarcating what we consider meaningful and desirable.[128]

Dworkin defines critical interests as those involvements and concerns that make a life veritably better to satisfy interests that a person would be "mistaken and genuinely worse off" to ignore. One's convictions about what makes one's life good overall reflect one's critical interests. They guide our sense of the "general style of life" that we think is appropriate, and our sense of the choices that we think "are not only good at the moment but in character" for ourselves. A commitment to living by critical interests bespeaks an aspiration to "an integral, creative narrative" that portrays and expresses coherent choices of experiences, achievements, or a self-defining vision of a good life.[129] A person's convictions about his own critical interests are judgments about what it means for his own life to flourish. Dworkin claims that these convictions are best understood as a special application of a person's general commitment to the sanctity of life. That person "is eager to make something of his own life, not simply to enjoy it; he treats his own life as something sacred for which he is responsible, something he must not waste. He thinks it intrinsically important that he live well, and with integrity."[130]

I relate strong evaluations to critical interests as follows. Critical interests are the articulation of strong evaluations in terms of identity-defining commitments, projects, and goals. Formulating and living by critical interests requires stable traits of character. Virtues are the character traits by which one fosters a way of life that is integrated with and expressive of these commitments, projects, and goals. Creativity and self-love are the virtues by which one develops critical interests. The ethical imperative is that one ought to live by the critical interests one has formed. Fidelity, honesty, and resoluteness are but some of the virtues by which one does that. The virtues by which one cultivates and lives by critical interests are the attributes that together define a distinct personal character, by which I mean the inherent complex of dispositions that determine one's ethical and moral responses. As Ferrara puts it, the description of a character is an answer to the question: "What is peculiarly distinctive of my way of interacting with others?"[131] We can certainly speak of an authentic character or identity. As an ethical ideal, authenticity has its psychological and ethical constituents. But a robust notion of authenticity should capture the quality of a life that emerges from the engagement of that identity or character with the world. Authenticity effloresces from character and commitment. It is the ongoing engagement with the world, the way in which one lives an engaged life that stands for one's strong evaluations and critical interests. Authenticity is not just about one's self. It is a way of relating to, or living in, the horizons of significance that make up one's life world.

Critical interests and strong evaluations both inform one's personally evocative mode of living and contribute to the integrity and individuation of one's character. Both express aspirational ideals about the person one most wants to be. Taylor and Dworkin acknowledge that one can fail to live by strong evaluations and critical interests. Where Dworkin speaks of a vague and persistent sense that one is not living as one should, Taylor speaks of what is potentially a self-shattering "breakdown" and of being "spiritually out of joint."[132] These ideas have struck a chord with some of those who have written on psychotherapy as a generically ethical enterprise. Christopher claims that it is this sense of "being out of joint" with one's strong evaluations that leads persons to seek psychotherapy: "Quite often … we witness our patients profoundly struggle with these 'deepest evaluations.' "[133] Tjeltveit claims that deep evaluations "are primarily (but not exclusively) those goods toward which therapy aims" and that we evaluate therapeutic outcome "by whether clients achieve those good ends."[134]

Our efforts to respond to the demands of the world comprise a challenging performance requiring skill. Authenticity means that one's life is good because one is meeting this challenge well by responding to the demands of the world through the lenses of our critical interests and strong evaluations. Authenticity can thus be responsive to both our self-regarding ethical responsibilities and our other-regarding moral ones. It is a mode of living that characterizes our identity-defining engagements with self and other. In conceiving facets of an integrated self, Jahoda noted the importance of a "unifying outlook on life" that guides one's actions and feelings in the process of shaping a future. It also inspires a strong "investment in living."[135] The latter notion connotes an affirmative participation in living through an animated range of engagements "with other people and the things of this world, the objects and activities that [one] considers significant … with work, ideas, and interests."[136]

Construed in my terms, authenticity is a mode of invested living that reflects aspects of positive mental health in the fulfillment of identity-conferring projects through engagement with the world. This broader, more inclusive notion of authenticity has strong affinities with Varga's. As an ethical ideal, authenticity has been widely conceptualized as an existential praxis of the self to achieve a good life, i.e., that one should be true to oneself and lead a life that expresses what the person takes herself to be and to stand for. Rather than limit authenticity to notions of a uniquely discovered or created self, I follow Varga's lead in connecting it "to the (wholehearted) manner in which we engage with our lives" and integrate them through living by values, commitments, and projects that we endorse as central to our self-understanding. To betray these projects is to betray oneself.[137]

A wholehearted mode of responsiveness to what we care about does not emerge in a normative vacuum. It transpires from "our responsiveness to inter-subjectively constituted values and orientations, without which we would not be genuine moral agents."[138] Hence Varga's insistence that authenticity cannot be understood without reference to culturally shaped horizons or collective fields of significance that are constituted by distinctions of worth. While a person is embedded in these fields with others, they are the context within which she takes a personal orientation through her strong evaluations about what is good, or valuable, or what should be done, or what she should oppose or endorse. The virtues, profile modes of ethical response, and identity-conferring projects of an authentic life cannot be reduced to the inner life of any one person. They emerge instead from the interpersonal collaboration of communication and meaning-making. An authentic way of living is thus embedded in "historical-cultural" fields of significance in which the making of choices becomes meaningful. These fields or horizons of significance provide the vital sources of our agency.[139]

Varga and Taylor stress the same point: it is through being embedded in these fields that we are in dialogue about what really matters to us and what we really want to live for. As a way of living, authenticity is about situating ourselves in these fields of significance and worth through wholehearted commitments that articulate some of their aspects. Living an authentic life cannot be separated from our responsiveness to interactions with others through which our background contexts of significance are explored. An authentic life involves a lucid responsiveness to the normative force of locally constituted values and public conceptions of good. Hence the occasional feeling that living by our commitments and strong evaluations is overwhelmingly necessary and that we are responding to the claim that some distinctions of worth make on us—to the call of values that are larger than our own projects. The wholehearted commitments and identifications of authentic living are not inherently hostile to public values. This invites serious reconsideration of the standard notion that there is a hostile relation between authenticity and morality.[140] The patient must find his own way to an authentic mode of living. The therapist can challenge and encourage those efforts, but it is the patient who works out her own authenticity with diligence.

## 6.7 Conclusion

Healing projects take work, and one recovers in no small measure by dint of one's efforts. The project is aimed at recovering personal unity through self-respect and self-love. Patients have both other- and self-regarding responsibilities for doing this work. The healing project begins as the patient develops an alliance with the therapist. It becomes less dependent as the patient develops a stronger alliance with herself and works at recovery on her own. This independent work becomes the patient's project of self-regarding care. It reflects efforts to manage treatment and restore self-unity that the patient is responsible for making on her own behalf. The patient's responsible efforts can involve the cultivation of virtues that are contextual to the healing project. The patient cultivates specific virtues by which the project is conducted with the goal of recovery. These healing virtues can meet both other- and self-regarding responsibilities, e.g., the patient has to be perseverant in her efforts to work with the psychiatrist as well as in her efforts to work on her own. Once a threshold level of self-unity is restored, the patient continues to cultivate recovery virtues by which it is sustained. These are the virtues of self-respect and self-love that are focused largely on meeting the responsibility the patient has to herself.

I have discussed a plurality of patient-centered virtues in chapters three and five in addition to the catalogue of patient virtues noted above. Healing virtues enable the working through, and recovery virtues evince a new sense of control, meaning, and purpose by which a patient can surpass a life that is vitiated by the problems that led him to seek therapy. Healing virtues like creative flexibility, open-mindedness, and intellectual sobriety can be construed as epistemic if their psychotherapeutic targets are reliable, justified beliefs and modes of inquiry with a strong warrant for truth. Swanton's virtues of focus, dialogue, and constraint integration can arguably subsume these virtues. Healing virtues such as perseverance, hopefulness, healing curiosity, and respect for the healing project can be construed as generically ethical if their targets are better ways of treating oneself and others. Courage and trustfulness are other healing virtues I have not discussed in detail that might also be articulated in generic ethical terms. As psychotherapy can demand an unsparing confrontation with painful experience, it thus takes courage, confidence, and resolution to meet this demand to be honest. The realistically hopeful and perseverant patient needs to trust the resolve of her therapist to assist in her recovery. But she must also trust in her own resolve to care for herself and surmount the vicissitudes most healing projects present. This implies trusting her self-efficacy, i.e., her belief in her ability to succeed in challenging situations by coordinating skills to attain desired therapeutic goals.[141] This can require creative flexibility in responding to altered circumstances and setbacks.

I have posited recovery virtues as therapeutic goals. They emerge from the patient's efforts to attain the targets that those virtues aim at. The patient's primary focus is attaining the targets, since the virtues won't emerge unless those targets are consistently hit in a good enough way. Self-respect and self-love can be seen as virtues to be cultivated in their own right if the patient is striving to overcome deficiencies in self-regard. The patient's efforts to work through her problems are aimed at the states of well-being those virtues target. I want now to examine four modes of psychotherapy in terms of the triadic analysis, two of which aim in part to facilitate a patient's quest for authenticity.

## Notes

1. For a modified version of this chapter, in which I expand patient responsibilities beyond psychotherapy, see Duff R. Waring, "Patient Responsibilities in a Psychiatric Healing Project," in *The Oxford Handbook of Psychiatric Ethics*, eds. John Z. Sadler, Werdie (C.W.) Van Staden, and W.K.M. Fulford (Oxford: Oxford University Press, 2015), 1402–1418.
2. **W.W. Meissner**, *The Therapeutic Alliance* (New Haven: Yale University Press, 1996), 83.
3. *Dorland's Illustrated Medical Dictionary* (2004), s.v. "therapeutic alliance." I do not examine the ethical issues around treatment refusal. I focus exclusively on consenting patients who choose to adhere to a treatment regimen. I use the term adherence instead of compliance "to incorporate the broader notions of concordance, cooperation [negotiation] and partnership" (E.Vermeire, H. Hearnshaw, P. Van Royen, and J. Denekens, "Patient Adherence to Treatment: Three Decades of Research. A Comprehensive Review," *Journal of Clinical Pharmacy and Therapeutics* 26 (2001): 339).
4. **Meissner**, *The Therapeutic Alliance*, 6–7.
5. **A.D. Weissman**, *The Existential Core of Psychoanalysis: Reality, Sense and Responsibility* (Boston: Little Brown, 1965), 223.
6. **Meissner**, *The Therapeutic Alliance*, 208–209.
7. Cf. **Jennifer Radden** and **John Z. Sadler**, *The Virtuous Psychiatrist: Character Ethics in Psychiatric Practice* (Oxford: Oxford University Press, 2010), 137.
8. Cf. **Radden** and **Sadler**, *The Virtuous Psychiatrist*, 128.
9. **Radden** and **Sadler**, *The Virtuous Psychiatrist*, 137. Radden and Sadler propose the following six virtues: persistence, courage, honesty, hopefulness, flexibility, and trustfulness.
10. Cf. **Andrea C. Westlund**, "Selflessness and Responsibility for Self: Is Deference Compatible with Autonomy?" *Philosophical Review* 112 (2003): 495; cf. Barbro Froding, "On the Importance of Treating Oneself Well," *Polish Journal of Philosophy* 4 (2010): 13.
11. **Barbro Froding**, "Hope as a Virtue in an Aristotelian Context," *Philosophy, Psychiatry, & Psychology* 19 (2012): 184.
12. **Maureen M. Kelley**, "Limits on Patient Responsibility," *Journal of Medicine and Philosophy* 30 (2005): 190.
13. American Medical Association, "On Patient Responsibilities," *Code of Ethics*, Section E-10.02, 1993 (updated June 1998, December 2000, and June 2001).
14. **Leonard C. Groopman**, **Frank G. Miller**, and **Joseph J. Fins**, "The Patient's Work," *Cambridge Quarterly of Health Care Ethics* 16 (2006): 44.
15. **Groopman, Miller,** and **Fins**, "The Patient's Work," 45.
16. **J.S. Beck**, *Cognitive Therapy: Basics and Beyond*, 2nd ed. (New York: Guilford, 2011).
17. **Kelley**, "Limits on Patient Responsibility," 191.

18. **Duff R. Waring**, "The Virtuous Patient," *Philosophy, Psychiatry, & Psychology* 19 (2012): 25–36. Copyright © 2012 The Johns Hopkins University Press. This article was first published in *Philosophy, Psychiatry, & Psychology* 19.1 (2012), 25-35. Reprinted with permission by Johns Hopkins University Press.
19. **Kelley**, "Limits on Patient Responsibility," 197–200.
20. **Groopman, Miller,** and **Fins**, "The Patient's Work," 49–50.
21. **Thomas E. Hill Jr.**, *Autonomy and Self-Respect* (Cambridge: Cambridge University Press, 1991), 43.
22. Cf. **Ronald Dworkin**, *Sovereign Virtue: The Theory and Practice of Equality* (Cambridge, MA: Harvard University Press, 2000), 485 (note 1), 241, 242, 245, 253, 259, 270–271; Ronald Dworkin, *Justice for Hedgehogs* (Cambridge, MA: The Belknap Press of Harvard University Press, 2011), 13–14, 191–218
23. Cf. **Christine Swanton**, *Virtue Ethics: A Pluralistic View* (Oxford: Oxford University Press, 2005), 135–136.
24. Cf. **Hill Jr.**, *Autonomy and Self-Respect*, 23.
25. **Meissner**, *The Therapeutic Alliance*, 176.
26. **Hill Jr.**, *Autonomy and Self-Respect*, 152, 154.
27. **W.D. Falk**, "Morality, Self, and Others," in *Morality and the Language of Conduct*, eds. Hector-Neri Castaneda and George Nakhnikian (Detroit: Wayne State University Press, 1963), 31–32, 40, 48.
28. **Falk**, "Morality, Self, and Others," 53.
29. **Falk**, "Morality, Self, and Others," 50.
30. **Falk**, "Morality, Self, and Others," 49, 51.
31. **Falk**, "Morality, Self, and Others," 63–64.
32. **Falk**, "Morality, Self, and Others," 63–64.
33. **Falk**, "Morality, Self, and Others," 64.
34. **Harry G. Frankfurt**, *The Reasons of Love* (Princeton: Princeton University Press, 2004), 71.
35. **Groopman, Miller,** and **Fins**, "The Patient's Work," 47.
36. **Groopman, Miller,** and **Fins**, "The Patient's Work," 47.
37. **Swanton**, *Virtue Ethics*, 68–76.
38. **Dworkin**, *Justice for Hedgehogs*, 13–14.
39. **Dworkin**, *Justice for Hedgehogs*, 13.
40. **Dworkin**, *Justice for Hedgehogs*, 205.
41. If we have goodwill toward others, then arguably we also want them to assume responsibility for themselves for their own benefit, i.e., we do believe that persons should try to respect and love themselves. As Hill Jr. puts it in *Autonomy and Self-Respect*, 24: "It is as if we take a moral interest in a person's setting and living by their own values …We care for their having the satisfaction of a good opinion of themselves … Perhaps the moral interest is in each person living as an autonomous agent, where 'autonomy' implies both personal integration and forming values beyond comfort, least resistance etc."
42. **Falk**, "Morality, Self, and Others," 49.

43. **Frankfurt**, *The Reasons of Love*, 84.
44. **Frankfurt**, *The Reasons of Love*, 81–82.
45. Cf. **Falk**, "Morality, Self, and Others," 30.
46. **Dworkin**, *Justice for Hedgehogs*, 15.
47. **Froding**, "On the Importance of Treating Oneself Well," 19.
48. **Dworkin**, *Justice for Hedgehogs*, 204, 206, 208, 213.
49. Cf. **Andrea** C. Westlund, "Selflessness and Responsibility for Self: Is Deference Compatible with Autonomy?" 497.
50. **Meissner**, *The Therapeutic Alliance*, 6, 175, 176, 184.
51. **Meissner**, *The Therapeutic Alliance*, 185.
52. **Mike W. Martin**, *From Morality to Mental Health: Virtue and Vice in a Therapeutic Culture* (Oxford: Oxford University Press, 2006), 29.
53. While I endorse key ideas of the so-called "recovery movement," I do not subscribe to its apparent agnosticism on how to reconcile patient autonomy and accountability. Nor would I support a rhetorical presumption that has been attributed to it by Pouncey and Lukens, i.e., that "all persons with mental illness are fully self-determining agents." I do not intend my analysis of patient responsibility to subvert the recognition that "severe mental illness can limit agency." See Claire L. Pouncey and Jonathan M. Lukens, "Madness Versus Badness: The Ethical Tension Between the Recovery Movement and Forensic Psychiatry," *Theoretical Medicine and Bioethics* 31 (2010): 94, 101.
54. **Nora. N. Jacobson** and **Diane Greenly**, "What is Recovery? A Conceptual Model and Explication," *Psychiatric Services* 52 (2001): 482–485; Larry Davidson, *Living Outside Mental Illness: Qualitative Studies of Recovery in Schizophrenia* (New York: New York University Press, 2003).
55. **Larry Davidson** and **J.S. Strauss**, "Sense of Self in Recovery from Severe Mental Illness," *British Journal of Medical Psychology* 65 (1992): 131–145.
56. **Groopman, Miller,** and **Fins**, "The Patient's Work," 44–52.
57. **William A. Anthony**, "Recovery from Mental Illness: The Guiding Vision of the Mental Health Service System in the 1990s," *Psychosocial Rehabilitation Journal* 16 (1993): 11–23.
58. **Morris Eagle**, *From Classical to Contemporary Psychoanalysis*, 238–239.
59. Cf. **Todd B. Kashdan** and **Jonathan Rottenberg**, "Psychological Flexibility as a Fundamental Aspect of Health," *Clinical Psychology Review* 30 (2010): 865–878.
60. **Swanton**, *Virtue Ethics*, 42–43.
61. **P. Paul Heppner** and **Dong-gwi Lee**, "Problem-Solving Appraisal and Psychological Adjustment," in *The Oxford Handbook of Positive Psychology*, eds. Shane J. Lopez and C.R. Snyder. 2nd ed. (Oxford: Oxford University Press, 2009), 346, 350–351.
62. Cf. **Ann S. Masten**, **J.J. Cutuli**, **Janette E. Herbers**, and **Marie Gabrielle J. Reed**, "Resilience in Development," in *The Oxford Handbook of Positive Psychology*, eds. Shane J. Lopez and C.R. Snyder. 2nd ed. (Oxford: Oxford University Press, 2009), 118.
63. **Albert Camus**, *The Myth of Sisyphus and Other Essays*, trans. Justin O'Brien (New York: Vintage Books, 1955).

64. Cf. **Kevin L. Rand** and **Jennifer S. Cheavens**, "Hope Theory," in *The Oxford Handbook of Positive Psychology*, eds. Shane J. Lopez and C.R. Snyder. 2nd ed. (Oxford: Oxford University Press, 2009), 324. Their analysis is based on Snyder's cognitive model of hope that is comprised of goals, pathways, and agency. See C.R. Snyder, *The Psychology of Hope: You Can Get There from Here* (New York: Free Press, 1994).
65. Cf. **Rand** and **Cheavens**, "Hope Theory," 324, 326.
66. I owe this point to Jennifer Radden.
67. **Davidson**, *Living Outside Mental Illness*, 46.
68. **Meissner**, *The Therapeutic Alliance*, 179.
69. **Martin**, *From Morality to Mental Health*, 188.
70. **Jerome D. Frank** and **Julia B. Frank**, *Persuasion and Healing: A Comparative Study of Psychotherapy*, 3rd ed. (Baltimore: Johns Hopkins University Press, 1993).
71. **Rand** and **Cheavens**, "Hope Theory," 329.
72. **Todd B. Kashdan** and **Paul J. Silvia**, "Curiosity and Interest: The Benefits of Thriving on Novelty and Challenge," in *The Oxford Handbook of Positive Psychology*, eds. Shane J. Lopez and C.R. Snyder. 2nd ed. (Oxford: Oxford University Press, 2009), 367–368, 370.
73. **Kashdan** and **Shiva**, "Curiosity and Interest," 370.
74. Cf. **Kashdan** and **Shiva**, "Curiosity and Interest," 371, 369.
75. **J. Halpern**, *From Detached Concern to Empathy: Humanizing Medical Practice* (New York: Oxford University Press, 2011), 114.
76. **Halpern**, *From Detached Concern to Empathy*, 112.
77. **Halpern**, *From Detached Concern to Empathy*, 113.
78. **Kashdan** and **Silvia**, "Curiosity and Interest," 371.
79. **Halpern**, *From Detached Concern to Empathy*, 113–114. For a discussion of healing curiosity and respect for the healing project as traits of the virtuous psychiatrist, see Radden and Sadler, *The Virtuous Psychiatrist*, 120, 136-139.
80. **Kashdan** and **Silvia**, "Curiosity and Interest," 371.
81. **Jahoda**, *Current Concepts of Positive Mental Health*, 30–35, 62–64.
82. **Radden** and **Sadler**, *The Virtuous Psychiatrist*, 138.
83. **Radden** and **Sadler**, *The Virtuous Psychiatrist*, 129.
84. **Swanton**, *Virtue Ethics*, 135–136, 11.
85. **Swanton**, *Virtue Ethics*, 135–136.
86. By contrast, Swanton defines self-love in Nietzschean terms as a bond that expresses one's "strength, vitality, and energy" in undistorted ways that should allow for both self-respect and respect for others (cf. *Virtue Ethics*, 134).
87. Cf. **Swanton**, *Virtue Ethics*, 135, 143–144, 185, 235.
88. **Aristotle**, *Nichomachean Ethics*, trans. Terrence Irwin (Cambridge: Hackett Publishing Company, 1985), 1166a5–1166b20, 1167b5.
89. **Julia Annas**, *The Morality of Happiness* (Oxford: Oxford University Press, 1993), 254
90. **Aristotle**, *Nichomachean Ethics*, 1168b20–1169a10.

91. **Annas**, *The Morality of Happiness*, 259, 261, 260.
92. **Frankfurt**, *The Reasons of Love*, 71, 78–80.
93. **John Lippitt**, *Kierkegaard and the Problem of Self-Love* (Cambridge: Cambridge University Press, 2013), 109.
94. **Frankfurt**, *The Reasons of Love*, 83.
95. **Lippitt**, *Kierkegaard and the Problem of Self-Love*, 96, 106.
96. **Frankfurt**, *The Reasons of Love*, 23.
97. **Lippitt**, *Kierkegaard and the Problem of Self-Love*, 107.
98. **Frankfurt**, *The Reasons of Love*, 86.
99. **Swanton**, *Virtue Ethics*, 100.
100. Cf. **Swanton**, *Virtue Ethics*, 145: "This is not to deny that in some contexts we can talk about the [specific] virtue of self-love, for example, in a context where an agent is striving to overcome a wide range of deficiencies in this area." Swanton does not elaborate on self-love as a contextual virtue. See also 143, note 42. She concentrates instead on self-respect and self-love as aspects of the profiles of all virtues, even those that are "not essentially self-regarding." On her account, some degree of love delimited by respect contour all virtuous responses to the demands of the world.
101. Cf. **Swanton**, *Virtue Ethics*, 100.
102. **Hagai Harari**, **Simone G. Shamay-Tsoory**, **Milli Ravid**, and **Yechiel Levkovitz**, "Double Dissociation Between Cognitive and Affective Empathy in Borderline Personality Disorder," *Psychiatry Research* 175 (2010): 277–279; Isabel Dziobek, Sandra Preissler, Zarko Grozdanovic, Isabella Heuser, Hauke R. Heekeren, and Stefan Roepke, "Neuronal Correlates of Altered Empathy and Social Cognition in Borderline Personality Disorder," *Neuroimage* 57 (2011): 539–548.
103. **Aaron Simmons**, "In Defense of the Moral Significance of Empathy," *Ethical Theory and Moral Practice* 17 (2014): 101–103. Simmons concedes at 106, note 3, that his argument will not convince a committed Kantian who believes that morality consists solely in doing one's duty out of respect for the moral law.
104. **Simmons**, "In Defense of the Moral Significance of Empathy," 104.
105. **Simmons**, "In Defense of the Moral Significance of Empathy," 105.
106. **Halpern**, *From Detached Concern to Empathy*, 129, 130.
107. **Halpern**, *From Detached Concern to Empathy*, 130–131.
108. Cf. **Jahoda**, *Current Concepts of Positive Mental Health*, 27–29.
109. Cf. **Jahoda**, *Current Concepts of Positive Mental Health*, 30–35.
110. Cf. **Jahoda**, *Current Concepts of Positive Mental Health*, 39–41.
111. **Michael F. Steger**, "Meaning in Life," in *The Oxford Handbook of Positive Psychology*, eds. Shane J. Lopez and C.R. Snyder. 2nd ed. (Oxford: Oxford University Press, 2009), 682.
112. Cf. **Steger**, "Meaning in Life," 682. For a full account, see R.F. Baumeister, *Meaning of Life* (New York: Guilford, 1991). For one account of a difference between self-efficacy and agency, see Rand and Cheavens, "Hope Theory," 324. They argue that self-efficacy is not a trait but a situation-specific assessment that one can effect a particular course

of action for a specific goal. By contrast, agency is a global, trait-like perception that one will carry out goal-directed actions for a wide range of goals. Agency thus reflects the intention to act as opposed to "simply perceiving the ability to do so."

113. Cf. **Steger**, "Meaning in Life," 680, 684.
114. **Richard G. Tedeschi** and **Lawrence G. Calhoun**, "Posttraumatic Growth: Conceptual Foundations and Empirical Evidence," *Psychological Inquiry* 15 (2004): 1–18.
115. Cf. **Christopher G. Davis** and **Susan Nolen-Hoeksema**, "Making Sense of Loss, Perceiving Benefits, and Posttraumatic Growth," in *The Oxford Handbook of Positive Psychology*, eds. Shane J. Lopez and C.R. Snyder. 2nd ed. (Oxford: Oxford University Press, 2009), 642, 647.
116. **Davis** and **Nolen-Hoeksema**, "Making Sense of Loss," 642.
117. Cf. **Dana S. Dunn, Gitendra Uswatte,** and **Timothy R. Elliott**, "Happiness, Resilience, and Positive Growth Following Physical Disability: Issues for Research, Understanding, and Therapeutic Intervention," in *The Oxford Handbook of Positive Psychology*, eds. Shane J. Lopez and C.R. Snyder. 2nd ed. (Oxford: Oxford University Press, 2009), 655–656, 658–659.
118. **Richard F. Summers** and **Jacques P. Barber**, *Psychodynamic Therapy: A Guide to Evidence-Based Practice* (New York: The Guilford Press, 2010), 214.
119. **Christine Swanton**, "The Notion of the Moral: The Relation Between Virtue Ethics and Virtue Epistemology," *Philosophical Studies* 171(1) (2014): 121–134.
120. **David Healy**, *The Suspended Revolution: Psychiatry and Psychotherapy Re-Examined* (London: Faber and Faber, 1990), 32.
121. **Radden** and **Sadler**, *The Virtuous Psychiatrist*, 106.
122. **Taylor**, *The Malaise of Modernity*, 29, 61, 63.
123. **Dworkin**, *Sovereign Virtue*, 270.
124. **Dworkin**, *Justice for Hedgehogs*, 261.
125. **Dworkin**, *Justice for Hedgehogs*, 204, 209.
126. **Charles Taylor**, *Sources of the Self: The Making of Modern Identity* (Cambridge, MA: Harvard University Press, 1989), 59.
127. **Charles Taylor**, "What is Human Agency?" in *Human Agency and Language: Philosophical Papers 1* (Cambridge: Cambridge University Press, 1985), 38–39, 35.
128. **Charles Taylor**, "The Moral Topography of the Self," in *Hermeneutics and Psychological Theory: Interpretive Perspectives on Personality, Psychotherapy, and Pathology*, eds. Stanley B. Messer, Louis A. Sass, and Robert L. Woolfolk (New Brunswick: Rutgers University Press, 1988), 298, 300.
129. **Ronald Dworkin**, *Life's Dominion: An Argument about Abortion, Euthanasia, and Individual Freedom* (New York: Vintage Books, 1993), 201–202, 205–206.
130. **Dworkin**, *Life's Dominion*, 215–216.
131. **Dworkin**, *Life's Dominion*, 78.
132. **Dworkin**, *Sovereign Virtue*, 270–271; Charles Taylor, "What is Human Agency?" 40; Charles Taylor, "The Moral Topography of the Self," 300.

133. **John Chambers Christopher**, "Hermeneutics and the Moral Dimension of Psychotherapy," in *Culture, Psychotherapy, and Counselling: Critical and Integrative Perspectives*, ed. Lisa Tsoi Hoshmand (Thousand Oaks, CA: Sage Publications, 2006), 187.
134. **Alan C. Tjeltveit**, *Ethics and Values in Psychotherapy* (London: Routledge, 1999), 195.
135. **Jahoda**, *Current Concepts of Positive Mental Health*, 40–41, 34-35.
136. **Jahoda**, *Current Concepts of Positive Mental Health*, 34-35.
137. **Somogy Varga**, *Authenticity as an Ethical Ideal* (New York: Routledge, 2012), 4–5, 7, 85.
138. **Varga**, *Authenticity as an Ethical Ideal*, 86.
139. **Varga**, *Authenticity as an Ethical Ideal*, 92, 93, 96, 97, 105. See also Taylor, *Sources of the Self*, 27.
140. **Varga**, *Authenticity as an Ethical Ideal*, 95, 98, 99, 110, 165 (note 5). See also **Charles Taylor**, "The Politics of Recognition," in *Multiculturalism: Examining the Politics of Recognition*, ed. Amy Guttman (Princeton: Princeton University Press, 1994), 25–73.
141. Cf. **James E. Maddux**, "Self-Efficacy: The Power of Believing You Can," in *The Oxford Handbook of Positive Psychology*, eds. Shane J. Lopez and C.R. Snyder. 2nd ed. (Oxford: Oxford University Press, 2009), 336.

# Chapter 7

# Four Psychotherapies and the Triadic Analysis

## 7.1 Introduction

I have argued that some psychotherapies can be understood as generically ethical treatments in cases that fit the triadic analysis, e.g., the case of Seneca's Angry Man, in which a combination of psychodynamic and cognitive behavioral therapies were used for both self-regarding ethical and other-regarding moral ends. Psychotherapies for a variety of disorders can be at least partially articulated in generically ethical terms. I will focus on four such therapies: existential, Kohutian self-psychological, cognitive behavioral, and mentalization-based.

Self-psychological and existential psychotherapies arguably evince a generic ethical/therapeutic overlap in their concerns with facilitating a patient's quest for authenticity. My next step is to show how cognitive behavioral therapy can be used to foster self-regarding ethical and other-regarding moral improvements in (1) tendencies of affective/emotional response; (2) a better understanding of how one should treat oneself and/or others; and (3) better patterns of behavior. To fit the triadic analysis, this would involve the affective, cognitive, and practical facets of ethical self-improvement through the cultivation of healing virtues. I construe mentalization-based therapy as a quintessential generic ethical treatment that aims to foster more than (1) through (3). It also aims to foster a psychological capacity that is a crucial facet of any generic ethical perspective.

## 7.2 Authenticity and Existential Psychotherapy

Existential psychotherapy (hereinafter EP) has grown steadily in Europe since the mid-1980s. I focus primarily on the British School as typified by van Deurzen because it has established itself as a leading institute for the training and accreditation of existential psychotherapists. I think the British School's approach to therapy is moving clearly toward some prescriptive value judgments that can be articulated in pluralistic, virtue ethical terms. Van Deurzen is the School's best-known exponent and offers an extensive account of its theory and praxis. I argue two points. First, van Deurzen's account can be understood as an exercise in delineating one's ethical/moral topography. EP often presents an easier fit with "a more philosophical exploration of how to live life in a constructive and meaningful way."[1] Second, it addresses an ethically value-laden problem, i.e., a loss of or confusion about the deep evaluations from which critical interests and an authentic way of living emerge. As we saw with the case of the Demoralized Woman, this problem can be articulated in self-regarding ethical terms.

Van Deurzen does not shy away from defining EP as having a secure foundation in ethics and philosophy.[2] Van Deurzen presents it as a non-medical, philosophical exploration that exhorts people to live well in accordance with their abilities, talents, standards, and ideals. While her approach to therapy is centered on exploring and refining a person's particular worldview and sense of self-regard, it is contextualized by a perspective "on life itself" that is broadly existential.[3] This perspective can be summarized as follows: life is absurd, i.e., it lacks an intrinsically coherent cosmological meaning that defines our purpose in a supportive universe. It is also seemingly chaotic and fraught with contradictions and hazards of living. Life is thus perpetually challenging our ability to deal with its inevitable suffering, disappointment, and adversity.[4] As she defines it, the existential position endorses the belief that persons have the capacity "to create meaning and order, in spite of seeming chaos and absurdity."[5] Life can be said to be "basically meaningful" because people "can create the meaning of their world by their own attitude to life."[6]

Van Deurzen insists on clarifying the four assumptions of EP with which prospective "clients" should agree. Absent this accord, the client will be unable to "engage fully with the therapeutic process."[7] (1) The human situation can make sense when people believe that they can create meaning by their own attitude to life. It is important for clients to believe in their ability to do this before commencing therapy. (2) However much people might be determined by circumstances, they still command a significant ability to determine how they ought to respond. (3) There are always unalterable, situational givens to human existence that limit our freedom of action. These limits can be physical, biological, social, or personal. (4) Clients are capable of enough reflection to gain insight into their way of living and to creatively manage their problems.[8]

Suitable candidates for EP would presumably have some degree of reflective ability and a motivation to improve their lot. At the very least, they have to be willing to work with the therapist to combat "a lack of will to live" with an effort "to find meaning in absurdity or suffering."[9] This approach assumes the central importance of the client's attitudinal and decision-making capacities.[10] Van Deurzen insists that only persons who commit to coming to terms with their lives will benefit from EP. They must also be willing and able to be fully and honestly engaged with the working through "of their own accord."[11] Confronting their sense of futility is the necessary first step in a quest for meaning. One might be dealing instead with an ethical crisis that is uniquely one's own and yet sufficiently troubling as to compromise psychological health.[12] The Demoralized Woman is one such example which I will revisit below.

How might EP fit the triadic analysis? What, if anything, does this approach involve in the way of cultivating virtues? Perhaps nothing at all. A person in therapy might resolve his uncertainty about the meaning of his life without becoming a more virtuous person. He might simply use the virtues he has to work through his quandary. But there might also be cases where a person strengthens virtues he already has or develops virtues he has lacked. Either way, the exemplary problem for EP is presented by the client who has lost touch with the meaning of his life. This problem epitomizes the paradigmatic existential complaint. In his dialogues with Medard Boss, Heidegger claimed that human beings are essentially in need of help because they are always in danger of losing themselves. To which Boss replied that many persons who lack the symptoms of any localized, psychical disorders seek psychotherapy because they no longer see meaning in their lives.[13] Taylor relates this to the breakdown of deep evaluations and ruptures in moral space. Hence the feelings of being "spiritually out of joint, of feeling lost, empty, and without meaning."[14]

We need a case where this exemplary problem fits the first part of the triad, i.e., a problem that can be articulated in virtue ethical terms. We would need a persistent state of normative enervation that deracinates one's sense of generic ethical space and the critical interests by which one defines oneself. Major depression can certainly do this, combining cognitive dysfunction, disordered moods, and the evisceration of positive self-regard. It is thus an officially recognized diagnostic category in which this exemplary problem is manifest. Even so, a person who is caught in its grip would have to sufficiently loosen its stranglehold on volition and will to meaning before engaging in existential psychotherapy. Van Deurzen offers numerous accounts of depressed persons who have participated successfully in EP but these seem to be persons who have either avoided or roused themselves from major depression's debilitating torpor and thus have sufficient capacity to engage with the praxis. A better fit with the first part of the triad would be a crisis profound enough to deplete one's meaningful sense of self, but without the anhedonia and disabled motivation of major depression. The case of the Demoralized Woman captures this crisis. This case gives us a problem in the form of an existential complaint that can be elucidated in generic ethical terms. Depending on its degree of disturbance, it can also be deleterious to the complainant's psychological health. I will explore how that case might fit the triadic analysis.

The second part of the triad consists of therapeutic goals that can be elucidated in virtue ethical terms and involve any or all of the following: (1) ethically desirable changes in tendencies of affective/emotional response; (2) a better understanding of how one should treat oneself or others; and (3) improved behavior. I think EP can accommodate these goals. If the client's problem is a debilitating loss of, or confusion about, deep evaluations and identity-conferring projects, then the desired outcome can include a set of character traits by which an ethically better way of self- and other-regarding life is cultivated and sustained. The therapeutic goal could be the sufficient attainment of a life well lived by the recovery virtues.

The aim of an existential working through is to assist persons in developing their unique talents for living in a way that is true to what they value; "to live life well by their own standards."[15] In helping persons to do this, EP aims at authenticity as an "ultimate goal."[16] Authentic living is about making clear, resolute, and well-informed choices in accordance with the values one recognizes as worth committing oneself to. One is called by and follows the direction that one's conscience indicates is the right one.[17] Authenticity is essentially being true to oneself by applying one's talents to the "art of living" in the ongoing "practice of shaping one's life after one's ideals."[18] Van Deurzen casts this idea in terms that are reminiscent of Taylor's notion that the grasp of some deep evaluations is akin to responding to the call of a motivating source that transcends us. EP aims to enable persons to "rediscover their inner connectedness" to encompassing ideals and values. These values can motivate persons to work through life's difficulties "with unerring purposefulness."[19] As Dworkin would put it, these discovered values can motivate persons to meet the challenges of living well with ethical integrity.

Van Deurzen circumscribes authenticity with moral limits. It is not a sufficient virtue unto itself if pursued in isolation and requires one to "find new criteria for deciding right and wrong."[20] It also requires trust in one's ability to make responsible "moral judgments" and discover "moral principles."[21] She sees ethical laws and principles as constituting a "limitation and boundary to human freedom."[22] These therapeutic goals can be articulated in virtue ethical terms. Authenticity is a mode of living well that requires a healthy bonding with oneself. I think we can refer to self-love as a specific recovery virtue "where an agent is striving to overcome a wide range of deficiencies" in this area.[23]

As for the third part of the triadic analysis, van Deurzen's account of psychotherapeutic praxis bears close scrutiny. The question here is whether her account accommodates efforts made by the patient to resolve the problems that involve the affective, cognitive, and practical facets of ethical self-improvement through the cultivation of certain virtues. I argue two claims to support the conclusion that it does. First, if the client's problem is a loss of, or confusion about, deep evaluations and critical interests, then the affective and cognitive aspects of ethical self-improvement are implicit in van Deurzen's account of the client's efforts in the working through of EP. Second, these efforts can involve the healing cultivation of honesty, perseverance, hopefulness, and virtues of practice. The recovery virtue of self-love will be no less apparent.

The praxis of EP involves a dialogical examination of how the clients live their lives, and a reflection on the meaning they give to their experience and on what they value and disvalue.[24] Although van Deurzen has not presented specific techniques or strategies by which this praxis is conducted, the broad outlines of her approach can be summarized as follows.[25] The therapist's praxis consists in challenging clients to deal with their problems by taking stock of their lives. Clients are directed toward an exploration and evaluation of four dimensions of their personal worldview. These are (1) the physical dimension, or the client's embodied relationship to the natural world; (2) the social dimension, or the client's relationships with others in the social domain; (3) the personal dimension, or the client's reflective sense of self-regard; and (4) the spiritual dimension, or the client's relationship with the beliefs, values, ideals, and principles that they live by. As therapy advances, this spiritual dimension can evolve into an exploration of the beliefs and values that clients aspire to live by.[26] The psychotherapist prods them to clarify their assumptions about the world on all four levels. The next step is to urge clients to recognize and, if need be, to determine their values. This is a necessary step in establishing the "ultimate and vital concerns" that make life meaningful and worthwhile for them. These concerns are expressed in the identity-conferring projects that clients aim to pursue. The third step is to establish the abilities and talents that clients can draw upon to realize their projects and achieve their objectives.[27] These initial steps reflect the starting point of virtue ethical reflection: a concern for one's life as a whole and how it is going.[28]

The existential psychotherapist comes across as more of a school-of-hard-knocks life coach than a physician or psychologist with expertise in a given therapeutic technique. There is a prescriptive didacticism to this approach that tends to "promote an existential outlook on life over and above such alternative standpoints as hedonism or new age optimism."[29] The attitude to be instilled in the client is one of hardy resilience coupled with a rough and ready self-empowerment. In their efforts to help clients face up to the challenge of living, existential psychotherapists have to rouse them from the guilt and despair of their passive withdrawal from life's inevitable risks and anxieties. "Tough logic can do far more for people in this position than understanding and holding of hands."[30] Prescriptively, van Deurzen's approach promotes the normative value judgment that it is better for clients to face up to life and meet its challenges directly than to "weakly" and "complacently" evade them. She thus values certain ways of being above others.[31] This has not been lost on her clients, one of whom felt "as if I was being measured against a theoretical perspective or belief, which did not take into account my very humanity, real, existential anxiety, about change and all that currently implies for me. I felt an ideology was being conveyed to me."[32]

The client's praxis consists initially of a willingness to openly discuss her problem in living. This involves the standard commitment to the process of working through with perseverance and honesty of disclosure. The client will have to face the problem by engaging in a repeated and varied examination of its facets and impact. She will also have to assess and elaborate on its meaning and magnitude, consider her options for dealing with it, and relate these to her abilities and limitations. First, the client must clarify her worldview in terms of the four dimensions of existence. This involves focusing on the client's life-world instead of isolating the problem from the situation in which it arises. Problems in living are not reduced to regressive meanings centered on "primitive" emotions and motivational forces. Rather, they are addressed as "wider moral and universal issues of meaning" that pervade our daily lives.[33] Clients must have a "fundamental commitment" to coming to terms with their way of being-in-the-world. Persons who want nothing more than symptom relief or the resolution of a specific problem "without this further touching on the rest of their existence … will not be well served by an existential approach."[34] Van Deurzen's idea is that once clients recognize the values that they really want to live by and let go of ones they find unsatisfactory, they can gain a new insight into the purpose of their life.[35] Second, clients must take stock of their values in all four dimensions in an effort to determine what ultimately matters to them. The idea here is that it is better to pursue a life lived in congruence with one's ultimate concerns and values.[36]

Note that a meaningful life is achieved in the personal dimension through evaluating one's self-regard. This can be explicated in virtue ethical terms as cultivating the self-love through which one forms a caring bond with identity-conferring values, critical interests, and projects. One is no longer detached from a coalescent sense of identity. Meaning is found on the spiritual level by discovering a sense of purpose.[37] Like Taylor, van Deurzen observes that it is the wider frameworks of meaning that clients often struggle with.[38] Indeed, challenging people to formulate a consistent frame of reference by which they can make sense of their inner experience in a chaotic world might be one of the main resources and curative factors of psychotherapy.[39] A working through that is based on this commitment would involve the application of some of the healing virtues we have already discussed: honesty, perseverance, hopefulness, and focus. If the problem in living involves problematic other- or self-regarding behavior, then the affective and cognitive aspects of moral self-improvement can also come into play.

## 7.3 The Demoralized Woman Redux

Let us reconsider the case of the Demoralized Woman, and the application of EP, in terms of the triadic analysis. Even assuming that there was an antecedent biochemical imbalance that caused her depression, she now presents a case of spiritual exsanguination; a pervasive, nonspecific malaise and a felt lack of meaning and purpose. Demoralization is usually portrayed as a "clearly defined syndrome of existential distress occurring in patients suffering from mental and physical illness, specifically ones that threaten life or integrity of being."[40] It was defined originally by Frank as a persistent inability to cope that is conjoined with feelings of helplessness, hopelessness, subjective incompetence, and loss of meaning and purpose in life.[41] While usually comorbid, it can occur alone without other disorders. It is not synonymous with anhedonia and is thus distinguished from depression, e.g., demoralized persons are unable to look forward to their future with pleasant anticipation, but they are able to experience pleasure generally and enjoy present moments.[42] Depressed persons lack motivation even when they know what an appropriate course of action might be. Demoralized persons are inhibited from action because of their uncertainty over what the appropriate course of action might be.[43] Depression can produce demoralization. Even after the anhedonic mood has remitted, the patient's ability to plan competent activity can be severely diminished because of the enduring change in self-image. This mode of attitudinal despair does not respond to antidepressants "because it is not the concurrent manifestation of a pathological mood; rather it is the secondary but now functionally autonomous cognitive residue of a past affective state."[44]

Demoralized persons feel they have lost, or are losing, "something critical to their sense of self."[45] In broader terms, their system of assumptions about the meaning and purpose of their lives in relation to others and their life-world has broken down. Where persons naturally seek competence, achievement, and meaning, demoralization challenges these aspirations and replaces them with feelings of helplessness and futility.[46] On my account, the Demoralized Woman has lost the sense of identity around which critical interests, deep evaluations, and an evolving system of meaningful connections between self, others, and life-world can cohere. Hence her subjective incompetence to engage in life with defining purpose. Her assumptions relevant to self-love and self-respect have been disconfirmed by the gradual exsanguination of her identity over the years of her depression.[47] Demoralization is essentially an ethical judgment, a "self-evaluation" that one is defeated by the hopelessness, loss of identity, and ultimately the despair that arises "from a loss of meaning and purpose."[48] The Demoralized Woman lacks a cohesive self to lovingly bond with and thus experiences subjective incompetence in responding to the challenge of living well.

We can thus articulate the Demoralized Woman's problem in self-regarding ethical terms. EP could assist her in delineating a generic ethical topography and situating herself in her own normative space, i.e., one defined by her own deep evaluations and critical interests. This is, I suggest, what we mean when we speak of a person's "quest for authenticity." How the person defines her self-worth and critical interests is up to her, but that she is worthy and capable of critical interests can be a commitment to the virtues of self-love and self-respect that psychotherapy may nurture. In these respects, the problem is one that can be articulated in self-regarding ethical terms.

Second, what would be the goals of a psychotherapy that aimed to ameliorate demoralization? The treatment aims for a state of positive mental health and an authentic mode of living that transcends symptom relief. In sum, the healthy bonding with herself that she currently lacks—a mode of being that is her best response to the challenge of living well and uniquely expressive of her identity-conferring values and projects. The desirable outcome state is one that can be prescriptively endorsed as better than the presenting problem state and can be articulated in virtue ethical terms as the acquisition of a better bond with herself through self-love, self-respect, and the ethical integrity of living by her critical interests.

Third, what would the psychotherapeutic praxis require of the Demoralized Woman? Van Deurzen's account could be clearer on this, but at least one existential psychotherapist who has been affiliated with the UK New School has related the efforts involved to a neo-Aristotelian framework of virtuous practical reasoning. According to Macaro, the patient's work is a demanding, perseverant exercise in translating discerning, creative reflection into repeated attempts at expressing self-defining values in habitual behavior. The Demoralized Woman will thus have to make her reflections specific and practical. This involves an applied, situated understanding of what is possible for herself given her interests, abilities, and the limitations she aims to surpass. She must then exercise her best open-minded judgment about formulating goals and taking the right steps to achieve them. The latter involves deciding which attitudes and habits to develop and which to suppress. There are three key steps to taking stock of her situation. She must (1) identify the areas in which she shows deficiency as well as the aspects of her character that she should develop in terms of her reflections on a satisfying life; (2) she must strive to ensure in an excellent or good enough way that she is taking the relevant considerations into account when deciding how to act in those areas; and (3) she must train herself to act on the right reasons so that her goal-oriented behavior becomes a natural expression of who she is and wants to be.[49] The virtue of creative flexibility would be crucial here. This working through would involve at least a threshold degree of character change. We can thus articulate the praxis of existential psychotherapy in the cognitive, affective, and behavioral terms of ethical self-improvement.

An existential therapeutic praxis for demoralization has been developed by James Griffith. Although he is not affiliated with van Deurzen's School, his approach is worth considering in its own right. The affinities with the turn to positive psychology have not gone unnoticed, especially in terms of its influence on psychotherapy.[50] Note also that construing patients' response to demoralization as in part a matter of strengthening character does not entail the idea that they either can or should initiate recovery without help. Subjecting them to this expectation "can be both useless and cruel."[51] Nor is the therapist's role limited to merely exhorting the patients' efforts.

Griffith's praxis amounts to a "program of action undertaken … to shape one's being as a person and how one chooses to live in relation to others."[52] It involves two modes of thinking: agency thinking covers beliefs and perceptions about one's capacities for effective action, while pathways thinking involves planning strategies for reaching one's goals. Both instill hope "as the sum of perceived capabilities ("I can do it") and … planning ("I know a way to do it") to reach a goal."[53] The first step is to foster agency thinking about hope for a desired future self "by relying on relational rather than individual qualities."[54] This involves the therapist as well as others to whom the patient might turn for support and assistance. The therapist's compassionate witnessing provides a "full hearing" of the patient's despair. Understanding and listening can often sufficiently quiet that despair and enable the beginning of "a different conversation about the future."[55] This conversation can "open a space" in which the patient can move beyond speaking about sources of despair to address potential sources of resilience, i.e., perceived strengths, competencies, and problem-solving skills that could enable steps toward a desired future. These sources are usually omitted in narratives that focus exclusively on suffering and they often reveal personal practices that the patient has used in the past to manage adversity. At the very least, they are personal practices the patient can envision using in the future. The goal of hopeful practices is a patient's resilient stance toward demoralization and sustaining a desired identity with relatedness to others. Hitting this target in an excellent or good enough way involves cultivating virtues of perseverance and hopefulness, and trust in oneself. The psychotherapist can help the demoralized patient to clarify critical interests and commitments that she might want to pursue in a desired future and support gradual but "deliberate steps" toward those ends.[56] Much will depend on whether the compassionate witnessing of the therapist will inspire the patient's dormant capacities for agency and pathways thinking.

EP will not instill authenticity but it can aim to ameliorate some psychological impediments to achieving it. The fulfillment of one's chosen identity by living reliably according to one's deep evaluations and critical interests is an ideal of positive mental health. Presented with the existential complaint of demoralization, there can be cases in which a psychotherapist can challenge, encourage, and support the patient in this project. Van Deurzen's brand of EP is quite amenable to an integrative analysis that sees ethics/morality and mental health to be conceptually and causally interwoven. One might read van Deurzen as endorsing a kind of meta-virtuous courage to live authentically through discovering and creating meaning in a harshly indifferent world.

## 7.4 Authenticity and Kohut's Self-Psychology

If there is a nexus between authenticity and positive mental health, then psychotherapy can have legitimate concerns with a patient's striving to articulate strong evaluations and live by identity-conferring values and commitments. Lacking such values and commitments can indicate a deficient bond with oneself and others and a pervasive sense of demoralization. This can indicate in turn deficiencies in self-love, self-respect, and other virtues from which an authentic way of living can emerge. Some psychodynamic practitioners have presented a lack of authenticity as an apposite problem for therapeutic redress. They often employ different notions of authenticity that are sketched out in greater or lesser detail. Issues of theory adherence to relevant philosophical accounts of authenticity, as well as questions about its generic ethical dimensions, are not always addressed as well as they could be, if at all. Still, they implicate a trend in the literature which sees authenticity as a therapeutic concern.[57] I argue that a challenge notion of authenticity is adumbrated in Kohut's self-psychologic therapy (hereinafter SPT).

By his own account, Kohut's SPT represented a new approach to psychoanalytic theory and praxis. I will avoid a lengthy exposition of his views on the pathogenesis of narcissistic personality disorder, childhood development, and transference. I will focus instead on those aspects of his theory that are relevant to authenticity and the triadic analysis. Kohut argued that pathological narcissism results from parental lack of empathy during a child's development. By not providing the child with appropriate empathic feedback, or mirroring, the child does not develop the ability to regulate self-esteem, and thus becomes an adult who vacillates between irrational overestimations of himself and feelings of inferiority. Furthermore, the adult cannot manage his fragile self-esteem and looks to others to provide the empathic feedback he did not receive as a child. He thus relies on others to make him feel valued. The therapist's empathy generates a therapeutic alliance within which the patient slowly acquires the ability to fill in developmental deficits by processing the positive experiences that occur during the sessions, e.g., feeling valued. The patient comes to examine his own perceptions of how he responds to himself and others and is gradually able to accept and work from the therapist's interpretations of his disorder without feeling rejected or condemned.[58] In fine, Kohutian analysts were to appreciate their patients' strivings and gratify their narcissistic needs during therapy with imaginative, empathic attentiveness. They should not attempt to compensate for any traumatic failures they may have experienced in childhood with extra measures of love and kindness. Rather, they should empathically immerse themselves in the scientifically observable manifestations of their patients' inner lives and use their psychological knowledge to "tactfully interpret and offer support for patients' strivings."[59]

Kohut's SPT might support a patient's quest for authenticity if only because his rendition of narcissistic personality disorder implies treating the demoralization that would paralyze it. We can still imagine cases that fit the triadic analysis but do not involve a quest for authenticity. Remember that after acquiring psychodynamic insights into the genesis and development of his problems, Seneca's Angry Man still needed a course of cognitive behavioral therapy to enable him to control his angry outbursts. This might be a recurring behavioral and emotional flaw in an otherwise authentic life. I argue below that mentalization-based therapy fits the triadic analysis and aims to instill a self- and other-regarding ability from which a generic ethical perspective can emerge. A patient who has learned to mentalize might become concerned about authenticity, but mentalization-based therapy does not involve efforts to support a patient's quest for it. Further, Kohut's stress on ambitions, achievements, and success may not rule out the social indoctrination of acceptable norms and ambitions. This could result in an uncritical acceptance of socially valued norms that would avoid the independent evaluation of critical interests and identity-conferring commitments that are especially right for me. All of which is to say that Kohut did not explicitly formulate a therapeutic ideal of authenticity. He did, however, formulate a psychotherapeutic approach that can be made compatible with one. This requires a supplementary analysis that elaborates (1) the problem for which psychotherapy is sought; (2) the desirable outcome or goal of the psychotherapy; and (3) the psychotherapeutic praxis that aims to bring that outcome about.

Kohut defined narcissistic personality disorder as a developmental defect that obstructs the formation of a cohesive and vital self. The "more circumscribed and colorful" symptoms range from perverse sexual fantasies to lack of sexual interest, disturbed capacities for work, inabilities to form and sustain significant relationships, and illegal activities. The pathological narcissist is convinced of his precious uniqueness and is seriously lacking in senses of humor and proportion. He is oversensitive to real or imagined slights, is easily hurt and offended, and plagued by "boundless" fears and worries. He also lacks empathy for the needs and feelings of others, and has tendencies towards serial lying, extravagant vanity, shame, irritability, attacks of uncontrollable rage, and persistent hypochondria. He is excessively prone to rapid emotional vacillations between "unbridled ambitions" and feelings of failure that fuel an intense need for others to supply him with self-esteem and emotional support. The more "vague" and diffuse" symptoms include depressed mood, feelings of emptiness, lack of initiative and zest, a persistent dullness of interpersonal experience, and a pervasive sentiment that one is not fully engaged in life. Any values and goals the patient does have seem "trite and uninspiring" and any success he has in living up to them feel "meaningless."[60]

The problem to be addressed in therapy can thus be articulated in self-regarding ethical and other-regarding moral terms. Kohut's pathological narcissist treats himself and others poorly. He has serious deficits in his moral regard for others and subjects them to reprehensible behavior and a conflicted, negative regard for himself that is full of self-contempt. He clearly lacks the affirmative, self-loving bond of having, and living by, identity-conferring standards, values, and projects that unify psychological well-being with personal coherence and ethical character, i.e., a cohesive bond with himself that is devoid of self-contempt. He is at odds with his fragmentary self and suffers from a "sense of inner uncertainty and purposelessness concerning wide sectors of his life."[61]

The broader, more diffuse symptoms indicate an emphasis on demoralization that is not reflected in the DSM-5 description of narcissistic personality disorder. They call to mind Dworkin's idea that estrangement from critical interests leads to a vague and persistent sense that one is not living as one should, and Taylor's idea that estrangement from strong evaluations can lead to a self-shattering "breakdown" and a sense of being "spiritually out of joint."[62] This paradigmatic existential complaint has been acknowledged as a major therapeutic concern in contemporary psychoanalysis.[63] Kohut's articulation of these symptoms was not idiosyncratic. Ever since Freud introduced the term "narcissism" in the 1920s, psychiatrists and psychoanalysts observed a sharp rise in the number of patients who complained about "vaguely defined discontents" such as loneliness, abandonment, worthlessness, emptiness, and boredom. These cases contrasted with the phobias and emotionally fraught paralyses that were exhibited by Freud's hysterical patients. Kohut tapped into one of the cultural currents of his time, writing as he did in the early years of what became known as "the decade of the new narcissism." Public interest in narcissism ran very high in the 1970s and was a recurring theme in cultural criticism, with Christopher Lasch's *The Culture of Narcissism* being a seminal text.[64]

Kohut defined the desirable outcomes or goals of SPT in terms that were thought by some to have existentialist overtones.[65] SPT aimed at firming up the self through stronger cohesion and a sharper delimitation of an internalized system of values by which the patient could pleasurably accept himself with a secure and positive regard. This would facilitate greater "devotion to cherished tasks and purposes" and self-confidence in relating to others without fear of rejection and humiliation. A deepening and refinement of the patient's abilities to esteem himself and others was crucial, as was an ability to devote himself consistently to "worthwhile and absorbing long-term goals" and "cherished ideals" that often determine the "major directions" of one's later life. These abilities would enable the patient to sustain a life involving loving relationships, restrained self-esteem, realistic ambitions, and meaningful work and achievement. SPT aims at the patient's forming and strengthening these ideals and goals. Once integrated into his "ego's realistic goal structure," these ideals and values would give "new meaning" to the patient's life. Kohut wrote approvingly of patients who develop a deeply "original" approach to living and working.[66] The principal indications of a "cure" include the removal or amelioration of the patient's hypochondria, lethargy, empty depression, and vulnerability to both grandiosity and self-deprecation. In broader terms, the patient will keenly experience joys in living and consider his life worthwhile, creative, and productive. The treatment of narcissistic personality disorder is successful when the patient's formerly fragmented, enfeebled self "has become sufficiently strengthened and consolidated to be able to function as a … self-propelling, self-directed, and self-sustaining unit which provides a central purpose to his personality and gives a sense of meaning to his life."[67]

This consolidation revolves significantly around a creative merging of the patient's ambitions and ideals with her talents and skills. Kohut saw the treatment of narcissistic personality disorder as especially relevant in late middle age, a "pivotal point" when many ask themselves whether they have been true to their own "innermost design."[68] Therapeutic transformations include "highly valued sociocultural attributes" such as empathy, creativity, humor, and wisdom. For example, creativity can range from an enhanced ability to perform tasks with "zestful initiative" to the emergence of "brilliantly inventive" artistic or scientific projects. Humor is a trait that brings balance to commitment, i.e., the patient's devotion to ideals and values would not be fanatical but informed instead by a sense of proportion that can be amusingly expressed.[69] I think these attributes could be articulated in pluralistic virtue ethical terms. Although Swanton saw creativity as a profile of the virtues, we might see it as a particular virtue to be cultivated in cases where it is blocked or frozen.[70]

In passages reminiscent of Jahoda, Kohut stresses a conception of positive mental health in relation to therapeutic goals. Mental health is more than the absence of neurotic symptoms. It is an ability, based on a firm, cohesive sense of self, to use one's skills and talents to live, love, and work successfully. A mentally healthy person is able to deal effectively with her environment in a manner consistent with her deepest purposes and highest ideals. Kohut did not propose unfailing consistency here, but degrees of improvement in this ability have a clear overlap with the purported benefits of engaging with SPT. He saw the possession of strong ideals as having great importance to the maintenance of emotional health.[71] Positive mental health for Kohut amounts to "healthy narcissism," a fine and positive inner state of which Kohut was an unabashed advocate. He was the leading exponent in the neo-Freudian analytic community of recasting self-love as a form of self-esteem. Where many saw narcissistic self-love in adults as a developmental arrest that impeded mature love of others, Kohut normalized self-love by folding it under his rubric of "healthy narcissism" and using the more neutral term "self-respect" instead. In a masterful account, Elizabeth Lunbeck shows how Kohut undermined the axiomatic association of narcissism with pathological self-absorption and vanity. Kohut's work "broadened narcissism's remit" by contrasting its pathologies, which had traditionally drawn the most attention, with healthy "aspirations to self-fulfillment" and a realistic but positive self-regard. Indeed, the creative strivings for self-realization and ambitious achievement that Kohut equated with healthy narcissism were seen to support the pursuit of "values, goals, and ideals" that could express the finer aspects of human nature.[72]

Kohut was less clear about the patient's contribution to the praxis that aims to bring these goals about. He did caution against disregarding the considerable influence of the patient's motivation, i.e., her wish to be relieved of her deficiencies and suffering. He also noted that some patients come to therapy with a belief that it will lead them away from grandiosity and toward greater personal security and restrained self-esteem.[73] If the patient's damaged sense of self could be restored, then her striving for a life lived in accordance with her deepest purposes, ideals, and ambitions would be further inspired and her abilities to effectively fashion such a life would be strengthened. We can impute the healing and recovery virtues into this process in ways that parallel their relevance to EPT. I think we can also attribute an implicit notion of responsive authenticity that captures aspects of the challenge model. Kohut defined mental health in large part as the capacity to self-assertively utilize one's talents and skills in accordance with one's ideals and values in the form of a life-plan. He saw the maintenance of a cohesive self and the implementation of this life-plan as a crucial, ongoing task. According to one of his closest colleagues, this task was nothing less than the imperative to "become what we are in the deepest layers of our being."[74] Narcissistic personality disorder stifles the patient's ability to formulate and live by such a plan. The patient is challenged by both the demands of the world and his demoralized, inchoate sense of self. For these reasons, we can see Kohut's self-psychology as supporting a patient's quest for authenticity. The demoralization of narcissistic personality disorder precludes an authentic way of living.

In theoretical terms, the broader benefits of Kohutian analysis can be articulated as roughly consonant with authenticity as an ethical ideal. In "experience-near" terms, those benefits implicate authenticity as a mode of living that is generated by a cohesive sense of self. While adumbrative ideas that implicate authenticity can be read out of Kohut's work, there is much that would have to be read into it to complete the sketch. Kohut did not refer to philosophical conceptions of authenticity and he was uncomfortable with the psychological notions of identity that were prevalent in his time. Nor did he acknowledge how his thinking might be laden with generic ethical values. Even so, one could argue that Kohut's cherished ideals and values are compatible with deep evaluations and critical interests. Indeed, if the ideals and values a patient cherishes are to be ones that inform a life that she can endorse as right for herself and her circumstances, then one could argue that they should reflect deep evaluations and critical interests. This argument would emphasize one's own independent reflection as opposed to uncritical acceptance of socially valued norms. One can then argue that Kohut's ambitions and goals are compatible with identity-conferring projects. If those goals and ambitions are to be true to a person's character, then they should be identity-conferring commitments. If we take Kohut at his word, his approach to self-restoration can engage the finer aspects of human nature. If cultivating strong evaluations and critical interests involves a sustained, higher-order reflective volition, then arguably Kohut's psychotherapy ought to engage with, if only by supporting, that effort.

A plausible parallel can be drawn between Kohut and Frankfurt: both would agree (1) that our combined capacities for self-reflection and commitment to self-defining projects goes a long way to making us persons and (2) that dedication to worthwhile projects generates much value and fulfillment in lives. Kohut's theories about the investment in living this dedication entails would also have to accommodate an idea held by leading proponents of authenticity, i.e., that a life cannot have this value and fulfillment without being connected to some projects that are seen as intrinsically worthwhile and not just as ways of maximizing good consequences.[75] I do not see a maximizing imperative in Kohut's work. He wanted his patients to experience "ego syntonic pleasure in their actions and ... successes," but his endorsement of a realistic goal system could well be used to put the brakes on maximization.[76] I also suspect he would be open to the findings of the positive psychology movement: that commitment to projects as worthwhile for their own sake is highly rewarding in ways that a deliberate commitment to maximizing good results is not. Finally, Kohut's emphasis on the self's development in relation to others might be articulated to accommodate Varga and Taylor's emphasis on our embeddedness in historical-cultural fields of significance, and the interpersonal collaboration of communication and meaning-making from which they emerge. This would require a very careful recasting of Kohut's realized nuclear self. As a therapeutic goal, I think a challenge model of authenticity is a congenial guest at Kohut's table.

## 7.5 Cognitive Behavioral Therapy

Cognitive behavioral therapy (hereinafter CBT) might seem an unlikely candidate for being a generically ethical treatment. Given that "CBT has become a large umbrella of interventions and techniques,"[77] we can speak of therapeutic approaches within the cognitive behavioral framework. The common feature of these approaches is a focus on "demonstrable behavioral outcomes achieved primarily through changes in the way an individual perceives, reflects upon, and in general, thinks about their life circumstances."[78] They assume that behavior is affected by cognition, that persons can alter and monitor their cognitive processes, and that changing cognitions will lead to changes in problematic behavior.[79] CBTs are designed to help patients "become aware of thought processes that lead to maladaptive behavioral responses and to actively change those processes in a positive way."[80] One can imagine many CBT cases in which praxis has nothing to do with self-regarding ethical or other-regarding moral improvement, let alone the cultivation of virtues. Someone might pursue CBT to redress frustrating patterns of thought and behavior that do not obstruct loving and respectful modes of relating to oneself and others, e.g., shyness, agoraphobia, and situational or separation anxieties. Far from being an exercise in strengthening character, CBT has been cast as an ideological platitude for the power of positive thinking and a "method of indoctrination into the pieties of American optimism."[81]

Whether CBT qualifies as a generic ethical treatment depends on the case. If (1) the problem CBT addresses can be elucidated in self- or other-regarding ethical terms, and (2) the goals of CBT involve any or all of the following: ethically desirable changes in (a) tendencies of affective/emotional response, (b) a better understanding of how one should treat oneself and/or others, and (c) better patterns of behavior, then (3) the efforts the committed patient makes to resolve the problem via CBT can involve the affective, cognitive, and practical facets of ethical self-improvement through the cultivation of certain virtues.[82] I argue that CBT qualifies as a generic ethical treatment for patients with at least three of DSM-5's Cluster B borderline personality disorders (hereinafter PDs), e.g., borderline personality disorder (hereinafter BPD), narcissistic personality disorder (hereinafter NPD), and antisocial personality disorder (hereinafter APD). These cases can fit the triadic analysis. The generic ethical/therapeutic overlap is even more obvious in forensic applications of CBT to antisocial personality disorder and criminal behavior, e.g., Moral Reconation Therapy and Social and Community Responsibility Therapy. The morally value-laden nature of these forensic applications is not implicit; they are among the most explicitly "moral" treatments on offer.

I argue that CBT can foster generic ethical growth in BPD, NPD, and APD patients that can be elucidated in virtue ethical terms. I will make this case by showing how these CBT cases fit the component parts of the triadic analysis. I will not rehash the previous arguments that these disorders can be elucidated in self-regarding ethical and other-regarding moral terms. The second part of the triadic structure is the desirable outcome or goal of the psychotherapy, i.e., ethically desirable changes in (1) tendencies of affective/emotional response; (2) a better understanding of how one should treat oneself and/or others; and (3) better patterns of behavior. Some modes of CBT were not designed explicitly as treatments aiming at generic ethical improvement. Their focus is limited ostensibly to symptom relief through cognitive restructuring and behavioral change. Charland would argue that "standard psychotherapy" for Cluster B personality disorders "may help and sometimes even be required for moral recovery, but it can never be sufficient on its own."[83] While Charland does not define the term, we might assume that "standard psychotherapy" does not require "a moral willingness and commitment to [character] change" through the "development of empathy" and dedicated honesty in the therapeutic alliance. These are Charland's "two milestones" that psychotherapies aimed at Cluster B personality disorders must pass to be successful. Charland cites Moral Reconation and Dialectical Behavioral therapies as contemporary initiatives that might sufficiently acknowledge these milestones.[84]

Charland has a point: CBT for disorders that cannot be plausibly construed as generic ethical problems would not require this moral willingness and commitment. But CBT for disorders that can be so construed arguably does. Consider the first milestone. CBT for the Cluster B personality disorders involves a therapeutic alliance that revolves around the "collaboration, congruence, empathy, and genuineness" of both therapist and patient.[85] Facilitating the patient's comfort level with honest self-disclosure is crucial to CBT for these disorders. It is difficult to see how the patient's work in self-monitoring, self-evaluation, and understanding the influence of negative schemas can proceed without a commitment to relating honestly in a therapeutic alliance.[86] A patient's outright dishonesty would scuttle the effort at cognitive restructuring. As for the second milestone, the development of empathy as a therapeutic goal is more pronounced in some Cluster B disorders than others. It is an explicit goal in CBT for NPD. "Key treatment goals" include: (1) recognizing and weakening maladaptive coping modes; (2) developing affect regulation skills; (3) increasing "respect and empathy for other's feelings, limits, [and] autonomy"; (4) increasing responsiveness to natural talents and strengths, and secure self-worth; and (5) increasing appropriate reciprocity. Successful treatment can be determined by evidence of "adaptive emotional self-care … [and] respectful social impulse control and reciprocity."[87] Clearly, these goals have self-regarding ethical and other-regarding moral dimensions.

The relevance of cultivating greater empathy in cases of BPD is evident, although it is possible that such patients might exhibit dissociation between cognitive and affective empathic capacities, i.e., the former capacity is diminished while the latter capacity is over-sensitized. If so, then BPD patients would need to strengthen the former and moderate the latter. Aside from a reduction of standard BPD symptoms, e.g., relationship and identity problems, emotional instability, emptiness, and fear of abandonment, key CBT goals include "Feeling safe with experiencing and expressing emotions and needs and with personally connecting to others" and the development of "a satisfying life on personal, social, and societal levels."[88] If empathy is essentially a dual ability to cognitively understand and affectively share the feelings of another, then a commitment to strengthening deficits in these abilities would seem implicit in connecting to others as part of a satisfactory life. The behavioral and interpersonal difficulties experienced by the BPD patient stem from emotional and cognitive dysfunction, with deficits in cognitive and affective empathy.[89] Typical core beliefs of BPD patients are that other persons are malevolent, cannot be trusted, will reject intimacy, and believe that the patient is bad and deserves punishment. While notorious for their emotional lability, many BPD patients think themselves into a self-protective mode of detachment, i.e., they do not connect with their own feelings or the feelings of others. The core beliefs are "that it makes no sense to feel emotions and to connect to others, that it is even dangerous to do so, and that being detached is the only way to survive and to control one's life."[90] These beliefs indicate deficits in cognitive and affective empathy and will hinder the patient's ability to accurately recognize and feel for others' emotional states. Indeed, these beliefs distort the patient's understanding of how others think and feel about him. A BPD patient's commitment to cognitive restructuring can thus be a commitment to strengthening his capacity for empathic concern.

The relevance of cultivating greater empathic concern in cases of APD can be implicative. This despite the fact that an impaired capacity for empathy is one of its signature symptoms. The standard goal of CBT with antisocial patients "should be the reduction of criminal and manipulative behavior."[91] Therapist and patient work together to change "the thinking patterns behind decision making that results in subsequent harm to self or others, while increasing decisions that lead to productive behaviors, prosocial outcomes, and ultimately a nondestructive life."[92] A "thinking pattern" of disregard for others is a notably challenging symptom to redress through self-monitoring and the restructuring of core beliefs. The first step is to get the patient to acknowledge his tendency to look out for himself and not think about how his actions affect others. The next step is to explore the impact of that tendency on his everyday life. A collaborative discussion with the therapist would examine how disregard for others has led repeatedly to poor decisions, damaged relationships, and criminal behavior.[93] Successful therapy would clearly involve improved empathic ability and a willingness to exercise it in relating to others. The aim is to move beyond emotional hardness and callous indifference to others to finer inner states of sympathy and understanding.

In sum, CBT for these three Cluster B personality disorders cannot avoid the implication that the effort patients expend to reduce symptoms involves making ethically and morally desirable changes to one's thoughts, feelings, and behavior. In these cases, CBT is applied in service to generic ethical self-improvement. The compulsive hand washer aims to free himself from a habit that impedes his ability to lead a more satisfactory life that is less riddled with anxiety. The BPD, APD, or NPD patient aims to free herself from patterns of cognitive, affective, and behavioral response that impede her ability to lead a more satisfactory life that is less riddled with generic unethicality, e.g., the morally objectionable treatment of others.[94] Decreasing the valence of dysfunctional schemas and replacing them with more benevolent ones cannot be soundly abstracted from changing and improving ways of relating to oneself and others. In such cases, CBT is a means by which a generic ethical "commitment to being patient and loving with both others and oneself"[95] can find therapeutic expression in a praxis that facilitates self-improvement. CBT for these personality disorders can accommodate Charland's moral willingness to change. Put another way, a person who aims at generic ethical self-improvement can use CBT to get there. Self-regarding ethical and other-regarding moral improvement involves affective, cognitive, and behavioral facets that CBT can aim to change for the better. On my account, "this remains true even if the theoretical vocabulary in which the therapeutic theory is couched makes little or no explicit mention of any such notions."[96]

CBT can be refined to make its generic ethical content ever more explicit. This is especially evident in forensic applications of CBT for criminal behavior. Patients with APD are among those "treatment resistant" persons for whom Moral Reconation Therapy (hereinafter MRT) is designed. It is "firmly grounded in the theoretical framework of cognitive behaviorism" and its therapeutic elements draw "a clear connection between thought processes and behavior."[97] The treatment goals of MRT are to raise patients from lower to higher levels of personality, identity, and moral development, i.e., enhanced moral reasoning and appropriate, responsible behavior toward self and others. It aims to "forge a connection" between enhanced moral reasoning skills and improved moral behavior.[98] MRT is "based upon the assumption that fully functioning, reasonably happy people have a strong sense of identity and that their behavior and relationships are based in relatively high levels of moral reasoning."[99]

Social and Community Responsibility Therapy (hereinafter SCRT) represents a "paradigm shift" from CBT approaches that focus egocentrically on helping patients resolve their psychological problems and distress. SCRT integrates this goal with a sociocentric focus on a "psychology of caring" and an emphasis on "enhancing moral values and strengthening moral character" by "developing thinking and behaviors that result in moral and social responsibility toward others, the community, and society as a whole."[100] It recognizes lack of empathy as an important component of the low self-control in antisocial behavior and the strong connection between empathy and prosocial moral comportment. It stresses "empathy building and training" as a "crucial component in … antisocial treatment and change."[101]

The Good Lives Model (hereinafter GLM) aims to help patients acquire the cognitive-behavioral skills to "achieve personally meaningful goals," to "make their way in the world," and to live their vision of a satisfactory life in a prosocial way. GLM emphasizes personal agency in its assumption that persons seek primary goods such as knowledge, excellence in play and work, "self-directedness," freedom from emotional turmoil, interpersonal and communal relatedness, creativity, and a meaningful, purposive life. It also assumes that patients' "sense of identity emerges from their basic value commitments, [and] the goods they pursue in search of better lives."[102] These goals explicitly involve ethically desirable changes in (1) tendencies of affective/emotional response; (2) a better understanding of how one should treat oneself and/or others; and (3) better patterns of behavior.

The third part of the triadic structure is the praxis of the patient that involves the affective, cognitive, and practical facets of ethical self-improvement through the cultivation of certain virtues. CBT approaches to these personality disorders stress the patient's responsibility for working on himself at least as much as they stress working with the therapist. The praxes of CBTs for personality disorders involve prolonged and focused efforts at changing core beliefs and the entrenched patterns of negative thought that inform self-defeating emotional responses and behaviors. Cognitive restructuring leads to social skills training in the restructuring of relationships with others.[103] This reflects the fundamental assumption of CBTs that the patient must effect substantial changes in his thinking before meaningful changes can be anticipated in behavior.[104] The "change techniques" by which these efforts are put into practice include developing cognitive and behavioral skills. The former include the self-monitoring and evaluation of automatic thoughts, reflexive attitudes and core beliefs, thought-recording to recognize and change errors in thinking, and the reinforcement of alternative thinking patterns. Given the nexus between thought and emotion, these are often combined with experiential techniques such as imagery rescripting that aim to bring problematic emotions "into active awareness" so they too can be evaluated, monitored, and hopefully reframed. The development of skills to help patients implement novel behaviors and acquire confidence in strengthening behavioral change can involve exercises in "anger management, assertiveness training, and relaxation."[105]

Whether the patient's work in CBT involves the cultivation of virtues depends on the extent to which the desired changes to the patient's psyche and behavior can be articulated as good qualities of character that are dispositions to respond to the demands of the world. More specifically, these qualities have to be developed into dispositions to respond (e.g., through fine inner states of respecting, loving, creating, appreciating, promoting, etc.) in a good enough or excellent way to "targets" in their fields, e.g., people, inner states, or actions. As such they are what virtues aim at, as when we say that the well-being of others is the target of beneficence, or the well-being of oneself is the target of self-love.[106]

If the demands of the world include the demand for self-improvement, then the healing and recovery virtues can aim at the targets that demand indicates, i.e., the desired changes to the patient's psyche and behavior that are improved ways of ethically relating to oneself and morally relating to others.

The PD patient's work in CBT aims to get things right in her thoughts, feelings, attitudes, and behavior toward herself and others. Getting things right involves hitting the targets of the healing virtues by replacing PD symptoms with internal targets such as benevolent schemas that evince proper caring for oneself. External targets include respectful and empathic behavior toward others. I regard the recovering PD patient's efforts toward improved performance in living as an expression of the healing virtues that inform them. The BPD patient who cultivates perseverance and creative flexibility in changing self-defeating patterns of thought and behavior will hopefully begin to treat herself and others with greater forbearance. The performance in living of a recovered PD patient is arguably not a state of affairs distinct from the virtues of self-love, respect, and empathic concern for others that inform it. Again, healing virtues like perseverance, honesty, and creative flexibility enable the patient to work toward recovery and gradually acquire other virtues, such as self-love and empathic concern. Once established as "deep" qualities of character, they also enable the patient to sustain recovery.[107]

Wanberg and Milkman recount the case of Larry. They explicate the praxis of his psychotherapy in cognitive behavioral terms that are supplemented by the sociocentric focus of SCRT. I want to re-interpret their case in virtue ethical terms that are consonant with their focus on a psychology of caring and the development of morally responsible thinking and behavior. Larry is a thirty-one-year-old blue-collar worker with a history of antisocial behavior that began in his teens. Past problems included substance abuse and criminal convictions for breaking and entering and driving while intoxicated. He was later convicted of grand theft and burglary. While serving a year in prison, he completed a CBT[-SCRT] program for offenders with conjoint substance abuse problems.[108] Over the course of a successful therapy, SCRT patients learn to identify and map their core beliefs from which the automatic thoughts that lead to criminal behavior and substance abuse emerge. They can then practice the cognitive restructuring skills through dialogue or role-playing to change problematic thought patterns. This prepares them for dealing with high-risk situations that trigger self-defeating behavior by countering the beliefs and cognitions that inform it. These techniques are supplemented by training in social skills that orients patients to respecting the rights of others and acting on concern for their welfare.[109] Fostering consideration for others through cognitive and affective empathy is crucial here.

The vignette begins after Larry is released from prison. He is clean and sober, holding down a job, and completing his first year of parole. It revolves around the following incident: Larry's car stalls while he is driving to an appointment with his parole officer. Feeling angry and hopeless, he called Tim, a former partner in crime, for assistance. When Tim arrived, Larry was late for his appointment which also meant he would be late for work. This was an exigent situation for Larry and he thought of getting high to ease the pressure. He had missed two previous appointments for legitimate reasons but his parole officer was displeased and threatened to return him to prison if it happened again. Larry knew he had done nothing wrong, at least not yet. His frustration incited a slew of automatic thoughts expressing negative core beliefs ("Bad things happen to me, I've never had a fair chance"). He was initially gripped by the thought that his parole officer would confirm his core beliefs and cut him no breaks ("I'm going back to prison"). Tim reinforced this belief ("He'll put you in the slammer") and enticed him to escape to LA where they could resume criminal activity. Larry thought he might "Just as well split."[110]

Larry had learned numerous techniques for identifying his core beliefs, monitoring his automatic thoughts and their attendant emotional and behavioral responses, and formulating prosocial, morally respectful alternatives. These skills enabled him to stop automatic thoughts about getting high and fleeing with Tim and counter them with a different perspective that restructures the situation in morally responsible terms, e,g., that he would disappoint the people who had helped him if he ran away, and that getting high would hinder his ability to respond constructively to the situation. Reflecting empathically is an acquired skill that involves thinking from another's point of view ("What will this do to my wife?"). He also learned about working to punish negative thoughts and reward positive ones ("Punish: 'I'm going with Tim. But then I'll end up back in prison for sure,' Reward: 'My kid's going to need a good dad. I don't want to go back to prison. That's better for everybody'").[111]

Larry could recognize this as a high-risk situation in which his negative core beliefs and automatic thought patterns could predominate and rationalize irresponsible behavior. His understanding that these beliefs had to be countered enabled other thoughts to stem the tide. He thought of the effect his actions would have on his pregnant wife. Where he had treated other women badly in the past, he felt that he owed his wife for the way she supported his efforts to change. She didn't deserve to be hurt and abandoned. He saw that his child would need a committed father. He acknowledged his respect for his parole officer and his counsellor in the CBT-SCRT program, and wondered why he hadn't called his support group sponsor. He also reassessed Tim as "a loser."[112] These thoughts enabled him to consider prosocial and morally responsible alternatives. He applied his newly acquired cognitive behavioral skills to his situation and told Tim that he would not run from it. He then set up meetings with his parole officer and therapist.[113]

Larry's case can illustrate the relevance of healing virtues to the application of these skills. Strengthening his capacity for honesty enabled Larry to forgo deception, confront his self-defeating cognitions, and candidly disclose them. In reconceiving different ways to think, feel, and behave according to prosocial values, he had to work hard at developing imaginative flexibility and open-mindedness. The modification of behavioral strategies and core beliefs, and the shifting of mindsets and behavioral repertoires, is crucial to responding to situational demands and defeating strategies that compromise prosocial functioning. Larry needed to see beyond his embedded core beliefs and not think about the situation in terms that confirmed them. This involves envisioning, or looking into, alternate values and interpretations that open his mind to different perspectives. Here too, perseverance involves both protracted effort and the ability to endure adverse events by way of flexible response. To meet the demands of the world in prosocial terms, Larry needs to persistently evince an ability for flexible, creative, and positive adaptation. Cultivating hopefulness enables him to believe that he can find prosocial pathways to desired goals and summon the motivation to follow them. The exploratory striving and mindful immersion of healing curiosity facilitate the depth of self-invigilation demanded by SCRT. Larry needs to be curious about how he might move beyond his core beliefs and live a life outside of them. This involves a positive, mindful orientation to a future in which his core beliefs are no longer relied upon as self-fulfilling prophecies. Respect for the healing project will intersect with Larry's project of self-regarding care as he assumes the primary responsibility for using SCRT skills to reconceive high-risk situations.

These virtues work in synthesis with the three virtues of practice, i.e., the virtues of focus, the virtues associated with the integration of constraints to a problem's solution, and the dialogical virtues by which one aims at getting things right by acting virtuously overall in solving problems.[114] In Larry's case, as with Seneca's Angry Man, we can see them as dispositions of character that enable him to make the most of SCRT and facilitate attempts to resolve the problems that led him to seek it. If the triadic analysis applies, then they can be seen as instrumental to the working through and will vary in their state of development.

Larry needed virtues of focus so his problematic cognitions could be addressed. A shared attention with his therapist grounded his efforts to develop sufficient degrees of steadfast fixity in monitoring his core beliefs, tracking his automatic thoughts, and recording the patterns of behavioral and emotional response they would normally instigate. These efforts required "acumen, discipline, sensitivity,"[115] and perseverance. This kind of sustained self-invigilation can waver in the best of us, but for Larry, an unreliable and wavering focus could facilitate a relapse into the self-defeating and other-disregarding behavior that led him to prison. A committed engagement with SCRT was how he worked through a dialogical process of feedback, learning, and modification by which virtues of focus could be cultivated and strengthened to effect a good enough solution to his problems in living.[116]

Larry also needed the virtues required for integrating constraints to a problem's solution. These involve creativity, depth of understanding, commitment to valid information, and insight. Others include dispositions to assemble relevant data, to examine and evaluate assertions made during therapy, to trust the therapist's expertise, to admit mistakes, and to modify beliefs on the basis of evidence. In these ways, he developed "the imaginative and analytic virtues required to facilitate constraint integration."[117] SCRT helped him to re-evaluate his core beliefs and automatic thoughts as self-defeating but amenable to modification. Finally, Larry needed "virtues of dialogue" to participate adequately in therapy. He had to contribute his own thoughts to the ongoing conversation of how he should go about the task of countering his negative cognitions and replacing them with prosocial ones.[118]

The recovery virtues of self-love, empathic concern, and respect for others are no less relevant. Larry needs to forge, and bond with, a different constellation of values and core beliefs that afford him the coherence of ethical integrity. There is arguably a sense in which Larry feels unworthy of the good things that could befall him. His embedded cognitions close off his appreciation of how he might bring them about. While he recognizes that his son needs a good father, he needs the positive self-embrace that affirms his ability to be that father. He understands that his wife deserves a good husband, but he needs to bond with himself in such a way as to become that husband. Recognizing another person's needs is not the same as meeting them, and that is precisely what Larry needs to feel he is worthy of doing. His embrace of those identity-conferring commitments needs to be devoid of self-contempt. Self-love can thus inform, and perhaps empower, empathic concern and respect for others. Larry's appreciation of how his actions affect others, and his growing ability to sympathize with their feelings, indicate an expansion of his self-identity: he is becoming the kind of person who is open and responsive to others in ways that his negative cognitions did not permit. More to the point, he wants to be that person. In bonding better with himself, he finds better ways of bonding with others. Larry's case thus fits the triadic analysis. We have a problem that can be elucidated in self- and other-regarding ethical terms, and psychotherapeutic goals that can be elucidated in virtue ethical terms. The efforts Larry makes to work through his problems involve the affective, cognitive, and behavioral facets of generic ethical self-improvement. This working through can be seen as a concerted effort to replace character faults with character strengths or virtues.

## 7.6 Mentalization-Based Therapy

Bateman and Fonagy's mentalization-based psychotherapy (hereinafter MBP) is claimed to be a uniquely apposite approach to the core deficit of BPD.[119] In broad terms, if recovery from BPD is possible by means of MBP, "then it must be effecting specifically [ethical and] moral changes for the better."[120] In more specific terms, I argue that MBP cases can fit the triadic analysis. Lacking the capacity for mentalization is a generic ethical problem since it reflects a dysfunctional relationship with oneself and others. The therapeutic goal is the strengthening of a valued capacity to relate ethically to oneself and morally to others. As such, the efforts the committed MBP patient makes to recover from BPD involve the affective, cognitive, and practical facets of generic ethical self-improvement. I also think these efforts involve the cultivation of healing virtues. The restoration of mentalization also involves the recovery virtues of self-love and empathic concern and respect for others.

There is first the problem for which psychotherapy is sought. As the leading proponents of MBT, Bateman and Fonagy do not contest the DSM criteria of BPD, e.g., they regard impulsivity as a key feature. They describe BPD as "a complex and serious mental disorder that is characterized by a pervasive pattern of difficulties with emotion regulation and impulse control and instability both in relationships and self-image."[121] They note the following features that are common to BPD patients: "all-or-nothing, or black or white thinking," intense feelings of shame, and disturbed cognitive schemata such as "the world is malevolent and dangerous," "I am powerless and vulnerable," and "I am essentially unacceptable and uncared for." The clinical presentation of BPD patients often includes violent physical (and emotional) attacks on themselves or others. They also lack a coherent, unified sense of self that generates pervasive feelings of "emptiness" and an often "compulsive search for meaning."[122]

Bateman and Fonagy surpass the DSM by proposing a more nuanced understanding of BPD that reflects their theoretical focus on normal human self-development in the context of a person's early attachment relationships. They view an agentive sense of self and others (i.e., a sense of persons as thinkers of thoughts and doers of things) as an achievement determined by childhood developmental factors. Understanding the origins of BPD requires an understanding of how that developmental process can go wrong. Given the clinical consensus that BPD patients are markedly insecure in their sense of attachment to themselves and others, Bateman and Fonagy posit a relationship between the way a person's early attachment environment is experienced and the later manifestation of BPD symptoms. The attachment experience, or the close proximity in infancy to another person, is a necessary condition for generating the infant's psychological capacity for interpersonal interpretation. This capacity is a means of processing experience via emotional regulation, attentional control, and mentalization. Acting together, these components enable a person to collaborate productively with others. In order to exercise this capacity, a person needs a symbolic representational system for mental states and the ability to selectively activate states of mind in accordance with particular intentions. This attentional control is not limited to one's sense of self. A person needs to appreciate that others have this capacity and hence their own states of mind and intentions that will often differ from one's own. It follows for Bateman and Fonagy that disruption of early affectional bonds will generate maladaptive attachment patterns and undermine the interpersonal interpretive capacity that they see as crucial to normal psychosocial development. They place the component of mentalization "at the pinnacle" of this self-regulatory capacity. It involves understanding the actions of oneself and others in terms of intentional mental states, e.g., desires, feelings, and beliefs, to which I would add values. "In effect, mentalizing refers to making sense of each other and ourselves, implicitly and explicitly in terms of mind states and mental processes."[123]

When we mentalize our own or others' actions, we think about mental states as separate from but potentially causing them. The point is to go beyond observable phenomena, i.e., surface behavior, to account for our own or others' actions in terms of beliefs, desires, preferences, plans, and values.[124] Mentalization can be self-regarding, e.g., "How do I feel about the way she feels about me?" It can also be other-regarding, e.g., "How does she feel about the way I feel about her?" or "How and why might she be thinking or feeling about her behavior towards me?" Mentalization "acts as a buffer between feeling and action [by] helping the individual form a deeper understanding of others, to recognize his own and others' misunderstandings, to consider if others or his own motivation or reaction is deceitful and manipulative or honest and true, and to moderate interpersonal and emotional distance."[125] It is our ability to consciously or subconsciously read the minds of others with an open mind of our own. If my early attachment experience involved good enough mirroring, then I can extend to others the respect and understanding that my primary caregivers afforded to myself. Mentalization enables us to give others, and ourselves, the benefit of the doubt without jumping to unreflective conclusions that are based on surface appearances. Consider the following example: I agree to meet a colleague at a designated time. He arrives late and is brusque in speech and manner. Much will depend on context and the background of our past interactions but if I can adequately mentalize, then I can distinguish ostensibly rude speech and manner from a variety of mental states that might inform it. Without giving it much thought, I may "read his mind" with secure confidence as him being annoyed with himself for being late. Mentalizing is thus an acquired focus by which one can stop, listen, look, and explore a range of intentional mental states that make another's actions meaningful in the way he intends them to be.[126] It is not about unreflectively letting another's actions speak for themselves, since I am aware that the surface presentation might be at odds with the mental state behind it. Nor is it about force-fitting the meaning of another's actions to my own preconceived ideas of what another's actions must mean, e.g., "people don't respect me."

Bateman and Fonagy regard an inability to mentalize as the core dysfunction in BPD. If my early attachment experience involved deficient mirroring, if I did not experience my attachment environment as secure because my primary caregivers did not afford a soothing and respectful understanding to myself, then I might become seriously limited in my ability to extend respect and understanding to others. "The caregiver's failure to provide a relationship in the context of which mentalization and the sense of self as a psychological entity can develop leads to the persistence of the more primitive modes of psychic reality."[127] We might think again of Iris Murdoch: my mind will be much less open to empathic and respectful mentalization if it is constantly active in fabricating an anxious, self-preoccupied, and often falsifying veil of hostility that obfuscates my moral vision.[128] If I am unable to mentalize, then I will not distinguish ostensibly rude speech and manner from a variety of mental states that might inform it. Without giving it much thought, and with considerable insecurity, I may equate my colleague's ostensibly rude speech and manner with actually rude speech and behavior. I am unaware that the surface presentation might be at odds with the mental state behind it. I thus force-fit the meaning of my colleague's actions to my own preconceived ideas of what his actions must mean, e.g., "he does not respect me."

The self- and other-regarding aspects of BPD can be easily articulated as problematic in generic ethical terms. Bateman and Fonagy agree with Freud in holding that the infant's sense of self should be sustained by the loving caregiver in such a way that it can become self-loving. The sign of a self that lacks self-love is shame.[129] Persons who lack the interpretive capacity to understand their own mental states "are not only deficient in self-love," but also lack an "authentic, organic self-image."[130] This leads them to experience the gnawing inner emptiness noted above, which generates in turn their besetting search for a meaningful life. An inability, or defensive unwillingness, to see other persons as having their own mental states precludes empathic concern, or identification with their suffering, interests, beliefs, and desires.[131]

The goal of MBT is to facilitate mentalization to enable the patient to form a more stable, robust sense of self and develop secure relationships with others. The initial aims are to stabilize the impulsivity that results from the uncontrolled affect that characterizes BPD, and help patients to develop a strengthened ability to identify emotions and their appropriate expression with others. This will hopefully stimulate a patient's increasing ability to mentalize. Long-term goals include the enhancement of personal integrity, responsibility, and interpersonal function.[132] In BPD, the impediments to mentalization are most prominent in intimate relationships. By strengthening the ability to mentalize, the patient will discover more about how she thinks and feels about herself, how she responds to others, and understand how "errors" in understanding influence her problematic behavior. While mentalization has an essential self-regarding dimension, its relevance to other-regarding moral concern is crucial: "Understanding the behavior of others in terms of their likely thoughts, feelings, wishes and desires is a major developmental achievement."[133] Good mentalization also involves a number of features that indicate enhanced respect for and empathy with others, e.g., absence of paranoia, a desire to reflect on how others think and feel, an acceptance that others can have different perspectives on the same situation, a "genuine" and "generous" interest in the thoughts and feelings of others, and an openness to discovering and forgiving differences in how they think and feel.[134]

The joint praxis of therapist and patient that aims to realize these goals consists of close reflective attention on the patient's mind in individual and group therapy sessions. The therapist explores and puts forward her own understanding of the patient's current state of mind. The purpose is to stimulate the patient to use his own mind to better understand his mental states and those of others, including the therapist's. This is a process of joint and focused attention by which the patient's mental states are scrutinized. The mentalizing therapist constructs an evolving image of the patient in her own mind that she communicates during the sessions. This communication helps the patient understand what the therapist feels (about the patient) and why the therapist feels as she does. The patient has to find himself in the therapist's mind and vice versa "if the two together are to develop a mentalizing process. Both have to experience a mind being changed by a mind."[135] The working alliance in psychotherapy is essential to establishing the "virtuous" synergetic cycle between a secure relationship and the recovery of mentalization. The patient feels secure when understood by the therapist, which in turn facilitates the exploration of the therapist's mind that allegedly enables the patient to begin finding himself. Psychotherapy is a relational context in which the borderline patient comes to feel safe in exploring the mind of another in order to find his own mind within it. If this dialogical exploration is beneficial, then the patient learns to allocate more mindful space to look searchingly into the thoughts and feelings of others. Improvements in ability to interpret other's mental states without the obfuscating influence of inflexible attitudes and emotional lability "may generate a far more benign interpersonal environment."[136] The development of mentalization depends on the patient's interaction with the benign, reflective, and empathic mind of the therapist. The patient finds himself first in the therapist's mind and later in his own as he integrates the therapist's image (of the patient) as part of his (the patient's) own self-image. "The therapist's respect for minds generates the patient's respect for self, respect for other and ultimately respect for human narrative."[137]

When considering the work in facilitating mentalization that patients are responsible for, it seems that there are dispositional traits they must apply in effecting it. The work of paying close attention to the patient's mind involves much in the way of monitoring and evaluating thoughts, feelings, and patterns of emotional and behavioral response. It is not surprising that a joint focus on enhancing mentalization is seen by MBT proponents as a foundational common thread throughout diverse psychotherapies.[138] CBT, for instance, has been construed as "providing highly structured ways of practicing mentalizing" that entail "adaptive and flexible mental activity compatible with moral and ethical considerations."[139] Working toward the recovery of mentalization demands a "pro-mentalizing attitude of inquisitiveness," e.g., "asking instead of assuming what someone thinks and feels," coupled with "tentativeness … open-mindedness," and "grounded imagination."[140] The healing virtues would all apply to this praxis, with healing curiosity, respect for the healing project, and imaginative flexibility being especially relevant to the pro-mentalizing attitude.

I am not alone in thinking that strengthening the mentalizing capacity amounts to cultivating virtues. Allen extends "the intrinsic value of mentalizing into the relationship one has with oneself."[141] Optimal mentalizing requires a balance of distance and closeness, love and respect, and benevolent curiosity.[142] Allen posits the relevance of Swanton's notion of self-love, which he construes as a virtuous attachment relationship with oneself that promotes mentalizing, psychological strength, and vitality. As a "secure inner base," self-love enables us to invest fully in our projects and goals.[143] With due acknowledgement to Murdoch, Allen explains ideal mentalizing "as entailing a loving and compassionate view of oneself as one really is."[144] I won't elaborate further on the ethical relevance of self-love to recovering from BPD. Suffice it to say that I construe

MBT as having this self-regarding ethical dimension. I will focus instead on the other-regarding moral aspects of mentalizing.

The ability to imagine the other's inner states and reactions is an essential capacity for a fully moral sensibility. It captures much of what we mean when we say that morality is other-regarding. If you are seriously impaired in the capacity to be other-regarding, then you are seriously impaired in your capacity to be fully moral. The therapeutic goal is the restoration of a morally valued capacity. Since MBT is also a means to achieve that goal, it is plausibly construed as a generic ethical treatment. Mentalizing enables us to be open to other minds, able to take on other perspectives, and be influenced by "better ways of thinking feeling, and acting. In short, receptive mentalizing enables us to learn and grow through relationships, including psychotherapy relationships."[145] The sufficient attainment of mentalizing capacity can be increasingly refined through intimate, mutual attention "potentially enhanced by knowledge gained through conversation."[146] Allen suggests that a rich and accurate capacity to mentalize will most likely occur in the context of an accepting, benevolent perspective that is ideally "a loving sense of connection" to another person's reality.[147]

Allen construes mentalizing as a virtue that BPD patients must work to sustain.[148] Mentalization has also been equated with the cognitive and affective dimensions of empathy. Bateman and Fonagy assert a clear overlap between mentalization and "higher order forms of empathy" that involve "an imaginative capacity" to work with "representations of shared experience" in an effort to match the emotional reactions of others with our own.[149] Allen claims that empathy might be the most important single facet of mentalizing.[150] Mentalization and empathy both involve an appreciation of the mental states of others but empathy adds facets of "sharing in those mental states and having empathic concern for others." While empathy is essentially other-regarding, mentalization is equally self- and other-regarding.[151] "The crux of mentalizing," notes Allen, "is having another person's mind in mind—or your own."[152] In self-regarding terms, cultivating mentalization enables self-love. In other-regarding terms, it enables empathic concern. Taken together, generic ethics "is unimaginable without mentalizing."[153]

## 7.7 Conclusion

The healing virtues can inform the standard praxes of these four psychotherapies in cases that fit the triadic analysis. To meet the demands of the healing project, which evolve into demands for self-care, the committed patient will need to cultivate them in the working through. Virtuous engagement with the strategies and techniques of these therapies better enables patients to realize their benefits. A commitment to honesty is essential, as are perseverance and hopefulness, especially for long-term psychotherapy. It is difficult to imagine a PD patient benefitting from the self-monitoring, evaluation, and cognitive restructuring exercises of CBT without perseverance, healing curiosity, and creative flexibility. Breaking self-defeating and deeply entrenched patterns of thought and behavior is not done credibly by rote. Summers and Barber have recognized the relevance of virtuous patient engagement with psychodynamic praxis in a way that can be extended to the approaches discussed above. For the patient's engagement with the working through to be effective, "treatment may need to build strengths while it diminishes problems."[154] Character development can be crucial to effective psychotherapy if only because many of the problems it aims to redress "typically sap individuals of their [character] strengths."[155] Consider again the depleted empathic capacity of the APD patient, or the deficits of self-love and cognitive flexibility in NPD and BPD. If PDs sap virtuous character strengths, then successful psychotherapy would sufficiently restore them. Where the presenting problems have a significant generic ethical overlap, successful psychotherapy entails excellent or good enough improvement in the way one treats oneself and others. Extreme cases of depression or demoralization aside, patients will usually come to therapy with some capacity for the healing virtues intact. Hence the attention paid by contemporary psychodynamic therapists to assessing the patient's character strengths as well as his pathology.[156] Since patients and therapists need to work together, therapists will want some idea of the patients' capacities for doing their work in the healing project.

Summers and Barber also recognize the relevance of virtuous character strengths that enable therapists to do their work in the healing project. Each therapist will come to that work with some strengths that will help them do it. They aver that the therapist who develops her own character strengths will increase her ability to help patients develop theirs.[157] Many of their points can be applied with slight modification to the patient's engagement with the working through. They note, for instance, that because therapists never know all of the relevant data, and because "life throws curveballs" at therapists and patients alike, "flexibility in conceptualization, perception, and behavior is important" in avoiding outdated perceptions of their patients. We can note also that the patients' flexibility in the healing project can enable them to avoid outdated perceptions of themselves. Where the therapists' curiosity enables increased understanding and facilitates the exploration of patients' narratives, the patients' curiosity can enable increased understanding of themselves.[158] Although Summers and Barber were referring specifically to therapists, I would extend the following ideas to patients: "The very work of doing therapy challenges character strengths and provokes self-reflection, and for many this results in further strength development."[159] They cite hope, flexibility, and curiosity as character strengths that help therapists to be effective, and they are likely increased after "long hours of attention, concern, and facilitating optimism."[160] I cite them as healing virtues that are likely increased through perseverance. A patient's committed engagement with any of the four psychotherapies discussed above can be a virtuous exercise in striving to manifest qualities that better enable them to work through PDs by way of generic ethical improvement.

## Notes

1. **Mick Cooper**, *Existential Therapies* (London: Sage Publications, 2003), 142.
2. **Emmy van Deurzen**, *Existential Counselling and Psychotherapy in Practice*, 2nd ed. (London: Sage Publications, 2002), 213.
3. **Van Deurzen**, *Existential Counselling*, 25, 23.
4. **Van Deurzen**, *Existential Counselling*, 6–7, 18, 19.
5. **Van Deurzen**, *Existential Counselling*, 6.
6. **Van Deurzen**, *Existential Counselling*, 6.
7. **Van Deurzen**, *Existential Counselling*, 2.
8. **Van Deurzen**, *Existential Counselling*, 6, 10–11, 18.
9. **Van Deurzen**, *Existential Counselling*, 136.
10. **Van Deurzen**, *Existential Counselling*, 2.
11. **Van Deurzen**, *Existential Counselling*, 3.
12. **Van Deurzen**, *Existential Counselling*, 8–9, 11, 13–14, 21.
13. **Martin Heidegger**, *Zollikon Seminars: Protocols–Conversations–Letters*, ed. Medard Boss, trans. Franz Mayer and Richard Askay (Evanston, IL: Northwestern University Press, 2001), 157, 160.
14. **Charles Taylor**, "The Moral Topography of the Self," in *Hermeneutics and Psychological Theory: Interpretive Perspectives on Personality, Psychotherapy, and Psychopathology*, eds. Stanley B. Messer, Louis A. Sass, and Robert Woolfolk (New Brunswick: Rutgers University Press, 1988), 300.
15. **Van Deurzen**, *Existential Counselling*, 25.
16. **Van Deurzen**, *Existential Counselling*, 25.
17. **Van Deurzen**, *Existential Counselling*, 43, 48.
18. **Van Deurzen**, *Existential Counselling*, 87.
19. **Van Deurzen**, *Existential Counselling*, 87.
20. **Van Deurzen**, *Existential Counselling*, 50.
21. **Van Deurzen**, *Existential Counselling*, 88, 91.
22. **Van Deurzen**, *Existential Counselling*, 11.
23. Cf. **Christine Swanton**, *Virtue Ethics: A Pluralistic View* (Oxford: Oxford University Press, 2003), 145.

24. **Emmy van Deurzen** and **Raymond Kenward**, *Dictionary of Existential Psychotherapy and Counselling* (London: Sage Publications, 2005), 71.
25. **Cooper**, *Existential Therapies*, 112.
26. **Van Deurzen**, *Existential Counselling*, 62–92.
27. **Van Deurzen**, *Existential Counselling*, 94, 125.
28. **Julia Annas**, *The Morality of Happiness* (Oxford: Oxford University Press, 1993), 124.
29. **Cooper**, *Existential Therapies*, 117.
30. **Van Deurzen**, *Existential Counselling*, 54.
31. **Cooper**, *Existential Therapies*, 117; Emmy van Deurzen, *Everyday Mysteries: Existential Dimensions of Psychotherapy* (London: Routledge, 1997), 70.
32. **Van Deurzen**, *Everyday Mysteries*, 281.
33. **Van Deurzen**, *Everyday Mysteries*, 183.
34. **Van Duerzen**, *Existential Counselling*, 3.
35. **Van Duerzen**, *Existential Counselling*, 94–105.
36. **Van Duerzen**, *Existential Counselling*, 109, 139.
37. **Van Deurzen**, *Everyday Mysteries*, 101.
38. **Van Deurzen**, *Everyday Mysteries*, 183.
39. **Van Deurzen**, *Everyday Mysteries*, 124.
40. **David M. Clarke** and **David W. Kissane**, "Demoralization: Its Phenomenology and Importance," *Australian and New Zealand Journal of Psychiatry* 36 (2002): 734.
41. **Clarke** and **Kissane**, "Demoralization: Its Phenomenology and Importance," 733. See also Jerome Frank, "Psychotherapy: The Restoration of Morale," *American Journal of Psychiatry* 131 (1974): 271–274.
42. **Clarke** and **Kissane**, "Demoralization: Its Phenomenology and Importance," 736, 739.
43. **John M. de Figueiredo**, "Depression and Demoralization: Phenomenologic Differences and Research Perspectives," *Comprehensive Psychiatry* 34 (1993): 309. Clarke sees demoralization as a subtype of depression: David M. Clarke, "Depression, Demoralization, and Psychotherapy in People Who Are Medically Ill," in *The Psychotherapy of Hope: The Legacy of Persuasion and Healing*, eds. Renato D. Alarcon and Julia B. Frank (Baltimore: Johns Hopkins University Press, 2012), 125–157.
44. **Donald F. Klein** and **J.M. Davis**, *Diagnosis and Drug Treatment of Psychiatric Disorders* (Baltimore: Williams and Wilkins, 1969), 175–176.
45. **Clarke** and **Kissane**, "Demoralization: Its Phenomenology and Importance," 737.
46. **Clarke**, "Depression, Demoralization, and Psychotherapy in People Who Are Medically Ill," 139.
47. Cf. **John M. de Figueiredo** and **Jerome D. Frank**, "Subjective Incompetence: The Clinical Hallmark of Demoralization," *Comprehensive Psychiatry* 23 (1982): 355.
48. **Clarke** "Depression, Demoralization, and Psychotherapy in People Who Are Medically Ill," 144.
49. **Antonia Macaro**, *Reason, Virtue and Psychotherapy* (West Sussex: John Wiley and Sons, 2006), 31, 33, 38, 44–45, 79.

50. **James L. Griffith** and **Anjali Dsouza**, "Demoralization and Hope in Clinical Psychiatry and Psychotherapy," in *The Psychotherapy of Hope: The Legacy of Persuasion and Healing*, eds. Renato D. Alarcon and Julia B. Frank (Baltimore: Johns Hopkins University Press, 2012), 161.
51. **Griffith** and **Dsouza**, "Demoralization and Hope in Clinical Psychiatry and Psychotherapy," 164.
52. **Griffith** and **Dsouza**, "Demoralization and Hope in Clinical Psychiatry and Psychotherapy," 163.
53. **Griffith** and **Dsouza**, "Demoralization and Hope in Clinical Psychiatry and Psychotherapy," 161.
54. **Griffith** and **Dsouza**, "Demoralization and Hope in Clinical Psychiatry and Psychotherapy," 164.
55. **Griffith** and **Dsouza**, "Demoralization and Hope in Clinical Psychiatry and Psychotherapy," 166.
56. **Griffith** and **Dsouza**, "Demoralization and Hope in Clinical Psychiatry and Psychotherapy," 175.
57. **Claudio Neri**, "Authenticity as an Aim of Psychoanalysis," *American Journal of Psychoanalysis* 68 (2008): 325–349; William H.J. Martens, "A Theoretical Model of Fragile Authenticity Structure," *International Journal of Philosophical Practice* 2(3) (2004): 1–18; Leston Havens, "A Theoretical Basis for the Concepts of Self and Authentic Self," *Journal of the American Psychoanalytic Association* 34 (1986): 363–378; M. Guy Thompson, "Vicissitudes of Authenticity in the Psychoanalytic Situation," *Contemporary Psychoanalysis* 42 (2006): 139. See also M. Guy Thompson, "The Way of Authenticity and the Quest for Personal Integrity," *European Journal of Psychotherapy and Counseling* 7(3) (2005): 143–157.
58. **Jaimie Mclean**, "Psychotherapy with a Narcissistic Patient Using Kohut's Self Psychology Model," *Psychiatry* 4 (2007): 40–47.
59. **Elizabeth Lunbeck**, *The Americanization of Narcissism* (Cambridge, MA: Harvard University Press, 2014), 190, 194; Heinz Kohut, *The Restoration of the Self* (Chicago: The University of Chicago Press, 1977), 249, 266, 302, 311.
60. **Heinz Kohut**, *The Analysis of the Self: A Systematic Approach to the Psychoanalytic Treatment of Narcissistic Personality Disorders* (Chicago: The University of Chicago Press, 1971), 22–23, 62, 86, 150, 192–193, 229–230.
61. **Kohut**, *The Restoration of the Self*, 152.
62. **Ronald Dworkin**, *Sovereign Virtue*, 270–271; Charles Taylor, "The Moral Topography of the Self" 300.
63. **Morris N. Eagle**, *Recent Developments in Psychoanalysis: A Critical Evaluation* (New York: McGraw-Hill, 1984), 72–73.
64. **Lunbeck**, *The Americanization of Narcissism*, 38–39; Christopher Lasch, *Culture of Narcissism: American Life in an Age of Diminishing Expectations* (New York: Norton, 1978).
65. Cf. **Charles Hanly**, "Logical and Conceptual Problems of Existential Psychiatry," *The Journal of Nervous and Mental Disease* 173 (1985): 265. Hanly saw Kohut's self-psychology as part of a broad movement away from Freudian metapsychology and the instinctual unconscious, a movement that included existential psychology. Others

have drawn more explicit connections between existentialism and self-psychology, e.g., Mary L. Gottesfeld, "The Self-Psychology of Heinz Kohut: An Existential Reading," *Clinical Social Work Journal* 12 (1984): 283–287.

66. **Kohut**, *The Analysis of the Self*, 120, 296–297,108, 192, 258–259, 101, 325.
67. **Kohut**, *The Restoration of the Self*, 138–139, 284–285.
68. **Kohut**, *The Restoration of the Self*, 241.
69. **Kohut**, *The Analysis of the Self*, 299, 308, 324.
70. Cf. **Swanton**, *Virtue Ethics*, 161-173.
71. **Kohut**, *The Restoration of the Self*, 18, 283–284.
72. **Lunbeck**, *The Americanization of Narcissism*, 4, 55, 84–85.
73. **Kohut**, *The Analysis of the Self*, 192.
74. **Paul H. Ornstein**, "Heinz Kohut's Vision of the Essence of Humanness," in *Psychoanalytic Versions of the Human Condition: Philosophies of Life and Their Impact on Practice*, eds. Paul Marcus and Alan Rosenberg (New York: New York University Press, 1998), 215.
75. **John Davenport**, *Will as Commitment and Resolve: An Existential Account of Creativity, Love, Virtue, and Happiness* (New York: Fordham University Press, 2007), 472, 475–477.
76. **Kohut**, *The Analysis of the Self*, 299.
77. **Lori Seeler, Arthur Freeman, Raymond DiGiuseppe**, and **Damon Mitchell**, "Traditional Cognitive-Behavioral Therapy Models for Antisocial Patterns," in *Forensic CBT: A Handbook for Clinical Practice*, eds. Raymond Chip Tafrate and Damon Mitchell (Malden, MA: John Wiley and Sons, 2014), 15.
78. **Keith S. Dobson** and **Nasreen Khatri**, "Cognitive Therapy: Looking Backward, Looking Forward," *Journal of Clinical Psychology* 56 (2000): 908.
79. **Keith S. Dobson** and **L. Block**, "Historical and Philosophical Bases of the Cognitive-Behavioral Therapies," in *Handbook of Cognitive-Behavioral Therapies*, ed. Keith S. Dobson (New York: Guilford, 1988), 3–38. See also David B. Wilson, Leana Allen Bouffard, and Doris L. Mackenzie, "A Quantitative Review of Structured, Group-Oriented, Cognitive-Behavioral Programs for Offenders," *Criminal Justice and Behavior* 33 (2005): 173.
80. **Wilson, Bouffard,** and **Mackenzie**, "A Quantitative Review of Structured, Group-Oriented, Cognitive-Behavioral Programs for Offenders," 173. See also Donald H. Meichenbaum, "Cognitive-Behavioral Therapy in Historical Perspective," in *Comprehensive Textbook of Psychotherapy: Theory and Practice*, eds. Bruce Bongar and Larry Beutler (New York: Oxford University Press, 1995), 140–158.
81. **Gary Greenberg**, *Manufacturing Depression: The Secret History of a Modern Disease* (New York: Simon and Schuster, 2010), 316.
82. Cf. **Brad K. Wilburn**, "Moral Self-Improvement," in *Moral Cultivation: Essays on the Development of Character and Virtue*, ed. Brad K. Wilburn (Plymouth, UK: Lexington Books, 2007), 69–84.
83. **Louis Charland**, "Character: Moral Treatment and the Personality Disorders," in *The Philosophy of Psychiatry: A Companion*, ed. Jennifer Radden (Oxford: Oxford University Press, 2004), 74.
84. **Charland**, "Character: Moral Treatment and the Personality Disorders," 73.

85. **Daniel O. David** and **Arthur Freeman**, "Overview of Cognitive-Behavioral Therapy of Personality Disorders," in *Cognitive Therapy of Personality Disorders*, eds. Aaron T. Beck, Denise D. Davis, and Arthur Freeman. 3rd ed. (New York: The Guilford Press, 2015), 11.
86. **Denise D. Davis** and **Arthur Freeman**, "Synthesis and Prospects for the Future," in *Cognitive Therapy of Personality Disorders*, eds. Aaron T. Beck, Denise D. Davis, and Arthur Freeman. 3rd ed. (New York: The Guilford Press, 2015), 432, 435.
87. **Wendy T. Behary** and **Denise D. Davis**, "Narcissistic Personality Disorder," in *Cognitive Therapy of Personality Disorders*, eds. Aaron T. Beck, Denise D. Davis, and Arthur Freeman. 3rd ed. (New York: The Guilford Press, 2015), 313.
88. **Arnoud Arntz**, "Borderline Personality Disorder," in *Cognitive Therapy of Personality Disorders*, eds. Aaron T. Beck, Denise D. Davis, and Arthur Freeman. 3rd ed. (New York: The Guilford Press, 2015), 374.
89. **Isabel Dziobek, Sandra Preissler, Zarko Grozdanovic, Isabella Heuser, Hauke R. Heekeren**, and **Stefan Roepke**, "Neuronal Correlates of Altered Empathy and Social Cognition in Borderline Personality Disorder," *Neuroimage* 57 (2011): 539–548.
90. **Arntz**, "Borderline Personality Disorder," 372–373.
91. **Damon Mitchell, Raymond Chip Tarfrate**, and **Arthur Freeman**, "Antisocial Personality Disorder," in *Cognitive Therapy of Personality Disorders*, eds. Aaron T. Beck, Denise D. Davis, and Arthur Freeman. 3rd ed. (New York: The Guilford Press, 2015), 350, 352.
92. **Mitchell, Tarfrate,** and **Freeman**, "Antisocial Personality Disorder," 359.
93. **Mitchell, Tarfrate,** and **Freeman**, "Antisocial Personality Disorder," 360.
94. **Charland**, "Character: Moral Treatment and the Personality Disorders," 72.
95. **Charland**, "Character: Moral Treatment and the Personality Disorders," 72.
96. Cf. **Charland**, "Character: Moral Treatment and the Personality Disorders," 73.
97. **Wilson, Bouffard,** and **Mackenzie**, "A Quantitative Review of Structured, Group-Oriented, Cognitive-Behavioral Programs for Offenders," 180.
98. **Gregory L. Little** and **Kenneth D. Robinson**, "Moral Reconation Therapy: A Systematic, Step-By-Step Treatment System for Treatment Resistant Clients," *Psychological Reports* 62 (1988): 135–136, 144–147.
99. **Gregory L. Little** and **Kenneth D. Robisnson**, "Effects of Moral Reconation Therapy upon Moral Reasoning, Life Purpose, and Recidivism among Drug and Alcohol Offenders," *Psychological Reports* 64 (1989): 84.
100. **Kenneth W. Wanberg** and **Harvey B. Milkman**, "Social and Community Responsibility Therapy (SCRT): A Cognitive-Behavioral Model for the Treatment of Substance-Abusing Judicial Clients," in *Forensic CBT: A Handbook for Clinical Practice*, eds. Raymond Chip Tafrate and Damon Mitchell (Malden, MA: John Wiley and Sons, 2014), 253, 264.
101. **Wanberg** and **Milkman**, "Social and Community Responsibility Therapy," 266.
102. **Clare-Ann Fortune** and **Tony Ward**, "Integrating Strength-Based Practice with Forensic CBT: The Good Lives Model of Offender Rehabilitation," in *Forensic CBT: A Handbook for Clinical Practice*, eds. Raymond Chip Tafrate and Damon Mitchell (Malden, MA: John Wiley and Sons, 2014), 438–439.

103. **Wanberg** and **Milkman**, "Social and Community Responsibility Therapy," 252.
104. **Glenn D. Walters**, "Applying CBT to the Criminal Thought Process," in *Forensic CBT: A Handbook for Clinical Practice*, eds. Raymond Chip Tafrate and Damon Mitchell (Malden, MA: John Wiley and Sons, 2014), 112.
105. **Marije Keulen-de Vos, David P. Bernstein,** and **Arnold Arntz**, "Schema Therapy for Aggressive Offenders with Personality Disorders," in *Forensic CBT: A Handbook for Clinical Practice*, eds. Raymond Chip Tafrate and Damon Mitchell (Malden, MA: John Wiley and Sons, 2014), 76. See also Daryl G. Kroner and Robert D. Morgan, "An Overview of Strategies for the Assessment and Treatment of Criminal Thinking," in *Forensic CBT: A Handbook for Clinical Practice*, eds. Raymond Chip Tafrate and Damon Mitchell (Malden, MA: John Wiley and Sons, 2014), 96, 103. See also Wanberg and Milkman, "Social and Community Responsibility Therapy," 262–266.
106. **Swanton**, *Virtue Ethics*, 19–30.
107. Cf. **Christine Swanton**, "Comments on Intelligent Virtue: Rightness and Exemplars of Virtue," *Journal of Value Inquiry* 49 (2015): 311, 313.
108. **Wanberg** and **Milkman**, "Social and Community Responsibility Therapy (SCRT)," 254.
109. **Wanberg** and **Milkman**, "Social and Community Responsibility Therapy (SCRT)," 263–266.
110. **Wanberg** and **Milkman**, "Social and Community Responsibility Therapy (SCRT)," 254.
111. **Wanberg** and **Milkman**, "Social and Community Responsibility Therapy (SCRT)," 254–256, 262.
112. **Wanberg** and **Milkman**, "Social and Community Responsibility Therapy (SCRT)," 255.
113. **Wanberg** and **Milkman**, "Social and Community Responsibility Therapy (SCRT)," 271.
114. **Swanton**, *Virtue Ethics*, 252.
115. **Swanton**, *Virtue Ethics*, 260, 258.
116. Cf. **Swanton**, *Virtue Ethics*, 260–261, 265.
117. Cf. **Swanton**, *Virtue Ethics*, 261.
118. Cf. **Swanton**, *Virtue Ethics*, 253, 258, 264.
119. **Anthony Bateman** and **Peter Fonagy**, *Psychotherapy for Borderline Personality Disorder: Mentalization-Based Treatment* (Oxford: Oxford University Press, 2004).
120. Cf. **Steve Pearce** and **Hanna Pickard**, "The Moral Content of Psychiatric Treatment," *The British Journal of Psychiatry* 195 (2009): 281.
121. **Bateman** and **Fonagy**, *Psychotherapy for Borderline Personality Disorder*, 1.
122. **Bateman** and **Fonagy**, *Psychotherapy for Borderline Personality Disorder*, 3–4, 56, 85.
123. **Bateman** and **Fonagy**, *Psychotherapy for Borderline Personality Disorder*, 55–56, 58.
124. **Bateman** and **Fonagy**, *Psychotherapy for Borderline Personality Disorder*, 70, 74.
125. **Bateman** and **Fonagy**, *Psychotherapy for Borderline Personality Disorder*, 302.
126. **Anthony Bateman** and **Peter Fonagy**, *Mentalization-Based Treatment for Borderline Personality Disorder: A Practical Guide* (Oxford: Oxford University Press, 2006), 132–134.

127. **Bateman** and **Fonagy**, *Psychotherapy for Borderline Personality Disorder*, 84.
128. **Iris Murdoch**, *The Sovereignty of the Good* (London: Routledge, 1970), 84; cf. Swanton, *Virtue Ethics*, 113.
129. **Bateman** and **Fonagy**, *Psychotherapy for Borderline Personality Disorder*, 97; cf. Sigmund Freud, "On Narcicissm: An Introduction," in *The Standard Edition of the Complete Psychological Works of Sigmund Freud*, trans. and ed. James Strachey (London: Hogarth Press, 1914), 67–104.
130. **Batemen** and **Fonagy**, *Psychotherapy for Borderline Personality Disorder*, 85.
131. **Bateman** and **Fonagy**, *Psychotherapy for Borderline Personality Disorder*, 102.
132. **Bateman** and **Fonagy**, *Psychotherapy for Borderline Personality Disorder*, 163, 203, 221–223; Anthony Bateman and Peter Fonagy, *Mentalization-Based Treatment for Borderline Personality Disorder: A Practical Guide* (Oxford: Oxford University Press, 2006), 37.
133. **Bateman** and **Fonagy**, *Mentalization-Based Treatment for Borderline Personality Disorder: A Practical Guide*, 12.
134. **Bateman** and **Fonagy**, *Mentalization-Based Treatment for Borderline Personality Disorder: A Practical Guide*, 68; Anthony W. Bateman and Peter Fonagy, "Mentalization-Based Treatment of Borderline Personality Disorder," in *The Oxford Handbook of Personality Disorders*, ed. Thomas A. Widiger (Oxford: Oxford University Press, 2012), 774.
135. **Bateman** and **Fonagy**, *Mentalization-Based Treatment for Borderline Personality Disorder: A Practical Guide*, 93, 119.
136. **Bateman** and **Fonagy**, "Mentalization-Based treatment of Borderline Personality Disorder," 771–772.
137. **Bateman** and **Fonagy**, *Psychotherapy for Borderline Personality Disorder*, 220.
138. **Jon G. Allen**, "Mentalizing in Practice," in *Handbook of Mentalization-Based Treatment*, eds. Jon G. Allen and Peter Fonagy (Chichester, UK: Wiley and Sons, 2006), 3-30; Bateman and Fonagy, "Mentalization-Based Treatment of Borderline Personality Disorder," 771.
139. **Throstur Bjorgvinsson** and **John Hart**, "Cognitive Behavioral Therapy Promotes Mentalizing," in *Handbook of Mentalization-Based Treatment*, eds. Jon G. Allen and Peter Fonagy (Chichester, UK: Wiley and Sons, Ltd., 2006), 169, 161. Baterman and Fonagy note differences between MBT and CBT in *Mentalization-Based Treatment for Borderline Personality Disorder: A Practical Guide*, 160.
140. **Allen**, "Mentalizing in Practice," 17.
141. **Allen**, "Mentalizing in Practice," 23.
142. **Jon G. Allen**, "Psychotherapy: The Artful Use of Science," *Smith College Studies in Social Work* 78 (2008): 176.
143. **Jon G. Allen**, *Coping with Trauma: Hope through Understanding*, 2nd ed. (Washington, DC: American Psychiatric Publishing, 2006), 293, 246. See also Allen, "Mentalizing in Practice," 23.
144. **Allen**, "Mentalizing in Practice," 23. Allen refers to Murdoch's *The Sovereignty of the Good*.

145. **Allen**, "Mentalizing in Practice," 21.
146. **Allen**, "Mentalizing in Practice," 22.
147. **Allen**, "Mentalizing in Practice," 22–23.
148. **Allen**, "Mentalizing in Practice," 23.
149. **Bateman** and **Fonagy**, *Mentalization-Based Treatment for Borderline Personality Disorder: A Practical Guide*, 5.
150. **Allen**, "Mentalizing in Practice," 13.
151. **Lois W. Choi-Kain** and **John G. Gunderson**, "Mentalization: Ontogeny, Assessment, and Application in the Treatment of Borderline Personality Disorder," *American Journal of Psychiatry* 165 (2008): 1131.
152. **Allen**, "Psychotherapy: The Artful Use of Science," 174.
153. **Allen**, "Psychotherapy: The Artful Use of Science," 176.
154. **Richard F. Summers** and **Jacques P. Barber**, *Psychodynamic Therapy: A Guide to Evidence-Based Practice* (New York: The Guilford Press, 2010), 94.
155. **Summers** and **Barber**, *Psychodynamic Therapy*, 94.
156. **Summers** and **Barber**, *Psychodynamic Therapy*, 106.
157. **Summers** and **Barber**, *Psychodynamic Therapy*, 258.
158. **Summers** and **Barber**, *Psychodynamic Therapy*, 258.
159. **Summers** and **Barber**, *Psychodynamic Therapy*, 259.
160. **Summers** and **Barber**, *Psychodynamic Therapy*, 259.

Chapter 8

# Caveats, Summations, and Stones Left Unturned

Medication has no doubt played a central role in helping me manage my psychosis, but what has allowed me to see the meaning in my struggles—to make sense of everything that happened before and during the course of my illness, and to mobilize what strengths I may possess into a rich and productive life-is talk therapy. People like me with a thought disorder are not supposed to benefit much from this kind of treatment, a talk therapy oriented toward insight and based on a relationship. But I have.

Ellyn R. Saks, *The Centre Cannot Hold: My Journey through Madness.*[1]

The notion that virtues are relevant to psychotherapeutic praxis is not widely shared in the clinical community. There are, however, some signal acknowledgements. Wallwork claims that an analyst's "virtues are indispensable" to realizing the internal goods of psychoanalytic praxis. He cites empathic respect, benign and tolerant curiosity, emotional honesty, openness and humility, and self-control as virtues that facilitate an interpersonal and intrapsychic environment propitious to the analytic process. These "process virtues" are taught by the example of training analysts and supervisors, and foster the patient's capacities to self-reflect. Wallwork insists that an appreciation of the analyst's role-specific virtues "is needed to bring ethics to center stage from their isolation at the boundaries where they guard against boundary violations."[2] Radden and Sadler's role-specific psychiatrist virtues can easily be applied to those who do psychotherapy.[3] Summers and Barber argue for the relevance of therapist and patient virtues in psychodynamic praxis. Following the typology of Peterson and Seligman, they cite wisdom, courage, humanity, justice, temperance, and transcendence as virtues that are each composed of three to five character strengths, e.g., creativity, open-mindedness, and curiosity for the virtue of wisdom, and forgiveness, humility, and self-regulation for the virtue of temperance. This typology is applied to both therapist and patient. Since the problems that bring patients to psychotherapy typically diminish various character strengths, the therapist needs to work with the patient to revitalize them. Patients can also bring undiminished character strengths to therapy that can facilitate their work in building a therapeutic alliance, initiating processes of change, and maintaining resilience after cessation of treatment. The therapist's virtues facilitate this work by contributing to a "flexible, emotional, open, reflective" alliance.[4] Fowers argues for the relevance of Aristotelian virtue ethics to psychotherapeutic praxis, which he sees as advancing personal development and well-being that is ultimately aimed at flourishing in society.[5] I have also noted Allen's construal of Swanton's bonding virtue of self-love as the secure attachment with oneself that enables optimal, i.e., benevolent mentalization.[6] I have thus been navigating territory that has been explored by others and continues to be charted. I conclude by noting some of the parameters and limitations of my analysis.

I implicate a number of issues that have been explored elsewhere in greater detail. We know, for instance, that psychotherapy works but there is ongoing debate about how. This controversy pivots on two models of therapeutic dialogue: the medical model and the contextual one. The medical model holds that psychotherapy works by inducing theory-specific treatment effects for patients with specific diagnoses. Think of these as interaction effects that would be delivered by the key techniques of the psychotherapy. These effects are held to reflect adherence to a treatment protocol which supposedly ensures that the unique techniques of the psychotherapy are faithfully applied.[7] The contextual model challenges the idea that there are techniques unique to any psychotherapy. Jerome Frank's pioneering account delineated the common features of the therapeutic relationship and context shared by all psychotherapies, which features arguably contribute to their success. The contextual model proposed by Wampold holds that psychotherapy induces benefits via pan-theoretical common factors shared by any mode of therapeutic dialogue, e.g., the therapist–patient alliance, the therapist's allegiance to a theoretical orientation, and the patient's belief in it.[8]

A comprehensive engagement with this debate is beyond my current scope. With its emphasis on hope, Frank's account might be more amenable than it seems initially to the cultivation of healing virtues as therapeutic factors. The patient's belief in the tenets of the particular psychotherapy they endorse might be construed in normative terms as the result of an inquiry regulated by epistemic virtues, i.e., patients should evaluate their plausibility and justificatory warrant. In triadic analysis cases, psychotherapy is as much about generic ethical improvement and education as it is about alleviating psychological distress. The contextual model shifts the emphasis on the main contributing factor in successful treatment from what therapists supposedly know about their patients to what they do with them, i.e., to how they relate to patients in a therapeutic alliance. Since that alliance only works interpersonally, I offer a qualified focus on what the patient does.

My account applies to patients who commit to psychotherapy in an ongoing effort to better know themselves and to affect ethically desirable changes (1) in their tendencies of affective/emotional response; (2) in their understanding of how one should treat oneself and/or others; and (3) in their patterns of behavior. These cases can revolve significantly around the self-regarding responsibility of patients to find the right values to live by. A quest for authenticity aspires to self-knowledge. Self-knowledge of one's core aspects, holistic self-understanding, or even beliefs with a strong warrant for being possibly true, are not completely separable from the effort to affect ethically desirable changes in (1) through (3). Insofar as they reflect facets of who you are and who you strive to be, you have to know something about yourself to choose the right values to live by. Truth counts for many patients who commit to changing themselves for the better. Or as Camus put it, "if not truth itself, at least the effort toward truthfulness."[9] In those cases that can be explicated in virtue epistemic and ethical terms, this effort is at least moderately demanding. While my account does not entail perfectionism, the patient's ongoing efforts would require sufficient degrees of perseverance. My analysis would exclude the many patients who seek therapy only to rid themselves of annoying traits or habits that do not diminish generic ethical character strengths or take moral advantage of others. Someone who wants to overcome a fear of public speaking or wide-open spaces may otherwise be living quite authentically with sufficient degrees of self-love and empathic respect for others.

While I have proclaimed the idea that truth matters to many psychotherapy patients, I do not think it always matters at any cost. Hence my reluctance to assume that self-knowledge is always good for someone. It may come at a cost that is too great for some to bear. One idea behind psychodynamic therapy is that acquiring knowledge of how and why one became disturbed enables one to start containing one's problems instead of being contained by them.[10] But there might be instances of self-knowledge that you can live without. Knowing why you changed for the worse does not entail that you will change for the better. Apparently, some people are better able to do the latter when they know the former. But suppose that re-examining your past is not the way to get beyond it; suppose that such effort would further mire your past in the present. There seems little point in roiling in dark waters if it won't help you drain the swamp. There can also be cases where self-knowledge should wait; where the immediate focus should be on changing harmful behaviors to protect self and others. If one has a compulsion to behave abusively, then successful efforts at self-control might clear a more propitious space for reflection on one's core aspects. They might also better enable one to face a later psychodynamic exploration with confidence. Seneca's Angry Man might have preferred to start with cognitive behavior therapy to contain his symptoms. Much will depend on how patients want to contain their problems. Those who see their problems as coextensive with their symptoms may have little motivating interest in psychodynamic exploration.

I concede that some talking cures can contribute to what Lasch termed a "culture of narcissism" and I regard this as a problem that a reconceived psychotherapy must address.[11] But I deny that psychotherapy will necessarily make that contribution and argue that it can and should be avoided. Acknowledging the close connections between some psychotherapeutic praxes and the moral improvement of one's other-regarding attitudes and behavior is arguably one way to do this.[12] A virtue ethical conception of psychotherapy might be well suited to reminding us that our developmental capacities will not be adequately realized without some degree of intimate and communal involvement with others. I see no necessary connection between psychotherapy and the promotion of an atomistic, unencumbered self and the amorality, instrumental rationality, and self-absorption of Rieff's "psychological man." Like Rieff, I regard the "triumph of the therapeutic" as a perilous victory and am not without sympathy for what he termed a "therapy of commitment," although I think the communitarian implications of that notion can be modified by a more liberal and pluralistic approach to virtue ethics.[13] That approach "requires a normative picture of what a good human being should be like" and thus requires endorsing "some conceptions of the good."[14] As such, "it provides a rationale for seeking to make people into new, self-governing versions of themselves while respecting their rights to their own plans and beliefs."[15] I find this line of thought to be echoed currently in Dworkin's attempt to recapture an ethic of self-affirmation from which responsibilities to others are derived.[16]

I am wary of easy assumptions that contemporary concerns about "self-discovery" and "psychic growth" represent "unseemly self-absorption" in "private life at the expense of public life."[17] There might be much that is wrong with our socio-cultural influences that psychotherapy can help us to understand. The view that contemporary society does much to hinder the development of healthy private life merits careful consideration. If psychotherapy can acknowledge and delineate how socialization can reproduce "political domination at the level of personal experience," then psychotherapy need not intensify the malady it could aim to alleviate.[18] The social phenomenology of R.D. Laing was intended to inform a psychotherapy that aimed to clarify any interpersonal or social origins of a patient's suffering.[19] I think there is still much work to be done here. As per Woolfolk and Murphy, I see the "relation between psychotherapy and culture" as "one of reciprocal influence. Psychotherapy absorbs and reflects the culture of which it is a part while, at the same time, it places its own distinctive imprint on that culture."[20] A psychotherapeutic relationship might be one in which cultural influences on the psyche are questioned, as opposed to reinforced. It might also provide a temporary "haven from a heartless world"[21] and enable patients to develop the character strengths to better deal with it.

I agree with those who claim that virtue ethics has not been brought to its knees by the situationist critique.[22] Some question whether the concept of character is viable enough to sustain virtue ethics. Situationists conclude that their empirical findings seriously undermine the existence of character traits, let alone the virtues. Other philosophers have questioned whether this critique is viable enough to sustain that conclusion. Situationists arguably fall short of both refuting the existence of virtues (i.e., it does not follow from the fact that some people add badly that there are no sums) and offering relevant empirical evidence that people do not exhibit them with cross-situational consistency. Sreenivasan contends that the behavioral measures they use to generate empirical data about character traits do not properly operationalize virtuous ones.[23] Situationists might be successful in refuting character traits that license predictions on the basis of objective, normatively insensitive behavioral measures that are taken from the "widest range of measures minimally associated with the trait[s] by common sense."[24] But this is not the conception of character traits that virtue ethicists endorse. A virtue is more than a single-track disposition to perform acts of a certain type, e.g., benevolent ones. It is rather a multi-track disposition involving a complex mindset of "fine inner states" that inform an array of emotional responses, desires, motivations, reasons, and values. We arguably lack the relevant empirical evidence to vindicate the situationists' claim that "not enough people have any virtues."[25] I side with Swanton: situationist personality psychology "has not removed virtue ethics from the moral-theoretic landscape."[26]

The connections I have made to the positive psychology movement are adumbrative and indicate the need for further empirical study and conceptual elaboration. A more detailed engagement with this issue is also beyond my current scope. I settle here for noting some cogent reservations about this burgeoning movement. Critics argue that positive psychology might become "another passing fad" unless it pays greater attention to foundational issues, e.g., "how we can speak to questions of human character and the good life in a pluralistic society, and how we can clarify the nature of human agency and responsibility despite some quite different views of them across cultures."[27] These issues are also relevant to current work in virtue ethics. Positive psychologists and philosophers alike should avoid "hastily" and "naively" universalizing their "particular cultural preferences and ideals as good for or applicable to all human communities," e.g., the "one-sided individualism" of North American society "with its stress on personal autonomy and individually-defined fulfillment."[28] A culturally sensitive and socially critical positive psychology may yet achieve gains in understanding the means of better human and community development. Much remains to be seen, as positive psychology "is a work in progress and in flux."[29] My own worst case scenario would see positive psychology become the New Age alternative to cosmetic psychopharmacology: where Prozac can make you better than well, cultivating virtues can make you better than good. I am not convinced it has to come to that.

I close with some brief remarks on psychotherapy's relevance to the era of biological psychiatry. The biopsychiatric approach arguably minimizes the relevance of lived experience in favour of a detached, often reductionist third-person emphasis on biochemical etiology. At least one recent critique has concluded that contemporary biopsychiatry is a "spectacular failure."[30] If biopsychiatry has lost sight of lived experience as an explanandum in its own right, then a truly humanized psychiatry needs to utilize first-person phenomenology in the therapeutic encounter.[31] Psychotherapy can balance a focus on the biochemical treatment of mental disorders with a renewed dialogical focus on a phenomenology of personal meaning. Much of that meaning will involve a patient's ethical evaluation of how her life is going, and where it should be going overall.

Psychotherapy can reveal much about persons that is not virtuous, but it might also show how virtues can heal. Yeats wrote of the heart's rag and bone shop, the place to which we descend when our ladders to better states of mind are lost, and the place from which all such ladders begin.[32] Healing virtues might enable patients to build new ladders and leave the rag and bone shop behind.

## Notes

1. **Ellyn R. Saks**, *The Center Cannot Hold: My Journey through Madness* (New York: Hyperion, 2007), 331.
2. **Ernest Wallwork**, "Ethics in Psychoanalysis," in *Textbook of Psychoanalysis*, eds. Glen O. Gabbard, Bonnie E. Litowitz, and Paul Williams. 2nd ed. (Washington, DC: American Psychiatric Publishing, 2012), 357–360.
3. **Jennifer Radden** and **John Z. Sadler**, *The Virtuous Psychiatrist: Character Ethics in Psychiatric Practice* (Oxford: Oxford University Press, 2010).
4. **Richard F. Summers** and **Jacques P. Barber**, *Psychodynamic Therapy: A Guide to Evidence-Based Practice* (New York: The Guilford Press, 2010), 94–97, 258–259; Christopher Peterson and Martin E. Seligman, *Character Strengths and Virtues: A Handbook and Classification* (New York: Oxford University Press, 2004).

5. **Blaine J. Fowers**, "Psychotherapy, Character, and the Good Life," in *Critical Thinking about Psychology: Hidden Assumptions and Plausible Alternatives*, eds. Brent D. Slife, Paul J. Reber, and Frank C. Richardson (Washington, DC: American Psychological Association Press, 2005), 39–59.
6. **Jon G. Allen**, "Psychotherapy: The Artful Use of Science," *Smith College Studies in Social Work* 78 (2008): 159–187.
7. **Stanley B. Messer** and **Bruce E. Wampold**, "Let's Face Facts: Common Factors Are More Potent than Specific Therapy Ingredients," *Clinical Psychology: Science and Practice* 9 (2002): 22–23. For a more comprehensive analysis endorsing the contextual model, see Bruce E. Wampold, *The Great Psychotherapy Debate: Models, Methods, and Findings* (Hillsdale, NJ: Lawrence Erlbaum Associates, 2001).
8. **Jerome D. Frank** and **Julia B. Frank**, *Persuasion and Healing: A Comparative Study of Psychotherapy*, 3rd ed. (Baltimore: Johns Hopkins University Press, 1993); Messer and Wampold, "Let's Face Facts," 23.
9. Quoted in **Oliver Todd**, *Albert Camus: Un Vie* (Paris: Gallimard, 1996), 545.
10. I owe this point to Dr. Graeme J. Taylor.
11. **Christopher Lasch**, *The Culture of Narcissism: American Life in an Age of Diminished Expectations* (New York: W.W. Norton and Company, 1979).
12. **William J. Doherty**, *Soul Searching: Why Psychotherapy Must Promote Moral Responsibility* (New York: Basic Books, 1996). There is a distinctly communitarian perspective embedded in this account.
13. **Phillip Rieff**, *Freud: The Mind of the Moralist* (New York: Doubleday and Company, 1961) and *The Triumph of the Therapeutic: Uses of Faith after Freud* (Chicago: University of Chicago Press, 1987).
14. **Robert L. Woolfolk** and **Dominic Murphy**, "Axiological Foundations of Psychotherapy," *Journal of Psychotherapy Integration* 14 (2004):188.
15. **Woolfolk** and **Murphy**, "Axiological Foundations of Psychotherapy," 188.
16. **Ronald Dworkin**, *Justice for Hedgehogs* (Cambridge, MA: The Belknap Press of Harvard University Press, 2011), 13.
17. **Lasch**, *The Culture of Narcissism*, 30. I am grateful to an anonymous OUP reviewer for raising this point.
18. Cf. **Lasch**, *The Culture of Narcissism*, 30.
19. **Andrew Collier**, *R.D. Laing: The Philosophy and Politics of Psychotherapy* (New York: Pantheon Books, 1977).
20. **Woolfolk** and **Murphy**, "Axiological Foundations of Psychotherapy," 179.
21. **Lasch**, *The Culture of Narcissism*, 27.
22. **Duff R. Waring**, "Psychotherapy through the Prism of Moral Language," *Philosophy, Psychiatry, & Psychology* 19 (2012): 48. Copyright (c) 2012 The Johns Hopkins University Press. This article was first published in *Philosophy, Psychiatry, & Psychology* 19.1 (2012), 45–48. Reprinted with permission by Johns Hopkins University Press.
23. **Gopal Sreenivasan**, "Errors about Errors: Virtue Theory and Trait Attribution," *Mind* III(441) (2002): 54, 61–67.
24. **Sreenivasan**, "Errors about Errors: Virtue Theory and Trait Attribution," 64.

25. **Gopal Sreenivasan**, "The Situationist Critique of Virtue Ethics," in *The Cambridge Companion to Virtue Ethics*, ed. Daniel C. Russell (New York: Cambridge University Press, 2013), 311.
26. **Christine Swanton**, *Virtue Ethics: A Pluralistic View* (Oxford: Oxford University Press, 2003), 30-33.
27. **John Chambers Christopher**, **Frank C. Richardson**, and **Brent D. Sife**, "Thinking Through Positive Psychology," *Theory and Psychology* 18 (2008): 556.
28. **Christopher**, **Richardson**, and **Sife**, "Thinking Through Positive Psychology," 557.
29. For a detailed assessment from an Aristotelean perspective, see Kristjan Kristjansson, *The Virtues and Vices of Positive Psychology: A Philosophical Critique* (New York: Cambridge University Press, 2013), 230.
30. **Richard Bentall**, *Doctoring the Mind: Is Our Current Treatment of Mental Illness Really Any Good?* (New York: New York University Press, 2009), 264. See also Joel Paris, *Prescriptions for the Mind: A Critical View of Contemporary Psychiatry* (New York: Oxford University Press, 2009).
31. Cf. **Bill Fulford**, **Katherine Morris**, **John Sadler**, and **Giovanni Stanghellini**, "Past Improbable, Future Possible: The Renaissance in Philosophy and Psychiatry," in *Nature and Narrative: An Introduction to the New Philosophy of Psychiatry*, eds. Bill Fulford, Katherine Morris, John Sadler, and Giovanni Staghellini (Oxford: Oxford University Press, 2003), 1–41.
32. **William Butler Yeats**, "The Circus Animals' Desertion," in *The Collected Poems of W. B. Yeats*, ed. Richard J. Finneran (New York: Scribner Paperback Poetry, 1996), 346–347.

# Bibliography


**Adler, Alfred.** *Understanding Human Nature.* Translated by W.B. Wolfe. London: Allen & Unwin, 1932.

**Adshead, Gwen.** "Ethics in Psychotherapy." In *The Oxford Textbook of Psychotherapy*, edited by Glen O. Gabbard, Judith S. Beck, and Jeremy Holmes, 477–486. New York: Oxford University Press, USA, 2007.

**Allen, Jon G.** *Coping with Trauma: Hope through Understanding.* 2nd ed. Washington, DC: American Psychiatric Publishing, 2006.

**Allen, Jon G.** "Mentalizing in Practice." In *Handbook of Mentalization-Based Treatment*, edited by Jon G. Allen and Peter Fonagy, 3–30. West Sussex, UK: Wiley and Sons, 2006.

**Allen, Jon G.** "Psychotherapy: The Artful Use of Science." *Smith College Studies in Social Work* 78 (2008): 159–187.

**American Medical Association.** "On Patient Responsibilities." *Code of Ethics.* Section E-10.02., 1993 (updated June 1998, December 2000, and June 2001).

**American Psychiatric Association.** *Diagnostic and Statistical Manual of Mental Disorders.* 4th ed. Washington, DC: American PsychiatricPublishing, 1994.

**American Psychiatric Association.** *Diagnostic and Statistical Manual of Mental Disorders.* 4th ed. Text Revision. Washington, DC: American Psychiatric Publishing, 2000.

**American Psychiatric Association.** *Diagnostic and Statistical Manual of Mental Disorders.* 5th ed. Washington, DC: American Psychiatric Publishing, 2013.

**Annas, Julia.** *Intelligent Virtue.* Oxford: Oxford University Press, 2011.

**Annas, Julia.** *The Morality of Happiness.* Oxford: Oxford University Press, 1993.

**Anthony, William A.** "Recovery from Mental Illness: The Guiding Vision of the Mental Health Service System in the 1990s." *Psychosocial Rehabilitation Journal* 16 (1993): 11–23.

**Aristotle.** *Nichomachean Ethics.* Translated by Terrence Irwin. Cambridge: Hackett Publishing Company, 1985.

**Arntz, Arnoud,** "Borderline Personality Disorder." In *Cognitive Therapy of Personality Disorders*, edited by Aaron T. Beck, Denise D. Davis, and Arthur Freeman, 366–392. 3rd ed. New York: The Guilford Press, 2015.

**Axtell, Guy.** "Introduction." In *Knowledge, Belief, and Character: Readings in Virtue Epistemology*, edited by Guy Axtell, xi–xxix. New York: Rowman and Littlefield Publishers, 2000.

**Baier, Kurt.** *The Moral Point of View: A Rational Basis of Ethics.* Ithaca, NY: Cornell University Press, 1958.

**Bateman, Anthony** and **Peter Fonagy**. *Psychotherapy for Borderline Personality Disorder: Mentalization-Based Treatment.* Oxford: Oxford University Press, 2004.

**Bateman, Anthony** and **Peter Fonagy**. *Mentalization-Based Treatment for Borderline Personality Disorder: A Practical Guide.* Oxford: Oxford University Press, 2006.

**Bateman, Anthony** and **Peter Fonagy**. "Mentalization-Based Treatment of Borderline Personality Disorder." In *The Oxford Handbook of Personality Disorders*, edited by Thomas A. Widiger, 767–784. Oxford: Oxford University Press, 2012.

**Battaly, Heather D**. "Thin Concepts to the Rescue: Thinning the Concepts of Epistemic Justification and Virtue." In *Virtue Epistemology: Essays on Epistemic Virtue and Responsibility*, edited by Abrol Fairweather and Linda Zagzebski, 98–116. Oxford: Oxford University Press, 2001.

**Baumeister, Roy F.** *Meanings of Life*. New York: The Guilford Press, 1991.

**Beauchamp, Tom L.** and **James F. Childress**. *Principles of Biomedical Ethics*. 6th ed. Oxford: Oxford University Press, 2009.

**Beck, Judith S.** *Cognitive Therapy: Basics and Beyond*. 2nd ed. New York: Guilford, 2011.

**Behary, Wendy T.** and **Denise D. Davis**. "Narcissistic Personality Disorder." In *Cognitive Therapy of Personality Disorders*, edited by Aaron T. Beck, Denise D. Davis, and Arthur Freeman, 299–324. 3rd ed. New York: The Guilford Press, 2015.

**Bentall, Richard.** *Doctoring the Mind: Is Our Current Treatment of Mental Illness Really Any Good?* New York: New York University Press, 2009.

**Bieber, Irving**. "Psychoanalysis and Moral Values." In *Moral Values and the Superego Concept in Psychoanalysis*, edited by Seymour C. Post, 197–204. New York: International Universities Press, 1972.

**Binswanger, Ludwig.** *Being-in-the-World*. Translated by Jacob Needleman. New York: Harper and Row Publishers, 1968.

**Bion, Wilfred.** (1980). *Bion in New York and Sao Paulo*. Perthshire: Clunie Press, 1980.

**Bjorgvinsson, Throstur**, and **John Hart**. "Cognitive Behavioral Therapy Promotes Mentalizing." In *Handbook of Mentalization-Based Treatment*, edited by Jon G. Allen and Peter Fonagy, 157–170. Chichester, UK: Wiley and Sons, 2006.

**Bohart, Arthur C**. "Insight and the Active Client." In *Insight in Psychotherapy*, edited by Louis G. Castonguay and Clara E. Hill, 257–278. Washington, DC: American Psychological Association, 2002.

**Boniwell, Ilona**. "Perspectives on Time." In *The Oxford Handbook of Positive Psychology*, edited by Shane J. Lopez and Charles R. Snyder, 295–302. 2nd ed. Oxford: Oxford University Press, 2009.

**Bukowski, Charles.** *Ham on Rye*. Santa Rosa, CA: Black Sparrow Press, 1982.

**Camus, Albert.** *The Myth of Sisyphus and Other Essays*. Translated by Justin O'Brien. New York: Vintage Books, 1955.

**Cashman, Phillip.** *Constructing the Self, Constructing America: A Cultural History of Psychotherapy*. Cambridge, MA: Da Capo Press, 1995.

**Charland, Louis.** "Moral Nature of the DSM-IV Cluster B Personality Disorders." *Journal of Personality Disorders* 20 (2006): 116–125.

**Charland, Louis.** "Character: Moral Treatment and the Personality Disorders." In *The Philosophy of Psychiatry: A Companion*, edited by Jennifer Radden, 64–77. Oxford: Oxford University Press, 2004.

**Christopher, John C**. "Hermeneutics and the Moral Dimension of Psychotherapy." In *Culture, Psychotherapy, and Counselling: Critical and Integrative Perspectives*, edited by Lisa Tsoi Hoshmand, 179–203. Thousand Oaks, CA: Sage Publications, 2006.

**Christopher, John C., Frank C. Richardson,** and **Brent D. Sife.** "Thinking Through Positive Psychology." *Theory and Psychology* 18 (2008): 555–561.

**Choi-Kain, Lois W.,** and **John G. Gunderson.** "Mentalization: Ontogeny, Assessment, and Application in the Treatment of Borderline Personality Disorder." *American Journal of Psychiatry* 165 (2008): 1127–1135.

**Clarke, David M.** "Depression, Demoralization, and Psychotherapy in People Who Are Medically Ill." In *The Psychotherapy of Hope: The Legacy of Persuasion and Healing*, edited by Renato D. Alarcon and Julia B. Frank, 125–157. Baltimore: Johns Hopkins University Press, 2012.

**Clarke, David M.** and **David W. Kissane.** "Demoralization: Its Phenomenology and Importance." *Australian and New Zealand Journal of Psychiatry* 36 (2002): 733–742.

**Code, Lorraine.** *Epistemic Responsibility*. Hanover: University Press of New England, 1987.

**Code, Lorraine.** *What Can She Know? Feminist Theory and the Construction of Knowledge.* Ithaca, NY: Cornell University Press, 1991.

**Cohen, Elliot D.** and **Gale S. Cohen.** *The Virtuous Therapist: Ethical Practice of Counseling and Psychotherapy.* Pacific Grove, CA: Brooks Cole, 1998.

**Cohn, Hans W.** *Existential Thought and Therapeutic Practice: An Introduction to Existential Psychotherapy*. London: Sage Publications, 2002.

**Collier, Andrew.** *R.D. Laing: The Philosophy and Politics of Psychotherapy.* New York: Pantheon Books, 1977.

**Conrad, Dorothy C.** "Toward a More Productive Concept of Mental Health." *Mental Hygiene* 36 (1952): 456–473.

**Cooper, Mick.** *Existential Therapies.* London: Sage Publications, 2003.

**Crisp, Roger.** "Virtue Ethics and Virtue Epistemology." In *Virtue and Vice, Moral and Epistemic*, edited by Heather Battaly, 21–38. New York: John Wiley and Sons, 2010.

**Davenport, John J.** *Will as Commitment and Resolve: An Existential Account of Creativity, Love, Virtue, and Happiness.* New York: Fordham University Press, 2007.

**David, Daniel O.** and **Arthur Freeman.** "Overview of Cognitive-Behavioral Therapy of Personality Disorders." In *Cognitive Therapy of Personality Disorders*, edited by Aaron T. Beck, Denise D. Davis, and Arthur Freeman, 3–18. 3rd ed. New York: The Guilford Press, 2015.

**Davidson, Larry.** *Living Outside Mental Illness: Qualitative Studies of Recovery in Schizophrenia.* New York: New York University Press, 2003.

**Davidson, Larry** and **John S. Strauss.** "Sense of Self in Recovery from Severe Mental Illness." *British Journal of Medical Psychology* 65 (1992): 131–145.

**Davis, Denise D.** and **Arthur Freeman.** "Synthesis and Prospects for the Future." In *Cognitive Therapy of Personality Disorders*, edited by Aaron T. Beck, Denise D. Davis, and Arthur Freeman, 428–438. 3rd ed. New York: The Guilford Press, 2015.

**Davis, Christopher G.** and **Susan Nolen-Hoeksema.** "Making Sense of Loss, Perceiving Benefits, and Posttraumatic Growth." In *The Oxford Handbook of Positive Psychology*, edited by Shane J. Lopez and Charles R. Snyder, 641–650. 2nd ed. Oxford: Oxford University Press, 2009.

**Denis, Lara.** "Kant's Ethics and Duties to Oneself." *Pacific Philosophical Quarterly* 78 (1997): 321–348.

**Denis, Lara.** *Moral Self-Regard: Duties to Oneself in Kant's Moral Theory.* London: Routledge, 2001.

**DePaul, Michael** and **Linda Zagzebski**. "Introduction." In *Intellectual Virtue: Perspectives from Ethics and Epistemology*, edited by Michael DePaul and Linda Zagzebski, 1–12. Oxford: Oxford University Press, 2007.

**Diener, Ed.** "Positive Psychology: Past, Present, and Future." In *The Oxford Handbook of Positive Psychology*, edited by Shane J. Lopez and Charles R. Snyder, 7–12. 2nd ed. Oxford: Oxford University Press, 2009.

**DiGiuseppe, Raymond D.**, and **Raymond C. Tafrate**. *Understanding Anger Disorders.* New York: Oxford University Press, 2006.

**Dobson, Keith S.** and **Nasreen Khatri**. "Cognitive Therapy: Looking Backward, Looking Forward." *Journal of Clinical Psychology* 56 (2000): 907–923.

**Dobson, Keith S.** and **L. Block**. "Historical and Philosophical Bases of the Cognitive-Behavioral Therapies." In *Handbook of Cognitive-Behavioral Therapies*, edited by Keith S. Dobson, 3–38. New York: The Guilford Press, 1988.

**Doherty, William J.** *Soul Searching: Why Psychotherapy Must Promote Moral Responsibility.* New York: Basic Books, 1996.

**Dubyna, J.** and **C. Quin**. "The Self-Management of Psychiatric Medications: A Pilot Study." *Journal of Psychiatric and Mental Health Nursing* 3 (1996): 297–302.

**Dummett, Michael.** *Truth and Other Enigmas.* Cambridge, MA: Harvard University Press, 1978.

**Dunn, Dana S.**, **Gitendra Uswatte**, and **Timothy R. Elliott**. "Happiness, Resilience, and Positive Growth Following Physical Disability: Issues for Research, Understanding, and Therapeutic Intervention." In *The Oxford Handbook of Positive Psychology*, edited by Shane J. Lopez and Charles R. Snyder, 651–664. 2nd ed. Oxford: Oxford University Press, 2009.

**Dworkin, Ronald.** *Life's Dominion: An Argument about Abortion, Euthanasia, and Individual Freedom.* New York: Vintage Books, 1994.

**Dworkin, Ronald.** *Sovereign Virtue: The Theory and Practice of Equality.* Cambridge, MA: Harvard University Press, 2000.

**Dworkin, Ronald.** *Justice for Hedgehogs.* Cambridge, MA: The Belknap Press of Harvard University Press, 2011.

**Dziobek, Isabel**, et al. "Neuronal Correlates of Altered Empathy and Social Cognition in Borderline Personality Disorder." *Neuroimage* 57 (2011): 539–548.

**Eagle, Morris N.** "Psychoanalytic Interpretations: Veridicality and Therapeutic Effectiveness." *Nous* 14 (1980): 405–424.

**Eagle, Morris N.** *Recent Developments in Psychoanalysis: A Critical Evaluation.* New York: McGraw-Hill, 1984.

**Eagle, Morris N.** *From Classical to Contemporary Psychoanalysis: Critique and Integration.* New York: Routledge, 2011.

**Elliott, Carl.** "Caring About Risks: Are Severely Depressed Patients Competent to Consent to Research?" *Archives of General Psychiatry* 54 (1997): 113–116.

**Erikson, Erik H.** "Growth and Crises of the Healthy Personality." *Symposium on the Healthy Personality*, edited by Milton J.E. Senn, 91-146. New York: Josiah Macey Jr. Foundation, 1950.

**Falk, W.D.** "Morality, Self, and Others." In *Morality and the Language of Conduct*, edited by Hector-Neri Castaneda and George Nakhnikian, 25–68. Detroit: Wayne State University Press, 1963.

**Figueiredo, John M. de.** "Depression and Demoralization: Phenomenologic Differences and Research Perspectives." *Comprehensive Psychiatry* 34 (1993): 308–311.

**Figueiredo, John M. de** and **Jerome D. Frank.** "Subjective Incompetence: The Clinical Hallmark of Demoralization." *Comprehensive Psychiatry* 23 (1982): 353–363.

**Fingarette, Herbert.** *The Self in Transformation: Psychoanalysis, Philosophy and the Life of the Spirit.* New York: Harper and Row Publishers, 1965.

**Flaubert, Gustave.** *Madame Bovary.* Translated by Lydia Davis. New York: Viking Books, 2010.

**Fortune, Clare-Ann** and **Tony Ward.** "Integrating Strength-Based Practice with Forensic CBT: The Good Lives Model of Offender Rehabilitation." In *Forensic CBT: A Handbook for Clinical Practice*, edited by Raymond C. Tafrate and Damon Mitchell, 436–455. Malden, MA: John Wiley and Sons, 2014.

**Foucault, Michel.** *The History of Sexuality: An Introduction*, translated by Robert Hurley. New York: Vintage Books, 1978.

**Foucault, Michel.** *The Care of the Self: The History of Sexuality.* Vol. 3. Translated by Robert Hurley. New York: Vintage Books, 1986.

**Foucault, Michel.** "Technologies of the Self." In *Technologies of the Self: A Seminar with Michel Foucault*, edited by Luther H. Martin, Huck Gutman, and Patrick H. Hutton, 16–49. Amherst: University of Massachusetts Press, 1988.

**Foucault, Michel.** *The Hermeneutics of the Subject: Lectures at the College de France 1981–1982.* Edited by Frederic Gros. Translated by Graham Burchell. New York: Picador, 2005.

**Fowers, Blaine J.** "Psychotherapy, Character, and the Good Life." In *Critical Thinking About Psychology: Hidden Assumptions and Plausible Alternatives*, edited by Brent D. Slife, Paul J. Reber, and Frank C. Richardson, 39–59. Washington, DC: American Psychological Association Press, 2005.

**Fox Gordon, Emily.** *Book of Days: Personal Essays.* New York: Spiegal & Grau, 2010.

**Frank, Jerome D.**, and **Julia B. Frank.** *Persuasion and Healing: A Comparative Study of Psychotherapy.* 3rd ed. Baltimore: Johns Hopkins University Press, 1993.

**Frank, Jerome.** "Psychotherapy: The Restoration of Morale." *American Journal of Psychiatry* 131 (1974): 271–274.

**Frankfurt, Harry G.** *The Reasons of Love.* Princeton: Princeton University Press, 2004.

**Freud, Sigmund.** "On Narcicissm: An Introduction." In *The Standard Edition of the Complete Psychological Works of Sigmund Freud*, translated and edited by James Strachey, 67–102. Vol. 16. London: Hogarth Press, 1914.

**Freud, Sigmund.** "Fragments of an Analysis of a Case of Hysteria." In *The Standard Edition of the Complete Psychological Works of Sigmund Freud*, translated and edited by James Strachey, 1–22. Vol. 7. London: Hogarth Press, 1953.

**Freud, Sigmund.** "Identification." In *The Standard Edition of the Complete Works of Sigmund Freud*, translated and edited by James Strachey, 105–111. Vol. 18. London: Hogarth Press, 1953.

**Freud, Sigmund.** "On the Beginning of Treatment." In *The Standard Edition of the Complete Works of Sigmund Freud*, translated and edited by James Strachey, 121–144. Vol. 12. London: Hogarth Press, 1953.

**Froding, Barbro.** "On the Importance of Treating Oneself Well." *Polish Journal of Philosophy* 4 (2010): 7–21.

**Froding, Barbro.** "Hope as a Virtue in an Aristotelian Context." *Philosophy, Psychiatry, & Psychology* 19 (2012): 183–186.

**Fulford, Bill, Katherine Morris, John Sadler,** and **Giovanni Stanghellini.** "Past Improbable, Future Possible: The Renaissance in Philosophy and Psychiatry." In *Nature and Narrative: An Introduction to the New Philosophy of Psychiatry,* edited by Bill Fulford, Katherine Morris, John Sadler, and Giovanni Staghellini, 1–41. Oxford: Oxford University Press, 2003.

**Gabbard, Glen O.** "Major Modalities: Psychoanalytic/Psychodynamic." In *Oxford Textbook of Psychotherapy,* edited by Glen O. Gabbard, Judith S. Beck, and Jeremy Holmes, 3–14. Oxford: Oxford University Press, 2005.

**Garcia, Jorge L.A.** "Virtue Ethics." In *The Cambridge Dictionary of Philosophy*, edited by Robert Audi, 960–961. 2nd ed. Cambridge: Cambridge University Press, 1999.

**Gardiner, Stephen M.** "Review: Virtue Ethics: A Pluralistic View, by Christine Swanton." *Mind* 114 (2005): 207–212.

**Gay, Peter.** *Freud: A Life for Our Time.* New York: W.W. Norton and Company, 1998.

**Gediman, Helen K.,** and **Janice S. Lieberman.** *The Many Faces of Deception: Omissions, Lies, and Disguise.* New York: Jason Aronson, 1996.

**Gert, Bernard.** "Morality." In *The Cambridge Dictionary of Philosophy*, edited by Robert Audi, 586. 2nd ed. Cambridge: Cambridge University Press, 1999.

**Glannon, Walter.** "Responsibility, Alcoholism, and Liver Transplantation." *Journal of Medicine and Philosophy* 23 (1998): 31–40.

**Goldberg, Peter.** "Process, Resistance, and Interpretation." In *Textbook of Psychoanalysis,* edited by Glen O. Gabbard, Bonnie E. Litowitz, and Paul Williams, 283–302. 2nd ed. Washington, DC: American Psychiatric Publishing, 2011.

**Gottesfeld, Mary L.** "The Self-Psychology of Heinz Kohut: An Existential Reading." *Clinical Social Work Journal* 12 (1984): 283–287.

**Greenberg, Gary.** *Manufacturing Depression: The Secret History of a Modern Disease.* New York: Simon and Schuster, 2010.

**Greco, John** and **John Turri.** "Virtue Epistemology." *The Stanford Encyclopedia of Philosophy* (Spring 2011 Edition) , Edward N. Zalta (ed.), http://www.plato.stanford.edu/archives/spring2011/entries/epistemology-virtue. Accessed August 25, 2015.

**Greenson, Ralph.** *The Technique and Practice of Psychoanalysis.* New York: International Universities Press, 1967.

**Griffith, James L.** "Existential Inquiry: Psychotherapy for Crises of Demoralization." *European Journal of Psychiatry* 27(1) (2013): 42–47.

**Griffith, James L.** and **Anjali Dsouza.** "Demoralization and Hope in Clinical Psychiatry and Psychotherapy." In *The Psychotherapy of Hope: The Legacy of Persuasion and Healing*, edited by Renato D. Alarcon and Julia B. Frank, 158–177. Baltimore: Johns Hopkins University Press, 2012.

**Groopman, Leonard C., Frank G. Miller,** and **Joseph J. Fins.** "The Patient's Work." *Cambridge Quarterly of Health Care Ethics* 16 (2006): 44–52.

**Grosskurth, Phyllis.** *Melanie Klein: Her World and Her Work.* Cambridge, MA: Harvard University Press, 1987.

**Guignon, Charles B.** "Authenticity, Moral Values, and Psychotherapy." In *The Cambridge Companion to Heidegger*, edited by Charles B. Guignon, 268–292. 2nd ed. Cambridge: Cambridge University Press, 2006.

**Hacking, Ian.** *Rewriting the Soul: Multiple Personality and the Science of Memory.* Princeton, NJ: Princeton University Press, 1998.

**Hadot, Pierre.** "Reflections on the Idea of the 'Cultivation of the Self.'" In *Philosophy As a Way of Life*, edited by Arnold I. Davidson, 206–213. Oxford: Blackwel, 1995.

**Halpern, Jodi.** *From Detached Concern to Empathy: Humanizing Medical Practice.* New York: Oxford University Press, 2011.

**Handesman, Michael M., Samuel Knapp,** and **Michael C. Gottlieb.** "Positive Ethics: Themes and Variations." In *The Oxford Handbook of Positive Psychology*, edited by Shane J. Lopez and Charles R. Snyder, 105–114. 2nd ed. Oxford: Oxford University Press, 2009.

**Hanly, Charles.** "Logical and Conceptual Problems of Existential Psychiatry." *Journal of Nervous and Mental Disease* 173 (1985): 263–275.

**Hanna, Fred J.** and **Kaisa Puhakka.** "When Psychotherapy Works: Pinpointing an Element of Change." *Psychotherapy* 28 (1991): 598–607.

**Hanna, Kathleen M.** and **C.L. Decker.** "A Concept Analysis: Assuming Responsibility for Self-Care among Adolescents with Type-1 Diabetes." *Journal for Specialists in Pediatric Nursing,* 15 (2010): 99–110.

**Harari, Hagai, Simone G. Shamay-Tsoory, Milli Ravid,** and **Yechiel Levkovitz.** "Double Dissociation between Cognitive and Affective Empathy in Borderline Personality Disorder." *Psychiatry Research* 175 (2010): 277–279.

**Harris, George.** "Review: Virtue Ethics: A Pluralistic View, by Christine Swanton." *Notre Dame Philosophical Reviews* 2004.01.02. Accessed August 9, 2015. https://ndpr.nd.edu/news/23028-virtue-ethics-a-pluralistic-view-oxford/.

**Hartmann, Henz.** *Psychoanalysis and Moral Values.* New York: International Universities Press, 1960.

**Havens, Leston.** "A Theoretical Basis for the Concepts of Self and Authentic Self." *Journal of the American Psychoanalytic Association* 34 (1986): 363–378.

**Healy, David.** *The Suspended Revolution: Psychiatry and Psychotherapy Re-examined.* London: Faber and Faber, 1990.

**Heidegger, Martin.** *Zollikon Seminars: Protocols–Conversations–Letters.* Edited by Medard Boss. Translated by Franz Mayer and Richard Askay. Evanston, IL: Northwestern University Press, 2001.

**Heppner, Paul P.** and **Dong-Gwi Lee.** "Problem-Solving Appraisal and Psychological Adjustment." In *The Oxford Handbook of Positive Psychology*, edited by Shane J. Lopez and Charles R. Snyder, 345–356. 2nd ed. Oxford: Oxford University Press, 2009.

**Hill Jr., Thomas E.** *Autonomy and Self-Respect.* Cambridge: Cambridge University Press, 1991.

**Holtforth, Martin Grosse** et al. "Insight in Cognitive-Behavioral Therapy." In *Insight in Psychotherapy*, edited by Louis G. Castonguay and Clara E. Hill, 57–80. Washington DC: American Psychological Association, 2007.

**Horney, Karen.** "The Problem of Feminine Masochism." *Psychoanalytic Review* 22 (1935): 241–257.

**Horney, Karen.** *Neurosis and Human Growth: The Struggle Toward Self Realization.* New York: Norton, 1970.

**Hookway, Christopher.** "How To Be a Virtue Epistemologist." In *Intellectual Virtue: Perspectives from Ethics and Epistemology*, edited by Michael DePaul and Linda Zagzebsky, 183–202. Oxford: Oxford University Press, 2007.

**Hursthouse, Rosalind.** *On Virtue Ethics.* Oxford: Oxford University Press, 1999.

**Jacobson, Nora** and **Diane Greenly.** "What is Recovery? A Conceptual Model and Explication." *Psychiatric Services* 52 (2001): 482–485.

**Jahoda, Marie.** *Current Concepts of Positive Mental Health.* New York: Basic Books, 1958.

**James, William.** *The Varieties of Religious Experience.* New York: Image Books, 1978.

**Jopling, David.** "Placebo Insight: The Rationality of Insight-Oriented Psychotherapy." *Journal of Clinical Psychology* 57 (2001): 19–36.

**Jopling, David.** *Talking Cures and Placebo Effects.* Oxford: Oxford University Press, 2008.

**Kahr, Brett.** *D. W. Winnicott: A Bibliographical Portrait.* London: Karnac Books, 1996.

**Kant, Immanuel.** *Critique of Practical Reason.* Translated by Lewis W. Beck. Indianapolis: Bobbs-Merrill, 1956.

**Kant, Immanuel.** *Fundamental Principles of the Metaphysic of Morals.* Translated by Thomas K. Abbot. Amherst, NY: Prometheus Books, 1988.

**Kant, Immanuel.** *Practical Philosophy.* Translated and edited by Mary Gregor. Cambridge: Cambridge University Press, 1996.

**Karen, Robert.** "Shame." *Atlantic Monthly* 269(2) (1992): 40.

**Kashdan, Todd B.** and **Jonathan Rottenberg.** "Psychological Flexibility as a Fundamental Aspect of Health." *Clinical Psychology Review* 30 (2010): 865–878.

**Kashdan, Todd B.** and **Paul J. Silvia.** "Curiosity and Interest: The Benefits of Thriving on Novelty and Challenge." In *The Oxford Handbook of Positive Psychology*, edited by Shane J. Lopez and Charles R. Snyder, 367–374. 2nd ed. Oxford: Oxford University Press, 2009.

**Kelley, Kevin V.** and **Peter Caws.** "Psychoanalysis and Dynamic Therapies." In *Encyclopedia of Bioethics*, edited by Stephen G. Post, 2178–2185. 3rd ed. New York: Thomson Gale, 2004.

**Kelley, Maureen.** "Limits on Patient Responsibility." *Journal of Medicine and Philosophy* 30 (2005): 189–206.

**Kernberg, Otto F.** "The Psychotherapeutic Treatment of Borderline Personalities." *Psychiatry 1982: The American Psychiatric Association Annual Review*, edited by Lester Grinspoon, 470–486. Vol. 1. Washington, DC: American Psychiatric Press Inc., 1982.

**Keyes, Corey M.L.** "Toward a Science of Mental Health." In *The Oxford Handbook of Positive Psychology*, edited by Shane J. Lopez and Charles R. Snyder, 89–96. 2nd ed. Oxford: Oxford University Press, 2009.

**Klein, Donald F.** and **John M. Davis.** *Diagnosis and Drug Treatment of Psychiatric Disorders.* Baltimore: Williams and Wilkins, 1969.

**Kohut, Heinz.** *The Analysis of the Self: A Systematic Approach to the Psychoanalytic Treatment of Narcissistic Personality Disorders.* Chicago: University of Chicago Press, 1971.

**Kohut, Heinz.** *The Restoration of the Self.* Chicago: The University of Chicago Press, 1977.

**Kottler, Jeffrey.** "How Well Do We Know Our Clients?" In *Duped: Lies and Deception in Psychotherapy*, edited by Jeffrey Kottler and Jon Carlson, 9–14. New York: Routledge, 2011.

**Kristjansson, Kristjan.** *The Virtues and Vices of Positive Psychology: A Philosophical Critique*. New York: Cambridge University Press, 2013.

**Kroner, Daryl G.** and **Robert D. Morgan**. "An Overview of Strategies for the Assessment and Treatment of Criminal Thinking." In *Forensic CBT: A Handbook for Clinical Practice*, edited by Raymond C. Tafrate and Damon Mitchell, 87–103. Malden, MA: John Wiley and Sons, 2014.

**Landau, Russ Schafe.** *The Fundamentals of Ethics*. Oxford: Oxford University Press, 2010.

**Lanius, Ruth A., Eric Vermetten,** and **Clare Pain**, eds. *The Impact of Early Life Trauma on Health and Disease: The Hidden Epidemic*. Cambridge: Cambridge University Press, 2010.

**Laplanche, Jean** and **Jean-Bertrand Pontalis**. "Interpretation." In *The Language of Psychoanalysis*, translated by Donald Nicholson-Smith, 227–229. New York: W. W. Norton & Company, 1974.

**Lasch, Christopher.** *Culture of Narcissism: American Life in an Age of Diminishing Expectations*. New York: Norton, 1978.

**Lear, Jonathan.** "Avowal and Unfreedom." *Philosophy and Phenomenological Research* LXIX(2) (2004): 448–454.

**Levy, Stephen T.** and **Lawrence B. Inderbitzen**. (1992). "Neutrality, Interpretation, and Therapeutic Intent." *Journal of the American Psychoanalytic Association* 40 (1992): 989–1011.

**Lewis, Helen Block.** *Shame and Guilt in Neurosis*. New York: International University Press, 1971.

**Linley, Alex P.** et al. "Positive Psychology Applications." In *The Oxford Handbook of Positive Psychology*, edited by Shane J. Lopez and Charles R. Snyder, 35–48. 2nd ed. Oxford: Oxford University Press, 2009.

**Lippitt, John.** *Kierkegaard and the Problem of Self-Love*. Cambridge: Cambridge University Press, 2013.

**Little, Gregory L.** and **Kenneth D. Robinson**. "Effects of Moral Reconation Therapy Upon Moral Reasoning, Life Purpose, and Recidivism among Drug and Alcohol Offenders." *Psychological Reports* 64 (1989): 83–90.

**Little, Gregory L.** and **Kenneth D. Robinson**. "Moral Reconation Therapy: A Systematic, Step-By-Step Treatment System for Treatment Resistant Clients." *Psychological Reports* 62 (1988): 135–151.

**Logan, Linda.** "Selfless." *New York Times Magazine* April 28 (2013): 56–60.

**Lomas, Peter.** *Doing Good? Psychotherapy Out of Its Depth*. Oxford: Oxford University Press, 1999.

**London, Perry.** *The Modes and Morals of Psychotherapy*. 2nd ed. New York: Hemisphere Publishing Corporation, 1986.

**Lopez, Shane J.** and **Mathew W. Gallagher**. "A Case for Positive Psychology." In *The Oxford Handbook of Positive Psychology*, edited by Shane J. Lopez and Charles R. Snyder, 3–6. 2nd ed. Oxford: Oxford University Press, 2009.

**Luhrman, Tanya Marie.** *Of Two Minds: An Anthropologist Looks at American Psychiatry*. New York: Vintage Books, 2001.

**Lunbeck, Elizabeth.** *The Americanization of Narcissism*. Cambridge, MA: Harvard University Press, 2014.

**Macaro, Antonia.** *Reason, Virtue and Psychotherapy.* West Sussex: John Wiley & Sons, 2006.

**MacIntyre, Alasdair.** *After Virtue: A Study in Moral Theory*. 2nd ed. Notre Dame, IN: University of Notre Dame Press, 1984.

**MacKinnon, Christine.** "Knowing Cognitive Selves." In *Intellectual Virtue: Perspectives from Ethics and Epistemology*, edited by Michael DePaul and Linda Zagzebsky, 227–254. Oxford: Oxford University Press, 2003.

**Maddux, James E.** "Self-Efficacy: The Power of Believing You Can." In *The Oxford Handbook of Positive Psychology*, edited by Shane J. Lopez and Charles R. Snyder, 335–344. 2nd ed. Oxford: Oxford University Press, 2009.

**Mailer, Norman.** *The Spooky Art: Thoughts on Writing.* New York: Random House, 2004.

**Mailer, Norman.** "The Art of Fiction." In *The Paris Review Interviews*, edited by Philip Gourevitch, 397–425. Vol. 3. New York: Picador, 2008.

**Manion, Jennifer C.** "The Moral Relevance of Shame." *American Philosophical Quarterly* 39 (2002): 73–90.

**Margolis, John.** *Psychotherapy and Morality*. New York: Random House, 1966.

**Martens, William H.J.** "A Theoretical Model of Fragile Authenticity Structure." *International Journal of Philosophical Practice* 2(3) (2004): 1–18

**Martin, Mike W.** *From Morality to Mental Health: Virtue and Vice in a Therapeutic Culture.* Oxford: Oxford University Press, 2006.

**Martin, Mike W.** "Psychotherapy as Cultivating Character." *Philosophy, Psychiatry, & Psychology* 19 (2012): 37–39.

**Masten, Ann S., J. J. Cutuli, Janette E. Herbers,** and **Marie-Gabrielle J. Reed**. "Resilience in Development." In *The Oxford Handbook of Positive Psychology*, edited by Shane J. Lopez and Charles R. Snyder, 117–132. 2nd ed. Oxford: Oxford University Press, 2009.

**Matthews, Eric.** "Moral Vision and the Idea of Mental Illness." *Philosophy, Psychiatry, & Psychology* 6 (1999): 373–388.

**McLean, Jaimie.** "Psychotherapy with a Narcissistic Patient Using Kohut's Self Psychology Model." *Psychiatry* 4 (2007): 40–47.

**Meichenbaum, Donald H.** "Cognitive-Behavioral Therapy in Historical Perspective." In *Comprehensive Textbook of Psychotherapy: Theory and Practice*, edited by Bruce Bongar and Larry Beutler, 140–158. New York: Oxford University Press, 1995.

**Meissner, W.W.** *The Therapeutic Alliance*. New Haven: Yale University Press, 1996.

**Meissner, W.W.** *The Ethical Dimensions of Psychoanalysis: A Dialogue.* Albany: State University of New York Press, 2003.

**Messer, Stanley B.** and **Nancy McWilliams**. "Insight in Psychodynamic Therapy: Theory and Assessment." In *Insight in Psychotherapy*, edited by Louis G. Castonguay and Clara E. Hill, 97–30. Washington, DC: American Psychological Association, 2007.

**Messer, Stanley B.** and **Bruce E. Wampold**. "Let's Face Facts: Common Factors Are More Potent than Specific Therapy Ingredients." *Clinical Psychology: Science and Practice* 9 (2002): 21–25.

**Mill, John S.** *On Liberty*. Edited by Harry B. Acton. London: J.M. Dent and Sons, 1972.

**Miller, Ronald B.** *Facing Human Suffering: Psychology and Psychotherapy as Moral Engagement*. Washington, DC: American Psychological Association, 2004.

**Mitchell, Damon, Raymond C. Tafrate,** and **Arthur Freeman**. "Antisocial Personality Disorder." In *Cognitive Therapy of Personality Disorders*, edited by Aaron T. Beck, Denise D. Davis, and Arthur Freeman, 346–365. 3rd ed. New York: The Guilford Press, 2015.

**Montmarquet, James A.** "Epistemic Virtue." *Mind* 96(384) (1987): 482–497.

**Montmarquet, James A.** "An 'Internalist' Conception of Epistemic Virtue." In *Knowledge, Belief, and Character: Readings in Virtue Epistemology*, edited by Guy Axtell, 135–148. New York: Rowman and Littlefield Publishers, 2000.

**Montmarquet, James A.** "'Pure' Versus 'Practical' Epistemic Justification." *Metaphilosophy* 38, no. 1 (2007): 72–87.

**Moran, Richard.** *Authority and Estrangement: An Essay on Self-knowledge*. Princeton NJ: Princeton University Press, 2001.

**Moravscik, Julius.** "Understanding and Knowledge in Plato's Philosophy." *Neue Hefte fur Philosophie* 15/16 (1979): 53–69.

**Murdoch, Iris.** *The Sovereignty of the Good*. London: Routledge, 1970.

**Neri, Claudio.** "Authenticity as an Aim of Psychoanalysis." *American Journal of Psychoanalysis* 68 (2008): 325–349

**Newman, Cory F.** and **Jennifer L. Strauss**. "When Clients Are Untruthful: Implications for the Therapeutic Alliance, Case Conceptualization, and Intervention." *Journal of Cognitive Psychotherapy* 17(3) (2003): 224–252.

**Nozick, Robert.** *Philosophical Explanations*. Cambridge, MA: The Belknap Press of Harvard University Press, 1983.

**Nussbaum, Martha.** *The Therapy of Desire: Theory and Practice in Hellenistic Ethics*. Oxford: Oxford University Press, 1994.

**Ornstein, Paul H.** "Heinz Kohut's Vision of the Essence of Humanness." In *Psychoanalytic Versions of the Human Condition: Philosophies of Life and Their Impact on Practice*, edited by Paul Marcus and Alan Rosenberg, 206–232. New York: New York University Press, 1998.

**Paris, Joel.** *Prescriptions for the Mind: A Critical View of Contemporary Psychiatry*. New York: Oxford University Press, 2009.

**Pearce, Steve** and **Hanna Pickard**. "The Moral Content of Psychiatric Treatment." *The British Journal of Psychiatry* 195 (2009): 281–282.

**Peterson, Christopher** and **Martin E. Seligman**. *Character Strengths and Virtues: A Handbook and Classification*. New York: Oxford University Press, 2004.

**Pickard, Hanna.** "Responsibility without Blame: Empathy and the Effective Treatment of Personality Disorder." *Philosophy, Psychiatry, & Psychology* 18 (2011): 210.

**Pickard, Hanna.** "Responsibility without Blame: Philosophical Reflections on Clinical Practice." In *The Oxford Handbook of Philosophy and Psychiatry*, edited by K.W.M. Fulford, Martin Davies, Richard G.T. Gipps, George Graham, John Z. Sadler, Giovanni Stanghellini, and Tim Thornton, 1134–1154. Oxford: Oxford University Press, 2013.

**Potter, Nancy N.** "Oh Blame, Where Is Thy Sting?" *Philosophy, Psychiatry, & Psychology* 18 (2011): 225–230.

**Pouncey, Claire L.** and **Jonathan M. Lukens**. "Madness versus Badness: The Ethical Tension Between the Recovery Movement and Forensic Psychiatry." *Theoretical Medicine and Bioethics* 31 (2010): 93–105.

**Price, Jill.** *The Woman Who Can't Forget: The Extraordinary Story of Living with the Most Remarkable Memory Known to Science—A Memoir.* New York: Free Press, 2009.

**Quinn, Susan.** *A Mind of Her Own: The Life of Karen Horney*. New York: Summit Books, 1987.

**Radden, Jennifer.** "Virtue Ethics as Professional Ethics: The Case of Psychiatry." In *Working Virtue: Virtue Ethics and Contemporary Moral Problems*, edited by Rebecca L. Walter and P.J. Ivanhoe, 113–134. Oxford: Oxford University Press, 2007.

**Radden, Jennifer** and **John Z. Sadler**. *The Virtuous Psychiatrist: Character Ethics in Psychiatric Practice.* Oxford: Oxford University Press, 2010.

**Rado, Sandor.** "Fear of Castration in Women." *Psychoanalytic Quarterly* II(3–4) (1933): 425–475.

**Ramzy, Ishak.** "The Place of Values in Psychoanalytic Theory, Practice and Training." In *Moral Values and the Superego Concept in Psychoanalysis*, edited by Seymour C. Post, 205–225. New York: International Universities Press, Inc., 1972.

**Rand, Kevin L.** and **Jennifer S. Cheavens**. "Hope Theory." In *The Oxford Handbook of Positive Psychology*, edited by Shane J. Lopez and Charles R. Snyder, 323–334. 2nd ed. Oxford: Oxford University Press, 2009.

**Richardson, Frank C., Blaine J. Fowers**, and **Charles B. Guignon**. *Re-Envisioning Psychology: Moral Dimensions of Theory and Practice.* San Francisco: Jossey-Bass Publishers, 1999.

**Rieff, Phillip.** *Freud: The Mind of the Moralist.* New York: Anchor Books, 1961.

**Rieff, Phillip.** *The Triumph of the Therapeutic: Uses of Faith after Freud.* Chicago: University of Chicago Press, 1987.

**Riggs, Wayne D.** "Understanding 'Virtue' and the Virtue of Understanding." In *Intellectual Virtue: Perspectives from Ethics and Epistemology*, edited by Michael DePaul and Linda Zagzebski, 203–226. Oxford: Oxford University Press, 2007.

**Roazen, Paul.** (1972). "The Impact of Psychoanalysis on Values." In *Moral Values and the Superego Concept in Psychoanalysis*, edited by Seymour C. Post, 197–294. New York: International Universities Press, Inc., 1972.

**Roberts, Robert C.** and **W. Jay Wood.** *Intellectual Virtues: An Essay in Regulative Epistemology.* Oxford: Oxford University Press, 2007.

**Rodman, F. Robert**. *Winnicott: A Life and Work.* Cambridge, MA: Da Capo Press, 2003.

**Ross, W.D.** *The Right and the Good.* Oxford: Oxford University Press, 1930.

**Rousseau, Jean-Jacques.** *Confessions*. Translated by Angela Scholar. Oxford: Oxford University Press, 2000.

**Rush, Augustus J.** "Cognitive Therapy." In *The Psychotherapy Handbook*, edited by R. Herink, 91–94. New York: New American Library, 1980.

**Russell, Daniel.** "Aristotle on the Moral Relevance of Self-Respect." In *Virtue Ethics Old and New*, edited by Stephen M. Gardiner, 101–121. Ithaca, NY: Cornell University Press, 2005

**Saks, Elyn.** *Interpreting Interpretation: The Limits of Hermeneutic Psychoanalysis.* New Haven: Yale University Press, 1999.

**Saks, Elyn.** *The Center Cannot Hold: My Journey through Madness.* New York: Hyperion, 2007.

**Sangha, Sageeta.** "Review of Virtue Ethics: A Pluralistic View, by Christine Swanton." *Journal of Value Inquiry* 41 (2007): 373.

**Sartre, Jean-Paul.** *Saint Genet: Actor and Martyr*. Translated by Bernard Frechtman. New York: George Braziller, 1963.

**Sass, Louis A.** "The Self in Contemporary Psychoanalysis: Commentary on Charles Taylor." In *Hermeneutics and Psychological Theory: Interpretive Perspectives on Personality, Psychotherapy, and Pathology*, edited by Stanley B. Messer, Louis A. Sass, and Robert L. Woodfolk, 321–325. New Brunswick: Rutgers University Press, 1988.

**Scaturo, Donald J.** "Insight-Oriented Psychotherapy." In *The Corsini Encyclopedia of Psychology*, edited by Irving B. Weiner and W. Edward Craighead, 1–3. New York: John Wiley and Sons, 2009.

**Schwartz, Morris S.** and **Charlotte Green Schwartz**. "Mental Health: The Concept." In *International Encyclopedia of the Social Sciences*, edited by David L. Sills, 215–226. Vol. 1. New York: Macmillan, 1968.

**Segal, Hannah.** "The Curative Factors in Psychoanalysis." *International Journal of Psychoanalysis* 43 (1962): 212–217.

**Seeler, Lori, Arthur Freeman, Raymond DiGiuseppe,** and **Damon Mitchell**. "Traditional Cognitive-Behavioral Therapy Models for Antisocial Patterns." In *Forensic CBT: A Handbook for Clinical Practice*, edited by Raymond C. Tafrate and Damon Mitchell, 15–42. Malden, MA: John Wiley and Sons, 2014.

**Seneca**. *Dialogues and Essays*. Translated by John Davie. Oxford: Oxford University Press, 2007.

**Siegal, Allen M.** *Heinz Kohut and the Psychology of the Self*. New York: Routledge, 1996.

**Simmons, Aaron.** "In Defense of the Moral Significance of Empathy." *Ethical Theory and Moral Practice* 17 (2014): 97–111.

**Snyder, Charles R.** *The Psychology of Hope: You Can Get There from Here*. New York: Free Press, 1994.

**Sreenivasan, Gopal.** "Errors about Errors: Virtue Theory and Trait Attribution." *Mind* 3(441) (2002): 47–68.

**Sreenivasan, Gopal.** "The Situationist Critique of Virtue Ethics." In *The Cambridge Companion to Virtue Ethics*, edited by Daniel C. Russell, 290–314. New York: Cambridge University Press, 2013.

**Steger, Michael F.** "Meaning in Life." In *The Oxford Handbook of Positive Psychology*, edited by Shane J. Lopez and Charles R. Snyder, 679–688. 2nd ed. Oxford: Oxford University Press, 2009.

**Stein, Martin H.** "A Clinical Illustration of a 'Moral' Problem in Psychoanalysis." In *Moral Values and the Superego Concept in Psychoanalysis*, edited by Seymour C. Post, 226–239. New York: International Universities Press, 1972.

**Strupp, Hans H.** and **Suzanne W. Hadley**. "A Tripartite Model of Mental Health and Therapeutic Outcomes with Special Reference to Negative Effects in Psychotherapy." *American Psychologist* 32 (1977): 187-196.

**Summers, Richard F.** and **Jacques P. Barber**. *Psychodynamic Therapy: A Guide to Evidence-Based Practice*. New York: The Guilford Press, 2010.

**Swanton, Christine.** *Virtue Ethics: A Pluralistic View*. Oxford: Oxford University Press, 2003.

**Swanton, Christine.** "Satisficing and Perfectionism in Virtue Ethics." In *Satisficing and Maximizing: Moral Theoretic Perspectives in Practical Reasoning*, edited by Michael Byron, 176–189. Cambridge: Cambridge University Press, 2004.

**Swanton, Christine.** "The Definition of Virtue Ethics." In *The Cambridge Companion to Virtue Ethics*, edited by Daniel C. Russell, 315–338. New York: Cambridge University Press, 2013.

**Swanton, Christine.** "The Notion of the Moral: The Relation Between Virtue Ethics and Virtue Epistemology." *Philosophical Studies* 171(1) (2014): 121–134.

**Swanton, Christine.** "Comments on Intelligent Virtue: Rightness and Exemplars of Virtue." *Journal of Value Inquiry* 49 (2015): 307–314.

**Tangney, June Price, Jeff Stuewig,** and **Debra J. Mashek.** "Moral Emotions and Moral Behavior." *Annual Review of Psychology* 58 (2007): 345–372.

**Taylor, Charles.** "Self-Interpreting Animals." In *Human Agency and Language: Philosophical Papers 1*, 45–76. Cambridge: Cambridge University Press, 1985.

**Taylor, Charles.** "What is Human Agency?" In *Human Agency and Language: Philosophical Papers 1*, 15–44. Cambridge: Cambridge University Press, 1985.

**Taylor, Charles.** "The Moral Topography of the Self." In *Hermeneutics and Psychological Theory: Interpretive Perspectives on Personality, Psychotherapy, and Pathology*, edited by Stanley B. Messer, Louis A. Sass, and Robert L. Woolfolk, 298–320. New Brunswick: Rutgers University Press, 1988.

**Taylor, Charles.** *Sources of the Self: The Making of Modern Identity.* Cambridge, MA: Harvard University Press, 1989.

**Taylor, Charles.** "The Politics of Recognition." In *Multiculturalism: Examining the Politics of Recognition*, edited by Amy Gutman, 25–73. Princeton: Princeton University Press, 1994.

**Taylor, Charles.** *The Malaise of Modernity.* Toronto: House of Anansi Press, 2003.

**Taylor, Robert S.** "Kant's Personal Autonomy." *Political Theory* 33 (2005): 602–628.

**Tedeschi, Richard G.** and **Lawrence G. Calhoun.** "Posttraumatic Growth: Conceptual Foundations and Empirical Evidence." *Psychological Inquiry* 15 (2004): 1–18.

**Tessman, Lisa.** "Review of Virtue Ethics: A Pluralistic View, by Christine Swanton." *Philosophical Review* 114 (2005): 414–415.

**Thompson, Michael G.** "The Way of Authenticity and the Quest for Personal Integrity." *European Journal of Psychotherapy and Counseling* 7(3) (2005): 143–157.

**Thompson, Michael G.** "Vicissitudes of Authenticity in the Psychoanalytic Situation." *Contemporary Psychoanalysis* 42 (2006): 139–176.

**Timmermann, Jens.** "Kantian Duties to the Self, Explained and Defended." *Philosophy* 81 (2006): 505–530.

**Tjeltveit, Alan C.** *Ethics and Values in Psychotherapy.* London: Routledge, 1999.

**Tjeltveit, Alan C.** "The Good, the Bad, the Obligatory, and the Virtuous." *Journal of Psychotherapy Integration* 14 (2004): 149–167.

**Todd, Oliver.** *Albert Camus: Un Vie.* Paris: Gallimard, 1996.

**Trilling, Lionel.** *Sincerity and Authenticity.* Cambridge, MA: Harvard University Press, 1971.

**Trijsburg, Rutger Willem, Sjoerd Colijn,** and **Jeremy Holmes.** "Psychotherapy Integration." In *The Oxford Textbook of Psychotherapy*, edited by Glen O. Gabbard, Judith S. Beck, and Jeremy Holmes, 95–110. Oxford: Oxford University Press, 2005.

**Van Deurzen Emmy.** *Everyday Mysteries: Existential Dimensions of Psychotherapy.* London: Routledge, 1997.

**Van Deurzen Emmy.** *Existential Counselling and Psychotherapy in Practice.* 2nd ed. London: Sage Publications, 2002.

**Van Deurzen, Emmy** and **Raymond Kenward.** *Dictionary of Existential Psychotherapy and Counselling.* London: Sage Publications, 2005.

**Varga, Somogy.** *Authenticity as an Ethical Ideal.* New York: Routledge, 2012.

**Vermeire, E., H. Hearnshaw, P. Van Royen,** and **J. Denekens.** "Patient Adherence to Treatment: Three Decades of Research. A Comprehensive Review." *Journal of Clinical Pharmacy and Therapeutics* 26 (2001): 331–342.

**Vos, Marije Keulen-de, David P. Bernstein,** and **Arnold Arntz.** "Schema Therapy for Aggressive Offenders with Personality Disorders." In *Forensic CBT: A Handbook for Clinical Practice*, edited by Raymond C. Tafrate and Damon Mitchell, 66–83. Malden, MA: John Wiley and Sons, 2014.

**Wallwork, Ernest.** *Psychoanalysis and Ethics.* New Haven and London: Yale University Press, 1991.

**Wallwork, Ernest.** "Ethics in Psychoanalysis." In *The American Psychiatric Publishing Textbook on Psychoanalysis*, edited by Glen O. Gabbard, Bonnie E. Litowitz, Paul Williams, 349–366. 2nd ed. Washington, DC: American Psychiatric Publishing, 2012.

**Walters, Glenn D.** "Applying CBT to the Criminal Thought Process." In *Forensic CBT: A Handbook for Clinical Practice*, edited by Raymond C. Tafrate and Damon Mitchell, 104–121. Malden, MA: John Wiley and Sons, 2014.

**Wampold, Bruce E.** *The Great Psychotherapy Debate: Models, Methods, and Findings.* Hillsdale, NJ: Lawrence Erlbaum Associates, Publishers, 2001.

**Wanberg, Kenneth W.** and **Harvey B. Milkman.** "Social and Community Responsibility Therapy (SCRT): A Cognitive-Behavioral Model for the Treatment of Substance-Abusing Judicial Clients." In *Forensic CBT: A Handbook for Clinical Practice*, edited by Raymond C. Tafrate and Damon Mitchell, 252–278. Malden, MA: John Wiley and Sons, 2014.

**Waring, Duff.** "Why the Practice of Medicine Is Not a Phronetic Activity." *Theoretical Medicine and Bioethics* 21 (2000): 139–151.

**Waring, Duff.** "Psychotherapy Through the Prism of Moral Language." *Philosophy, Psychiatry, & Psychology* 19 (2012): 45–48.

**Waring, Duff.** "The Virtuous Patient." *Philosophy, Psychiatry, & Psychology* 19 (2012): 25–36.

**Waring, Duff.** "Patient Responsibilities in a Psychiatric Healing Project." In *The Oxford Handbook of Psychiatric Ethics*, edited by John Z. Sadler, Werdie (C.W.) Van Staden, and W.K.M. Fulford, 1402–1418. Oxford: Oxford University Press, 2015.

**Weiner, Irving B.** and **Robert F. Bornstein.** *Principles of Psychotherapy: Promoting Evidence-Based Psychodynamic Practice.* Hoboken, NJ: John Wiley and Sons, Inc., 2009.

**Weissman, Avery D.** *The Existential Core of Psychoanalysis: Reality, Sense and Responsibility.* Boston: Little Brown, 1965.

**Westlund, Andrea C.** "Selflessness and Responsibility for Self: Is Deference Compatible with Autonomy?" *Philosophical Review* 112 (2003): 483–523.

**Wiburn, Brad K.** "Moral Self-Improvement." In *Moral Cultivation: Essays on the Development of Character and Virtue*, edited by Brad K. Wilburn, 69–84. Plymouth, UK: Lexington Books, 2007.

**Williams, Bernard.** *Ethics and the Limits of Philosophy.* Cambridge, MA: Harvard University Press, 1985.

**Wilson, David B., Leana Allen Bouffard,** and **Doris L. Mackenzie.** "A Quantitative Review of Structured, Group-Oriented, Cognitive-Behavioral Programs for Offenders." *Criminal Justice and Behavior* 33 (2005): 172–204.

**Winslade, William J.** "Confidentiality." In *Encyclopedia of Bioethics,* edited by Stephen G. Post, 494–503. 3rd ed. New York: Thomson Gale, 2004.

**Wood, Alan.** "Duties to Oneself, Duties of Respect to Others." In *The Blackwell Guide to Kant's Ethics,* edited by Thomas E. Hill. Oxford: Blackwell Publishing, 2009.

**Woolfolk, Robert L.** *The Cure of Souls: Science, Values, and Psychotherapy.* San Francisco: Jossey-Bass Publishers, 1998.

**Woolfolk, Robert L.** and **Dominic Murphy.** "Axiological Foundations of Psychotherapy." *Journal of Psychotherapy Integration* 14 (2004): 168–191.

**Yeats, William B.** "The Circus Animals' Desertion." In *The Collected Poems of W. B. Yeats,* edited by Richard J. Finnera, 346–347. New York: Scribner Paperback Poetry, 1996.

**Zagzebski, Linda.** *Virtues of the Mind: An Inquiry into the Nature of Virtue and the Ethical Foundations of Knowledge.* Cambridge: Cambridge University Press, 1996.

**Zagzebski, Linda.** "Recovering Understanding." In *Knowledge, Truth, and Duty:* Essays on *Epistemic Justification, Responsibility, and Virtue,* edited by Mathius Steup, 235–251. New York: Oxford University Press, 2001.

**Zimmer, Richard B., Peter M. Bookstein, Edward T. Kenny,** and **Andreas K. Kraebber.** "Glossary." In *Textbook of Psychoanalysis,* edited by Glen O. Gabbard, Bonnie E. Litowitz, and Paul Williams, 567–587. 2nd ed. Washington, DC: American Psychiatric Publishing, 2011.

**Zinberg, Norman.** "Value Conflict and the Psychoanalyst's Role." In *Moral Values and the Superego Concept in Psychoanalysis,* edited by Seymour C. Post, 189–196. New York: International Universities Press, 1972.

# Index